KEN TAYLOR
DRAWN TO SPORT

Kenneth Taylor

Stephen Chalke

KEN TAYLOR
DRAWN TO SPORT

Stephen Chalke

FAIRFIELD BOOKS

Fairfield Books
17 George's Road, Fairfield Park, Bath BA1 6EY
Tel 01225-335813

First published 2006

ISBN 0 9544886 2 8

Page design by Niall Allsop

Printed and bound in Great Britain by Bath Press Ltd, Bath

Set in Garamond and Rotis Sans Serif

Contents

Index to Ken Taylor's art

Many of the drawings and paintings in this book are available from Ken Taylor, either as originals or as prints. Those who have bought his work include the Professional Footballers' Association, MCC, Surrey County Cricket Club and many private individuals. For further details, Ken can be contacted at The Red House, Stody, Melton Constable, Norfolk NR24 2EB.

On meeting Ken

I met Ken for the first time in February 1997. I was working on a book about county cricket in the 1950s, *Runs in the Memory*. The idea was to get players of that time to sit with me, tell their stories and relive their way of life, all in the context of a specially chosen match. It was my first book, and I had no contacts in the world of cricket so, whenever I met somebody, I would ask him to suggest other former players who might be good to interview. "Who would be a good person to meet from Essex? … and what about Yorkshire?"

It was Harold Rhodes in Derby who suggested Ken. The two of them had crossed paths while doing some coaching at Lord's and, though Harold did not know exactly where Ken lived, he pointed me in the right direction. "The last I heard of him, he was still teaching, somewhere in Norfolk."

A fortnight later, having tracked down Ken's phone number, I was following his directions to The Red House in Stody, a little village outside Holt. Even the bigger roads in North Norfolk lead nowhere much, with just a few little towns and villages nestling among farm fields and along the coast, and in February, with no holiday-makers, the whole place had something of an off-the-map feel to it. It was strange to think, as I peered up at wooden finger posts and negotiated narrow lanes, that I was journeying in search of memories of Yorkshire cricket in the 1950s.

Stody itself is little more than a hamlet. "If you get to the church," Ken had told me, "you've gone too far." And sure enough, I did get to the church. After three journeys up and down the road, I found a telephone kiosk and rang for help. It turned out that his house was back the way I had come, almost before the start of the village; I had missed it behind a hedge. By the time I arrived, I felt that I really had reached the back of nowhere.

It was a cold, clear morning, and he invited me into the main room, where a log fire burned. We talked about the game at Hove in 1959, when he had been one of a new generation of Yorkshire cricketers who had won the championship for the first time in a decade. He told me what an unselfish spirit their amateur captain Ronnie Burnet had created in the team, a spirit which reached its fullest flowering that afternoon at Hove when, casting off all inhibition, they scored a breathtaking 218 in 98 minutes.

Then he told me that he had spent his winters playing football for Huddersfield Town and how he had also been an art student, even winning a place at

The Slade. I found it hard to take in how somebody could pursue so many activities at such a high level at the same time, and my amazement was compounded when he mentioned almost in passing that his brother Jeff had studied for a Geography degree while playing First Division football and had gone on to be an opera singer, performing at Glyndebourne. Part of me was thinking, "This can't be right. He must be exaggerating." But of course he wasn't.

It was not the best interview I did for that book. He had a disconcerting habit of walking across to the fire so that his voice was too far from the tape recorder and, away from it all in Norfolk, he was clearly out of the habit of reminiscing with others about his sporting days. But there was an honesty and an insight in the things he said, very little of it revolving around his own achievements. I took to him.

He cooked me lunch, during which we chatted about the state of England. My visit took place in the last months of John Major's government, and I remember his saying how much damage Mrs Thatcher's policies had done to the industrial heart of Yorkshire and how unemployment had blighted a generation.

After lunch he asked if I would like to see his art work, and he led me into his studio. I don't know what I expected, but I was quite taken aback by what he laid before me: all these portraits in pastel of cricketers and footballers, together with the paintings of landscapes and buildings. It was a treasure trove, and I could not understand how someone who had so many talents could be so hidden away from the world.

I drove away in the late afternoon and, after further conversations with his team-mate Bryan Stott and with Sussex's Jim Parks, I sent him the completed chapter. It was the last one in the book, telling how Yorkshire had brought to a close Surrey's seven-year reign as county champions, and I called it 'The End of an Era'.

Three months later, the book was finished, and I started thinking about how to illustrate it. And my mind went back to that hour in his studio, to the portraits of cricketers he had shown me: the tousle-haired Fred Trueman, bristling with menace, and the free-flowing Denis Compton, his bat following through with panache. They were still alive in my imagination and, though I was 250 miles away in Bath and had no chance to inspect them again, I rang him to suggest the idea. Twelve full-page pictures, in black-and-white, one at the start of each chapter.

9

The book was a success, more so than I had dared to hope, and Ken's portraits drew many comments. Jack Russell was making quite a name for himself with his paintings, and Sussex's Martin Speight had just brought out a book of cricket pictures. But, apart from a limited edition of prints of four Yorkshire subjects, Ken's work had been hidden from view. And it was hard to know why. With his years at Huddersfield College and The Slade, he was a professionally trained artist, with a confidence of brush stroke and a distinctiveness of style.

He was delighted by the recognition – the glowing review from Michael Parkinson in the *Daily Telegraph*, the double page feature on him in the *Eastern Daily Press*, the phone call from Harold Pinter's secretary requesting a copy of his Len Hutton – and we joined forces on a second book, on the 1960s, *Caught in the Memory*. This time his portraits were reproduced in colour.

This second book received one extraordinary review, in the *Wisden Cricketers' Almanack*, in which the comic writer Peter Tinniswood went on for over a page, rising to a crescendo of delight and concluding: ''Read the book. Read the book, I beg you. I commend it wholeheartedly – and not least for the splendid illustrations by that fine Yorkshire stalwart of the 1960s, Mr Ken Taylor. He won't remember, but he once trod on my toe in the tea interval at Bramall Lane. He could grind my whole body into the ground without trace if he compels Mr Chalke to produce another volume about the 1970s.'

I decided not to take up that suggestion, working instead with individual subjects. Ken contributed four portraits to my book with Gloucestershire's 'Bomber' Wells and a striking jacket image for the one with his former team-mate Bob Appleyard, but the opportunity did not arise to use his work as fully as I had done in my first two volumes.

Then I suggested that we might join forces to produce something that displayed Ken's art more fully, and the idea of this book was born.

We have organised it as a cross between a scrapbook and an artist's workbook, with different subjects explored on each double page. Sometimes

End of the line
Weybourne, Norfolk

the art work leads, sometimes the writing. There are memorable matches relived, great characters recalled and reflections on a number of subjects: the differences between the two sports, the changes between then and now, the advantages and disadvantages of a life in which so many different talents are explored.

This last theme has intrigued me while writing the book. Our modern age, more perhaps than that of the 1950s, demands specialisation at an early age and has a built-in assumption that we are all striving to get to the top. Perhaps that is why today's cricket followers take so much to the commentary of Ken's Yorkshire team-mate Geoffrey Boycott, a sportsman who dedicated himself with a blinkered vision to extracting every ounce from what was quite a modest talent.

By contrast, Ken was endowed with great gifts and, in writing this book, I have been struck by the strength of some of the compliments I have discovered. Both E.W. Swanton and John Arlott thought that he was unlucky not to play cricket far more often for England, and Ray Wilson – his team-mate at Huddersfield Town – reckoned that he could have held his own without difficulty in the England football team. Indeed, the great Tommy Taylor – the Manchester United and England centre-forward, who was killed in the Munich air crash – singled him out as the most difficult centre-half he ever played against.

For many who knew him as a cricketer and footballer, there is a lingering feeling that he would have achieved much more if he had concentrated on one of them, and especially if he had not also been pursuing his art. There was a sense that, by August, he was looking forward to returning to football and, by March, he longed once more for the cricket. He even said to me on one occasion that he was glad he never went on an England cricket tour in winter, as he would have had to play three seasons of cricket in a row and that would have been too much.

So we look at his sporting life, and we conclude – as E.W. Swanton did – that he under-achieved, that his ambition was diluted by his spreading himself across so many activities. If he had had only one talent, like Geoffrey Boycott, he would have been forced to make more of it. And he would have got nearer to the top.

But it is not that simple. Ken has no regrets. If you offered him his time again so that he could reach greater heights in one sport at the expense of the other and of his art, I suspect that he would not take it. He enjoyed the variety.

To his team-mates he was 'a bit of a dreamer'. A brilliant fielder, an uncompromising centre-half, there was no problem with his concentration. But, away from the field of action, he often drifted into an imaginative world of his own, a world which had other dimensions than the number of runs he had scored that week or Huddersfield's position in the league table.

Inwardly, I suspect, he was less sure of his gifts than he should have been. He earned his living by making runs, and at times he found that a source of anxiety. And I think that his under-exposure as an artist – his contentment in the back lanes of Norfolk – stems in part from a reluctance to promote himself as aggressively as others in his situation might have done.

So, as the book has developed, I have found myself exploring several themes.

There is the comparison of then and now. A young reader will find it incredible that the equivalent of a Premier League footballer spent all week in an art studio, meeting up with his team-mates only on Saturdays, or a Yorkshire cricketer could pick up a bat after several weeks back at football and play a vital championship-winning innings. Today's sportsmen cannot come and go like this.

Here is a portrait of a man who straddled the worlds of art and sport, worlds which we tend to think very different. In this respect, the book gains a further dimension in taking in the life of Ken's brother Jeff, who moved without fuss between the concert platform and the muddy football field.

We can also reflect on the society that allowed two such boys, growing up in a working-class household among the smoking mills of Huddersfield, to discover such rich and varied outlets for their talents. They found their opportunities in wartime and in those years of great austerity that followed. I wonder: is our much more affluent society, with all its political drive for greater results, creating the same opportunities for the boys who now live in those streets?

So read the book how you like: a trip down memory lane, a chance to relish Ken's art, the life story of a man with an unusual array of talents or the starting point for a reflection on our present-day assumptions. Or perhaps you prefer just to enjoy some of the wonderful characters whom Ken knew. As somebody said to me, "Any book that contains both Bill Shankly and Brian Close won't go far wrong."

The first four sporting portraits

Ken has built up an extensive collection of portraits of footballers and cricketers, mostly from his own period of playing but some from more recent times. They are drawn in crayon on large sheets of coloured paper.

The seed of the idea for these portraits was sown some thirty years before he undertook the first of them. Ken was playing cricket at the end-of-season Scarborough Festival when a Yorkshire supporter came up and gave him 25 loose prints of Albert Chevallier Tayler's crayon drawings of Edwardian cricketers.

Published in 1905 under the title *The Empire's Cricketers*, the portraits were very popular in their time, and their style caught Ken's imagination.

Ranjitsinhji, by Chevallier Tayler

I really did like them. I think that they were probably done with the help of photographs, and many of the drawings look as if the photographs were posed. But they are of their particular age, and I've always treasured them. For years I meant to have a go myself and see what I could do with a similar kind of drawing.

Then, about ten years ago, we were doing a project at school on sports, and the kids were working from newspaper cuttings. And that spurred me on to get down to doing some myself. The *Yorkshire Post* gave me some old photographs, and I decided to do a set of four: Fred, Brian Close, Ray Illingworth and Dickie Bird.

I use a moss green paper, with a slightly woven texture, and a crayon, occasionally a felt pen. I like the feel of the crayon as you're drawing round the figure. And I like the fact that you can show the texture of the paper coming through the body. Sometimes a line will be enough to show the form. The Fred and Brian Close ones, particularly.

Ken produced 300 prints of each of the four, and they were well-received, not least by the subjects themselves. "I've got the one of me bowling hanging in my dining room," says Fred Trueman when he answers the phone. "I'm stood looking at it now, and it's absolutely marvellous, right down to the creases in my trousers. He's a top class artist, is Ken."

Brian Close agrees: "They are exceptional. He seems to have a great knack of catching both the concentration and the movement."

You've got to understand the form underneath the clothing. With doing anatomy at art school, you're aware of that. You know where the lumps and bumps of clothing are sticking out because of the bone structure which is underneath.

Knowing the players personally, it is easier for me to imagine their action. I work from a photograph, but I have a picture in my mind, like Fred running down the hill to bowl. Hopefully I can incorporate their personalities as well. Even though you're working from a photograph, you've got to be aware of the personality of the player you're drawing, the little idiosyncrasies.

It's not quite the same when I do a modern player. But when I'm drawing Derek Underwood, I'm facing him again. Or Colin Milburn, I'm at Sheffield and I'm fielding in the covers as he's belting the ball at me. "You seem to be everywhere," he said to me at one point. I can spend six or eight hours on one picture, and time just flies. It's a very happy time.

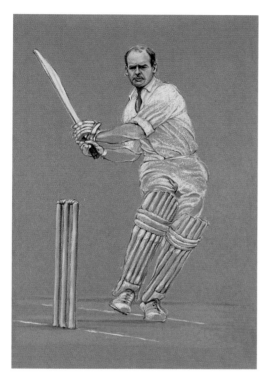

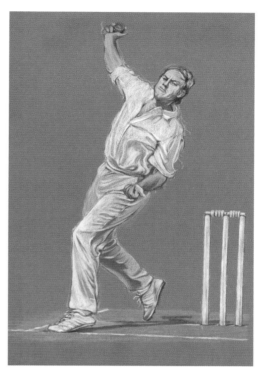

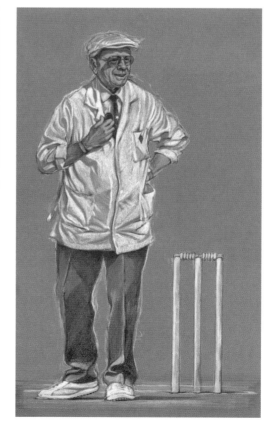

Clockwise from bottom left:
Fred Trueman, Brian Close, Ray Illingworth, Dickie Bird

The sporting facts and figures

KENNETH TAYLOR
Born Primrose Hill, Huddersfield, 21 August 1935

CRICKET
Debut for Yorkshire
24 June 1953 v. Northamptonshire at Headingley

He played a total of 313 first-class matches:
Yorkshire 303, Auckland 5, England 3, MCC 1,
E.W. Swanton's XI 1.

He played in 10 Gillette Cup matches, including the
1965 Final at Lord's when Yorkshire won the Cup.

He played in New Zealand in 1962/63, a member of
the Auckland side who won the Plunket Shield.

He toured the Far East in March and April 1963 as a
member of E.W. Swanton's Commonwealth Tour.

He scored 13,053 runs, including 16 centuries, took
131 wickets and held 150 catches.

He passed 1,000 runs in a season six times, with
1,494 in 1961 his best.

In his last ten years with Yorkshire (1959-68), they
won the championship seven times.

**He passed 150 in an innings on eight occasions,
all for Yorkshire:**
203* v Warwickshire, Edgbaston, 1961
178* v Oxford University, Oxford, 1962
168* v Nottinghamshire, Trent Bridge, 1956
163 v Nottinghamshire, Headingley, 1963
162 v Worcestershire, Kidderminster, 1967
160 v Australians, Headingley, 1964
159 v Leicestershire, Sheffield, 1961
153 v Lancashire, Old Trafford, 1964

He took five or more wickets in an innings once:
6 for 75 Yorkshire v Lancashire at Old Trafford, 1961

He played in three Test matches for England
v. India at Trent Bridge, 4-8 June 1959
v. India at Lord's, 18-20 June 1959
v. Australia at Headingley, 2-6 July 1964

FOOTBALL
Debut for Huddersfield Town
6 March 1954 v. Liverpool at Anfield

He played a total of 301 Football League matches:
250 for Huddersfield Town (1954-65) and
51 for Bradford Park Avenue (1965-67).

He appeared 18 times in the F.A. Cup for Huddersfield
Town and twice for Bradford Park Avenue.

He appeared once in the League Cup for Huddersfield
Town and three times for Bradford Park Avenue.

He scored 15 goals: 14 for Huddersfield Town and
one for Bradford Park Avenue.

From 1953/54 to 1955/56 Huddersfield Town played
in the First Division;
from 1956/57 to 1964/65 in the Second Division.

From 1964/65 to 1966/67 Bradford Park Avenue
played in the Fourth Division.

Between September 1955 and January 1958, he was
selected four times as a substitute for England Under-
23.

He scored three or more goals in a match once:
4 goals for Huddersfield Town against West Ham
United, 23 February 1957.

Early recognition

As early as November 1955, aged only 20, Ken appeared on the front cover of *Charles Buchan's Football Monthly*.

The profile inside the magazine included the following:

> His cool, studious type of play has caught the eye of F.A. selectors. Once experience has ripened his judgment, he will be England's centre-half.
>
> His sense of positional play is uncanny and he always tries to make good use of the ball – the sign of a great player in the making.

He was already in the England Under-23 squad, but a calf injury the following winter – coupled with the relegation of Huddersfield and the increasing distractions of cricket and art – prevented him from fulfilling the magazine's prediction.

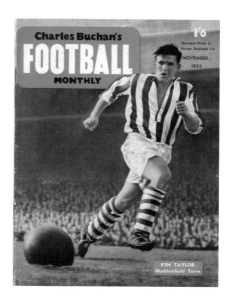

Huddersfield's Own Sportsman

By the autumn of 1957 Ken was both a Huddersfield Town footballer and a capped Yorkshire cricketer.

Such achievements did not generate a celebrity lifestyle, though on the morning of Saturday 7 September Ken did open the new Music Shop in King Street, Huddersfield. It was owned by Aub Hirst, a long-established bandleader in the town. "I didn't get any money for it. I just did it because they asked."

From there he went on to play against Rotherham United at Leeds Road.

Top of the Hit Parade that week was Paul Anka.

> *You and I will be as free*
> *As the birds up in the trees*
> *Oh, please, stay by me, Diana*

An innings to remember

The cover drive that brought up his double century against Warwickshire at Edgbaston in August 1961.

'An innings of much charm and character,' Ron Roberts called it in the *Daily Telegraph*. 'His on-driving was always impressive, and in the later stages his off-driving bore a certain resemblance to that of Hutton himself.'

Characteristically Ken has a clearer memory of his second innings. "I was run out for nought. I can see it now. The bowler was coming in from the pavilion end. I hit the ball to mid-on, shouted 'One' and went. I was running to the danger end, but Brian Bolus never moved. So I just ran straight off to the pavilion. From the sublime to the ridiculous."

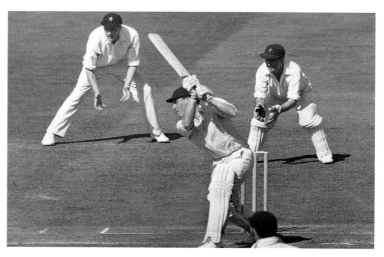

The Taylor family

Ken was the younger child of Harold and Amy Taylor of Primrose Hill, Huddersfield. His older brother, Jeffrey Neilson Taylor, was born on 20 September 1930, almost nine months to the day after his parents' wedding, and Kenneth – "No second name," he says. "I'm just plain Ken" – followed five years later.

Harold Taylor was an intelligent man. "He passed the exam to go to grammar school," Ken says, "but his parents couldn't afford to let him go." He spent the 1930s struggling, like so many working folk at that time, to find work. "He tried everything," Jeff says, "from hairdressing to gardening. I do remember him being on the dole for a while."

During the war, he worked nights at Highfield Gears, making parts for tanks and submarines, then in peacetime he became an engineer in a small mill, repairing looms and making sleys and healds. "The looms had long frames," Jeff explains, "with wooden bottoms and tops, and the wires between used to get bent and twisted. Dad had to repair them."

"This chap took him on," Ken says, "and promised to make him a partner. He used my father's brains, to design all these things, but he never kept his word."

Their father was a heavy smoker and he gradually developed emphysema – not just from the cigarettes but also from his time at Highfield Gears, where he had been engaged in dry stone grinding, with not enough water to wash the dust away. "He was on an oxygen cylinder at the end," Ken says. "It was desperate to see him; he died when he was only 69."

Their mother lived to a much greater age. "She was the driving force," Ken says. She had worked in a small factory, rolling hand-made cigars, before marrying at the age of 22, and after that she stayed at home, looking after her husband and the two boys – and her father when he came to live with them. "She had a very good voice. Jeff takes after her. She sang in the choir at the Buxton Road Methodist Chapel."

"You were an outsider if you didn't sing in Huddersfield at that time," Jeff says, "with all the church choirs and the choral societies. It's a very musical part of the world. When I was a boy, I went to chapel three times on a Sunday: choir in the morning, Sunday School in the afternoon, then choir again in the evening. Dad didn't go; he was a good man, I never knew him raise his hand or his voice, and we never had a drink in the house – but he didn't go to chapel. It was mother who was very keen on it. I sang in the choir with her and, after the evening service, we would go back to one of the houses. We'd sit round a piano and have a sing. Mam used to sing the old ballads like 'I'll Walk Beside You', but she could also sing George Formby and Gracie Fields songs."

They are happy memories, but Jeff does not think of his mother as a woman who was happy inside herself. "I don't know if it was of her own making. It was as though she wouldn't let herself be happy: the sort of person who saw a glass half empty rather than half full."

Their father may not have achieved as much in the worlds of education and work as he might have done if he had been born fifty years later, but he maintained high standards in everything he did. "He was the sort of person," Jeff says, "who, whatever he did, he did extremely well. He was a real perfectionist. He could do electrics. He could do woodwork. And when we were kids, if it snowed and we wanted a sledge, Dad would make it. And it would be better than anybody else's. There was a competitive feeling, and both Ken and I have got that."

"I'd sit indoors in the evening," Ken says, "making wooden kit aeroplanes and boats and tanks. Doing things, rather than watching telly as children do today."

The two boys took different talents from their parents: Jeff the singing from his mother, Ken the art and crafts from his father. But they were both keen sportsmen, and their father encouraged them in that.

Their father played cricket for Almondbury – a good fielder, as Ken would be – and soccer with his brother-in-law Jack. But war came, there was no time for such pursuits and – though Ken remembers him as "a games player, a very fit man" – neither of them has any memory of seeing him in action. "He was dead keen for us to play sport," Jeff says. "When I first signed for Huddersfield as a junior, he was with me. And he took Ken everywhere."

He was a proud parent, but he did not push for his boys to be selected – and, like most Huddersfield folk, neither he nor their mother were ones to express their feelings. "We weren't a touchy-feely family," Jeff says. "Dad would shake hands, that's all, and my mother would virtually push you away."

"Much later, when I was singing," Jeff tells, "I was doing a recital in St George's Hall, Bradford, a lunchtime recital with Keith Swallow on the piano. Dad couldn't come because he was working. So the night before, I took him to the rehearsal. I went right through the programme, and I sang it properly. He sat there as good as gold; he didn't even smoke. At the end he didn't say anything. Then, when we were going back in the car, he turned to me: 'By gum,' he said, 'young lad could play piano.'"

Another time he attended a concert at the Town Hall in Huddersfield – "and they put him in the Mayor's Box. He felt so uncomfortable and out of place, you've never seen anyone look so embarrassed."

"I can't remember my mother or father ever going out," Ken says, "to concerts or pictures or anything. They just stayed at home. My father went down to watch the football at Leeds Road, when Jeff and I were playing, but he only once came to see me playing cricket for Yorkshire. We were playing against Derbyshire at Chesterfield. Although there was a huge crowd, I saw him sneaking in through the gate. I don't think I did very well. I didn't really like anybody I knew coming to watch me."

It was his father who insisted on Huddersfield Town freeing Ken to play cricket at the ends of the football season. Even more significantly, it was his father who directed Ken towards a college education. He was a man of few words, but Ken can still repeat his advice: "You can't play games for ever."

Jeff and Ken, 1941
"We had new suits each Whitsuntide," Ken says. "All the children did in those days. You wore them all year, and nothing else was bought. They were made by a tailor called Waddington, because it was wartime and you couldn't buy ready-made clothes from the shops. After you'd got them, you'd go round to all your aunts and uncles, and they'd give you a penny or twopence for looking so smart."

Orchard Terrace

For the first eleven years of his life Ken lived at 31 Orchard Terrace, Primrose Hill, in South Huddersfield.

The house had two downstairs rooms. The front one was about twelve foot square, contained the piano and was kept neat for Sundays and special occasions. But the one at the back, which served as both kitchen and sitting-room, was always crowded, because that was where the fire was. A curtain in front of the back door kept out the draught.

Upstairs there were three small bedrooms: one for their parents, one – that you reached through the bathroom – for their grandfather, and the third where, throughout their time there, Ken and Jeff shared a bed.

Jeff was much too old to join in the games that Ken played with the other boys in the nearby streets. They kicked about a football, they played cricket in the ginnel at the back and they clambered down the hill, to the River Colne where they spent many hours, throwing stones into the water. "That's how I learnt to throw. Over the top so you don't put too much strain on your arm."

From such beginnings Ken became one of the outstanding fielders of his generation and in 1968, when the Yorkshire and Australian teams competed in throwing a cricket ball after close of play at Bramall Lane, he was the outright winner, with a distance of 114 yards, beating the Australian Paul Sheehan, who had been the favourite.

Jeff can remember the pre-war years when the family would occasionally go in Uncle Jack's car to see the illuminations at Blackpool, but for Ken – four years old at the outbreak of war, ten when it ended – there are no such memories: just a few entertainments in Greenhead Park during the 'Holidays at Home' weeks.

"People didn't move about during the war. After dark the streets were black. If you went out, you had to use a torch with an opening of only a quarter of an inch."

The air raid sirens were a regular occurrence. "The shelter we used was a disused mine, with lighting and seating, just down the hill. As soon as the siren went, we all marched down there. Once there was a huge bomb that dropped in the river and didn't explode. The people in the streets nearer the river had to be billeted farther up the hill, with people like ourselves. In the end they managed to get the bomb out."

"In some ways it was quite exciting," Jeff says. "We had to carry around our gas masks in their cardboard boxes, and on the way home from the shelter we would often pick up empty incendiary bomb canisters. They would be quite a prize."

"There were no bananas," Ken says. "Children of my age didn't know what they were like. We had to have them explained to us. And we had one orange a year, at Christmas. I remember one year we were on our way to the air raid shelter, and I'd forgotten my orange. I made my mother go all the way back for it."

"After the war," Jeff recalls, "I was able to get hold of a bar of dark chocolate with orange cream in it. It was the first time I'd tasted chocolate for years, and I've loved orange cream chocolate ever since."

"There was so much anxiety," Ken says. "The streets were full of families whose children had had to go off to war. Some of them, when they came back, had had a terrible time. Three doors down, one chap had been a prisoner-of-war, and he was shattered. … We had one huge street party when the war was over. It was a community."

The two boys were growing up. Jeff went off to grammar school; he started scoring goals galore in local football, and he performed as a boy soprano in the talent-spotting contests in Greenhead Park. His songs, like 'The Holy City', lifted the spirits of a beleaguered people.

And once again the scene was changed;
New earth there seemed to be;
I saw the Holy City
Beside the tideless sea.
Jerusalem! Jerusalem!
Sing for the night is o'er!
Hosanna in the highest!
Hosanna for evermore!

Meanwhile Ken settled into Stile Common School. He stayed there when, after the war, the family moved to Ingfield Avenue in Dalton, to a house which they rented from their Uncle Jack, where for the first time they had their own inside toilet and where the boys finally acquired separate beds. He could enjoy the latter part of his childhood in those hopeful years when people set about building a better world.

"I was a Saturday's child," Jeff says a little enviously. "I always had to work hard to achieve what I did. But somehow Ken had this happy knack that things happened for him. My mother always used to say, 'If Ken fell in cut, he'd come up smelling of roses.'"

When Jeff left home for National Service and university, it was Ken's turn to forge his way forward in the world of sport.

19

The ginnel at the back of Orchard Terrace

At the back of the house ran a ginnel, a passage which led from the
back doors to the outside toilets that they shared. All day in summer
Ken and the other boys would play cricket up and down the ginnel.
"It was a very narrow space," he says, "so I quickly learned to hit the
ball straight."

Aunt Emily's aspidistra

Drawn while at Huddersfield Art School

Aunt Emily was a great aunt, who lived one street away. "She was a lovely old lady, always welcoming, and my mother used to look in on her regularly. In those days everybody used to look after the elderly folk."

Ken remembers her grandmother clock, hanging from the wall with its pendulum swinging, the pair of pot dogs on the mantelpiece and, of course, the aspidistra. "Everybody had them in their front rooms." Through the window you can see the bungalow where the Carsons lived. Mr Carson managed the Theatre Royal, and their daughter Madeleine married another footballing cricketer, Chris Balderstone.

Professor Land

Henry Land was Ken's maternal grandfather. After his wife died, he moved in with the family, just before Ken was born, and he was there throughout the years of Ken's childhood.

He was an engineer in the mills, and before the war he earned some money on the side as 'Professor Land', magician and ventriloquist at children's parties, performing a Punch and Judy show that he often took on a Saturday to Blackpool beach.

From the age of four or five Jeff accompanied him on these trips to the seaside, taking the fifty-mile train ride there. "He had a collapsible booth, a square box with curtains, and he'd set out a tap mat. And I had to do a tap dance to get the crowd to gather round for his Punch and Judy. I've got a photo of me in a white satin suit and a top hat."

Jeff still possesses all the papier maché puppets that his grandfather had made, among them the dog, the crocodile and the hangman.

But neither Jeff nor Ken feels any fondness for him. "When he was on show," Jeff says, "he was charm personified but, when he was at home, he was an obnoxious bully, a typical Victorian martinet. I think in the end he really believed that he was a Professor. He never helped or did anything but cause trouble."

Or, as Ken puts it, "He was a ventriloquist. He amused the children at parties. But he didn't amuse us at home. He did nothing, only sit about. All we got from him was the smoke from his pipe."

"It was an evil-smelling twist," Jeff says, also a pipe-smoker. "He rubbed it himself. We spent most of our lives in that downstairs room with it."

"I remember finding a flute in the cupboard," Ken says. "He was supposed to have played it when he was younger, but I never heard him."

With their grandfather in the house, the rows soon started. One was so bad that he caused a schism between his four children: Jeff and Ken's mother and Auntie Phyllis on the one side, their two uncles on the other. "I sat on the back doorstep," Jeff remembers, "waiting for the shouting to stop." For the next thirty years, the two halves of the family would not speak. "Then they got too old and forgot what they'd been arguing about."

Sadly their own father, a quiet man with high standards in everything he did, finished up taking second place to his father-in-law. As an engineer in a munitions factory, he was not called up to fight, and this met with the disapproval of the old man.

"But," Ken says, "people didn't own their own houses. So there was no alternative to his living with us."

Their grandfather retired from work. He gave up the children's parties, passing the act to his son who became 'Professor Landson'; he grew more and more fixed to house and armchair.

During the war, Ken recalls, he never went down the shelter with them during raids: "He would sit on the corner of the street with an enamelled basin on his head and he'd just watch the planes flying over, dropping their incendiary bombs which would light up the place. Then the planes would come over with the big bombs. He wasn't particularly worried about being hit. It was like a firework display to him."

When the family moved to Dalton, he did sometimes spend months at Auntie Phyllis's house, but he always came back. And, when Ken went to Art College, he would become a regular subject for drawing practice.

"I used to draw him, draw him, draw him. He'd sit for hours in this cane chair. His clothes would fold into the same positions. He'd stand up, walk around, come back, sit down and everything would go back into the same position."

"I sold this picture at an exhibition. The woman who bought it came back a
month later and asked if she could swap it for something else. She said that
she'd put it on her wall and that, every time she looked at it, it made her feel sad.
I'm glad she brought it back. It's the only picture I've still got of my grandfather."

Huddersfield

The wool trade created the town of Huddersfield, with the River Colne providing soft water for the dyeing and bleaching. Specialising in worsted, like Bradford, the town also developed chemical and engineering industries and, as a result, in the 1930s it was less badly affected by the slump than Bradford.

A travel guide, written in 1950, refers to the town as 'industrial, smoky, crammed with mills and factories', and so much smoke was belched out of all the chimneys that dense smogs formed. "Sometimes," Ken says, "the conductors had to get out of the buses and walk in front of them, showing the way for the driver. The only time the air was really clear was in holiday fortnight, when the mills shut down."

Alas, some of the town's best architecture has not survived. The Cloth Hall was demolished in 1930, to be replaced by a cinema, and in the 1960s the Market Hall was pulled down. "It was a beautiful Victorian building, with arched windows and turrets, and they put in its place a flat-roofed thing that really spoiled the landscape. Halifax has done much better. They kept all their old buildings, like the Piece Hall and the theatre, and now it's a much nicer place to visit."

But for Ken Huddersfield was more than a set of buildings. It was a warm and friendly town, full of family and neighbours, "kind people who looked after each other. You could play out all evening, in the woods or by the river, and nobody would fear for you. Everybody knew who all the children were and, if you didn't behave yourself, it was reported back to your parents. I'd come home from school, and my mother used to say that I kicked the table leg and went straight out to play. And in summer I'd be out till it was dark."

Most of the families had lived in Huddersfield for several generations. "It was a working class town," Jeff says. "You were born there, you lived there and you died there."

But gradually – with the closing of the mills, the sweeping redevelopments of the 1960s and 1970s and the greater mobility that affluence brought – the old communities broke up. Jeff and Ken belonged to the first generation that began to move away.

The chimneys were pulled down. The mills became offices, industrial units and student flats. And the old population of Huddersfield, with its deep-felt sense of community, broke up, to be replaced by folk from all parts of the country and all parts of the world.

The Huddersfield skyline in the 1950s
Photographed by Ken from the corner of Orchard Terrace

The mill in Riley Street, 1977
For some the smoking mill chimneys represented a grim industrial age, where the air was constantly polluted and people worked long, hard hours. But for Ken they belonged to a thriving industrial landscape, an essential part of the Huddersfield where he grew up. "I felt very sad when they pulled all the chimneys down so I came back and drew this one."

Stile Common

On the face of it there was nothing very special about Stile Common School. It was an elementary school, like many others in England at that time. The younger pupils attended the infants' section in the middle of the building, then the boys and girls were separated out to the two ends. At the age of 11 the brightest went away to grammar schools, and the rest stayed put till they were 14 – though this was raised to 15 in 1948.

The school was opened in 1876, up on the hill above the centre of the town, and the building had undergone little change by the 1940s. The pupils no longer wrote on slate and the curriculum had expanded from the three Rs, but corporal punishment was still a regular part of the school's life, as Ken recalls.

> My first headmaster was a man called Bradley, and he had several canes, ranging from a thick, heavy one to a thin one. When you were going to be caned, you had to decide which one you wanted him to hit you with.

The school was just a couple of streets away from the Taylors' house in Orchard Terrace. Jeff was a pupil there and passed the 11-plus. He went on to Almondbury Grammar School and from there to University College, London.

But Ken was unable to follow in his footsteps. To the great disappointment of his teachers, he was not selected for a grammar school place.

> I felt a bit of a failure. And I know that Wally Heap our headmaster was upset about it; he went off to the examination board to find out why I hadn't passed.
> I realise now that I was dyslexic. As a child I was slow to read, and the 11-plus was all about speed. Although I could get things right, they told him that I hadn't done sufficient to pass. I'd only finished half the paper.

Ken stayed at Stile Common. And, by the happiest of chances, his talents were recognised by the headmaster Wally Heap, and he went from strength to strength.

"If he'd gone to grammar school," Jeff reckons, "he would have got lost. It turned out far better for him at Stile Common, especially with Wally Heap."

Heap had become head of the boys' section of the school in 1944, when Ken was ten years old. He was still a young man, in his thirties, prevented by a withered right arm from serving in the war, and he lifted the school with his vision and his infectious enthusiasm.

> He believed in finding the talent in each boy and nurturing it. Regardless of what you were good at, he

"The staff went up the steps to the right. We went up a slope on the left into the playground."

> was enthusiastic about it. He was a great motivator, like Bill Shankly was when he was manager at Huddersfield. When the war ended, all these men arrived as teachers, fit, young men who'd been in the forces, and all they wanted was to do their best for the children, to make the world better than it had been before the war. It was a happy environment altogether. I believe that there was even one term when we had 100% attendance.

Fortunately for Ken, out of all the activities in the school that Wally Heap encouraged, none was closer to his heart than cricket. He played in the local leagues, as a quick left-arm bowler, and he took every opportunity to set up cricket for the boys.

> All summer we played on a concrete strip at the top of the playground. No pads and a cork ball, up against a dustbin. You batted till you were out. You went in at break, then back at lunchtime, then again after school.

Jeff thinks that there were times when it went further than this. "Some afternoons I don't think

they even went back into school. Just as Bill Shankly was mad about football, so Wally Heap was about cricket."

Among the teachers who joined in the sessions was Colin Garthwaite, who played on Saturday afternoons as the professional at Cleckheaton. He was a good enough leg-spinner to have represented the Navy against the Army at Lord's in 1945, playing alongside Trevor Bailey against the likes of Freddie Brown and Charles Palmer, and his bowling gave Ken a grounding in playing leg-breaks that served him well in his years as a Yorkshire cricketer.

> Bowling with a cork ball on concrete, he got tremendous bounce and turn, and he taught me how to use my feet. "If you're going to play me," he'd say, "you'll have to get a lot nearer to where it pitches." After that, I could always play the ball that went away from me better than the off-spinner.

School matches were played at Primrose Hill Cricket Club. Stile Common won the Marshall Shield, for local schools, in each of Ken's last three years, and he progressed to play for the Huddersfield Schools, then the Yorkshire Schoolboys.

Eight for None!

Kenneth Taylor, the Stile Common schoolboy and Primrose Hill bowler, playing for his school in a Marshall Challenge Shield match against Netherton County School last evening, took eight wickets for no runs. Netherton were all out for nine, and six of this total were from extras.

His bat was given to him by Wally Heap, a man's bat with four inches sawn off the bottom and held together with electrical insulation tape, and there was a similar make-do-and-mend feel about the football equipment.

> Mr French, my class teacher, was also the Science teacher. He had a lift-up bench with a glue pot and one bunsen burner. That was the total equipment the Science Department had. And we used the glue pot for mending the cricket bats and the footballs.
> Most Friday afternoons in winter we played the staff at football on the local recreation field. We'd stitch up the ball, and we'd mark out the pitch with sawdust that we collected from the local cabinet maker, Robert Ayres.

Stile Common cricket team
Winners of the Marshall Shield
Colin Garthwaite, back left; Mr French, back centre; Wally Heap, back right.

Then there were the poetry sessions when Wally Heap's wife came in to school and stood before them in the classroom, delivering dramatic renditions of poems like John Masefield's 'Cargoes', Alfred Noyes' 'The Highwayman' and John Greenleaf Whittier's 'Barbara Frietchie'. The class then learned and recited them, and almost sixty years on Ken can still trip them off his tongue with gusto and relish.

The wind was a torrent of darkness among the gusty trees,
The moon was a ghostly galleon tossed upon cloudy seas,
The road was a ribbon of moonlight over the purple moor,
And the highwayman came riding –
Riding – riding –
The highwayman came riding, up to the old inn-door.

Ken's report for Christmas 1948 placed him second in a class of 39. The following year, he was second out of 46. His work was consistently good but, with no national curriculum or school league tables to create pressure, and with the staff – back from the war – happy to stay after hours, Ken's sporting potential had plenty of opportunity to be realised.

Wally Heap remained at Stile Common for thirty years, becoming headmaster of all three sections of the school in 1952 and headmaster of the primary school in 1958 when the older pupils went off to a new secondary school that was opened a mile away at Longley Hill.

In 1976, when the school celebrated its centenary, he spoke to the *Huddersfield Examiner*, revealing once more his passion for sport: "Although Stile Common is a district very close to the town centre, it has a tremendous village atmosphere of its own and the school has been an integral part of that. There was always a terrific liaison between the school and the local people, particularly with Primrose Hill Cricket Club who lent us their field for games, matches and sports days."

Among those encouraged to sporting success by the school were not only Jeff and Ken but also Arnold Hamer, who played cricket for Derbyshire, and Trevor Cherry, who played football for Huddersfield, Leeds and 27 times for England. "I took him down to Leeds Road for a trial," Ken says.

Football. Cricket. Even the Art. Ken's three great talents were all spotted by Wally Heap, and his life has owed so much to him, the dedicated master who was happy to work long hours, long years at the school up the hill and who made a difference to so many.

I always wanted to be like Wally Heap. I was guided towards teaching because I wanted to be like him.
He was the greatest influence on my life.

"Wally created Ken's career for him," Jeff says. "Any talent needs to be recognised and fostered, or it dies."

I wonder. How many talents like Ken's have been lost in schools where there was no Wally Heap?

I was very lucky.

STILE COMMON COUNTY EXIT SCHOOL.

REPORT FOR *CHRISTMAS* TERM 19*4 8*.

NAME :- Taylor Kenneth.
NUMBER IN CLASS :- 39.
POSITION :- 2

SUBJECT	MARKS POSSIBLE	MARKS ACTUAL	REMARKS.
ARITHMETIC:			
Mental	20	16	G.
Mechanical	20	14	G.
Problems	20	15	Absent.
ENGLISH:			
Reading	10	8	V.G.
Poetry	10	8	V.G.
General English	20	15	G.
Composition	20	13	V.G.
Writing		4	
HISTORY	20	18	V.G.
GEOGRAPHY	20	19	V.G.
SCIENCE	20	15	G.
ART	20	19	V.G.
PRACTICAL DRAWING	20	17	V.G.
HANDWORK	20	19	V.G.
TOTAL	240	200	

A very satisfactory term's work. Most of his work is of a very high order and extremely pleasing.

J. French. Class Teacher.

Head Teacher. W. Heap.

This is an excellent report, and I am pleased to note that Kenneth has maintained his usual standard. He must not be content until he has reached the top.
As a first class sportsman and school prefect, he is a very prominent member of the school.

29

A natural progression

At the age of ten Ken was playing on the wing in the Stile Common School football team that won the Turner Cup, and in his last two years at the school, when he was captain, the team won both the Turner and Crowther Cups and did not lose a match.

For four years he played for the Huddersfield Schoolboys' side. In one of his first games, in October 1946, when they beat Woodlesford, the newspaper described him as 'a junior Stanley Matthews, who was a great deal too much for the opposing full-back.'

From this he progressed to Leeds Road. He could not sign terms till he was 17, but he played as an amateur in their lower teams. Then in January 1952, at the age of sixteen, he was selected for an F.A. Youth side, to play at Villa Park, and in September of that year, now 17, he became a Huddersfield Town professional.

Cricket had more of a national structure, and Ken progressed in schoolboy sides from Huddersfield to Yorkshire to the North of England against the South and finally to represent England against Wales.

At the age of 11 Ken won a place in the Yorkshire Schoolboys' side. A year later Herbert Robinson – President of the Huddersfield and District Cricket League – attended the Stile Common Speech Day and presented him with his cap, and also a bat, which the *Huddersfield Examiner* said 'had been given by an anonymous donor.'

"I always assumed that it had been given by the school but, when I went to see Wally Heap, just before he died, he told me that my father had given it. I've no idea why he did it like that. Perhaps he couldn't afford to give Jeff something as well."

Another newspaper cutting tells of a Stile Common School Sports Day, held at Primrose Hill Cricket Club, in which Ken won the 160 yards, the 320 yards and the Cricket Ball Throw and was second in the High Jump, earning himself the title of Victor Ludorum.

The only photograph of the event is of the boys' team taking on the staff in the tug-of-war contest. The staff were the winners.

Huddersfield Schoolboys, 1949/50
Back row, left to right: Wright, Gill, Ladbrooke, Johnsey, Wilson, Bates, Wadsworth
Front row: Hildred, Taylor, Benfell, Dougherty

In the summer of 1949 the Yorkshire coach Arthur Mitchell came to Huddersfield and invited Ken to attend nets at the Fartown ground. "He gave a long talk at our school. I think it went over the heads of a lot of the boys. I remember one of them asking, 'What's a maiden over?'"

At Morley Ken made runs for Yorkshire Schoolboys against Lancashire. He came in to bat when Keith Kettleborough, later to play football for Sheffield United, was bowled, and he put on 44 in a partnership of 81 with his captain, Bryan Stott from the Airedale and Wharfedale Schoolboys' side. 'They gradually wore down Lancashire's attack and scored freely with some enterprising batting.'

The two were also picked, along with Bradford's Doug Padgett, to play for the North of England against the South at Denton in July, with Bryan Stott again captain. This time Ken made 51, the only half-century of the match, and the boys enjoyed a magical evening at the local Technical School, listening to Denis Compton and the New Zealand captain Walter Hadlee, who had come across after a day's Test cricket at Old Trafford.

In the match programme there was a message to the boys from England's Bill Edrich: 'I would like to wish you all a very successful and happy match, and may we see some of you in the Test teams of the future.'

They were thrilling days for the 13-year-old Ken. "It was the ambition of every boy in Huddersfield who played football, to play for Huddersfield Town, and it was the ambition of every boy who played cricket, to play for Yorkshire. And for me, it all seemed to happen as a natural progression."

Wally Heap immediately wrote to the *News Chronicle*, pressing for Ken's inclusion in their national coaching scheme, but the reply put him in his place. There were proper procedures to be followed, and 'we have no doubt that at the moment Taylor is in good hands.'

The next summer, his last at school, Ken captained the North of England team, now including Oldham's Geoff Pullar. Against the South at Morley – in front of 'The Old Firm', Jack Hobbs and Herbert Sutcliffe – he hit 64 and took three wickets for 37.

"It was that summer that my parents took me to Bournemouth for a week. It was the first holiday away that I'd ever had and, while I was there, I had to go to Harrow for a trial for an English Schoolboys side. My father took me. I'd never heard of Harrow. I had no idea where it was."

Ken played at Cardiff against the Welsh Schoolboys, making an unbeaten 21 in an all-out total of 87. Then in November he did receive a letter from the *News Chronicle*, saying that Jack Hobbs and Herbert Sutcliffe had picked him out for a trial.

The following summer he was scoring runs in the Yorkshire second eleven. He was now no longer a schoolboy, but he was still only 15 and he was picked again to represent the English Schoolboys against the Welsh. This time, according to one reporter, he 'walked to the historic wicket at Old Trafford and charmed the critical cricket professors in the pavilion with superb batsmanship.' Against Ruthin School's young Indian fast bowler Robert Duray-Aiyar and his leg-spinning school friend Bob Barber, he hit a 'masterful' 50, the reporter describing him as 'a natural ball player in the Compton pattern. … Some say his birth on August 21, 1935, was the most important event in Yorkshire since June 23, 1916'. There was an asterisk after this latter date, and at the bottom was the explanation: 'June 23, 1916: Len Hutton was born.'

Ken, together with Bryan Stott and Doug Padgett, were all – like the Master, Len Hutton – playing for the county before they turned eighteen. "They pushed you through at that time," he says. "It was a good way. If you're going to play, you don't want to be waiting till you're 20 or 21."

Brother Jeff

From Primrose Hill to Glyndebourne via the University of London and Fulham Football Club, Jeff's journey through life has been just as unusual as that of his younger brother Ken.

But as the older of the two, the first in the family to strike out from the West Riding, Jeff has had the greater struggle. Ken was five years younger and, with the example of a brother making his way in so many different spheres, he never felt self-conscious about being at times an art student, at times a rugged footballer.

Like Ken, Jeff was a gifted sportsman with an artistic temperament, and this marked him out from an early age. "My father always used to say that I was a bit of a loner. I've always been a dreamer; I used to bump into lamp posts when I was a small boy. I think Ken's the same. He's in his own world a lot of the time. He's got this ability to shut everything off."

But, where Ken stayed mostly in Yorkshire till he was 33 and thought nothing of his unusual mix of lives, Jeff left home at 18 and had to cope with an inner feeling that he was somehow not like everybody else around him.

"When I played football," he says, "I was the only player in the league with a degree. When I was at University and at the Royal Academy of Music, I was the only person who played professional football to pay for my studies. And when I appeared each week on television in 'Song Parade', I was the only one in the group who had an academic or a sporting background. I always got on well with everybody but somehow, wherever I was, I always felt different. Maybe that's why I never realised how good I was at anything."

Like Ken, though, he was good, very good – and from an early age, too.

In the winter of 1943/44, as a 13-year-old boy at Almondbury Grammar School, he played football not only for the school on Saturday mornings but for the junior Priestroyd Ironworks team in the Huddersfield Red Triangle League. As a quick and skilful centre-forward, taller than Ken would be but not quite as muscular, he scored 62 goals in nine matches and attracted not only a big write-up in the local paper but a visit from Alf Young, the coach at Huddersfield Town. By the end of the winter he had signed for Town as an amateur, and he was training with the older players.

"Priestroyd Ironworks played in the rec at the top of Newsome Road, a very bumpy pitch on a slope and always wet. All the pitches seemed to be on slopes – but that turned out to be good practice for later, when I was playing in the Football League. It was amazing

These Boys Have Something To Laugh About

TERRY CROWTHER (left) is goalkeeper for Priestroyd Ironworks, the wonder team of junior football in Huddersfield, with a record that can scarcely have been beaten.

They play in the Under 15 Section of the Red Triangle League, and in ten matches this season have scored 156 goals. TERRY has been beaten only once—and that was last Saturday. A goal record of 156—1 is phenomenal.

On the right is JEFF TAYLOR, like most of the team, a schoolboy. In nine games this season (he missed a match last Saturday because he was engaged in the Minor F.A. Trial) he has kicked 62 goals! This young centre-forward's best return was 13 (out of 23) against Birkby Youth, and he has had 9 (twice) and 8 goals in other games.

how many of the top grounds were sloping."

School was less impressed, the headmaster suspecting that in the school matches he was saving some of his strength for the afternoon – but "it wasn't true. I was young and fit and at that level I could easily manage both."

At the end of one season he broke a toe and found himself in plaster from the knee down, with a bracket and rubber heel to help him to walk. When the heel came off one day he went for help to the woodwork master, only to be refused – on the grounds that he had incurred the injury playing for Priestroyd Ironworks and not the school. He finished up back in hospital, having his leg re-plastered.

He became the school's outstanding young sportsman: captain of football and cricket, cross-country champion and Victor Ludorum on Sports Day. He also did well in the classroom, passing his Higher National Certificate and winning a place to study Geography at University College, London. And he starred in the school's productions of Gilbert and Sullivan: Ko-Ko in 'The Mikado' and Guiseppe in 'The Gondoliers'.

He left for London in the autumn of 1949 and, even after a year's National Service, he felt that he was an out-of-place Northerner in the strange and unwelcoming city. "On my first evening I was walking along Hendon Lane, lugging my huge case with all my worldly goods, and a police car stopped beside me and I was asked to open up the case. I remember wondering, 'What sort of place have I come to?'"

He was doing his football training in the mornings at Highbury and playing for the Huddersfield Reserves – until one Thursday when he received at his digs a short letter from George Stephenson, the Town manager:

You have been selected to play against Chelsea at Huddersfield, on Saturday November 12th. 1949 K.O. 2.30.p.m.
Please report to this ground at 1.45 p.m. prompt on that date.

The game was marred by gale force winds, accompanied by rain and sleet, prompting the Chelsea full-back Billy Hughes to describe the conditions as 'the worst I've ever met' but, with his side losing 2-0, Jeff scored a late goal that provided plenty of cuttings for his scrapbook.

He scored in four of his first five games, the exception being at Stoke where he was marked by the England centre-half Neil Franklin, though even on this occasion "I played so well that he went off in the second half with a twisted knee, from trying to catch me."

He was earning six pounds a week, five in summer, and, without a student grant, it was sufficient to support him through university. "To me it wasn't a job. I would have played for nothing."

At the start of his final year his professor advised him to cut back on his football in order to achieve a good degree result, and he asked George Stephenson to give him time off. But an alternative solution was offered: Jeff would be transferred to Fulham, also in the First Division, and that would allow him to stay in London.

In two years he had played 71 League and Cup games for Huddersfield and had scored 29 goals.

Fulham exchanged Len Quested, the England 'B'

wing-half, for him. Jeff thinks that there was also some money paid on top by Fulham. Such matters were kept secret from the players themselves, and there were certainly no agents involved. So it is impossible to say whether the value placed on Jeff was anywhere near the £34,500 British record for a transfer. All Jeff does know for sure is that he was made a signing-on payment of ten pounds.

It was November 1951. There was briefly talk that 15-year-old Ken might be part of the package, with the whole family moving to London, but their father was not interested. Ken needed to continue his training at Art School – and one day to play cricket for Yorkshire.

Fulham's Chairman was the comedian Tommy Trinder – "The day I signed, he invited me to his show at the Prince of Wales Theatre," Jeff says – and also on the board was Chappie D'Amato the band leader.

"There were good footballers there," he says, and he runs through the inside-forwards who provided for him: "Bobby Robson, a straightforward player, you could depend on him. Johnny Haynes, a very compact player, good with the ball and with great awareness. And Jimmy Hill: I liked him, but he was a great talker." And the club itself? "It wasn't at all like Huddersfield. It was more of a Christmas club really than a football club. A fun club. In many ways it suited me. I felt very much at home."

After university he signed up for the teacher training course at the Institute of Education, but his teaching practice at Chiswick Grammar School left him deciding that he was pursuing the wrong career. "They put me to teach a class of six sixth-form girls, and it frightened me to death. I didn't know anything about girls. All I'd done up to then was play football and been in the air force. I couldn't cope with it."

But his music was still developing. He remembers once hurrying off from a first-team match at Anfield to sing the baritone lead in 'Merrie England' with the Colne Valley Male Voice Choir, his first professional engagement, and at university he had been an active member of the Music Society, singing the Count in 'The Marriage of Figaro' and Escamillo in 'Carmen'. He went for an audition at the Royal Academy of Music and began training there as an opera singer. Fulham were relegated from the First Division in his first season, alongside Huddersfield, and, unlike his old side, they did not come straight back up. Somehow he was often injured, or losing his place to Bedford

Jezzard, and in three years he played only 33 matches – though he scored 14 goals.

"My real trouble," he says now, "was that I didn't realise how good a player I was. I had no idea how many clubs were interested in signing me when I left Town; I've only now been finding out. And perhaps I didn't spend enough time training. I always had something other than football to do."

Among the 'something other' was his blossoming friendship with Biddy Chevassut, a violin student at the Royal Academy, and in March 1954 they married, an innocent pair who spent their wedding night in a hotel at the foot of Box Hill before Jeff returned to Craven Cottage the next day for football training.

In August that year he followed his former Fulham manager Bill Dodgin to the nearby Third Division club Brentford, much to the disappointment of Chappie D'Amato who saw Jeff as a kindred spirit: 'As you well know,' he wrote, 'I have the highest regard for your ability as a serious singer – and the same goes for your football ability.'

Down in the lower reaches of the Football League he scored 34 goals in 94 games, but his career was effectively ended in December 1956 when he suffered a fractured cheekbone in a Cup tie against Crystal Palace. "In those days it was a tough game. There were no substitutes, and you didn't like the other side to see you were hurt. You'd get your nose broken, you'd have a patch put on it, and you'd go back out. At Huddersfield Roy Goodall, the trainer, would just come on with a bucket and a sponge. 'Get up, you're all right, get on.' That was your treatment."

That was essentially his treatment when his cheek bone was crushed. "It was all puffed out. They took me off, they had a look at it and sent me back out. In fact, I scored an equalising goal and got lots of letters afterwards, from people saying how much they admired me, but afterwards my face had blown up like a balloon. Biddy came into the dressing room, and she fainted. She had to be carried home."

By the most curious of coincidences, on the same afternoon at Vetch Field, Swansea, his younger brother Ken – who was now at The Slade and fitted in his football preparations on the Brentford training ground with Jeff – was stretchered off with the one serious injury of his career. The aluminium studs of the Swansea winger Cliff Jones tore into the muscle of his leg, leaving him with a deep wound which required twelve stitches on the outside and five in the muscle.

Jeff was sent for plastic surgery in East Grinstead. "I had to go down on my own on the train, and nobody in the club got in touch till Tuesday." He had an operation to pack out the cheek, and another to remove the packing; the severed nerve is still numb fifty years later. The advice he was given was clear: "If you want to be a singer, you must give up football."

"I was captain of Brentford at the time, enjoying my football. I didn't really want to give up."

In an attempt to persuade him to continue with them, the club pointed out that his pay would be going up by one pound a week, but his singing was now more important.

Fortunately, the chairman at Brentford was Vic Oliver, the comedian and violinist, and Jeff had already appeared on his radio variety show 'Band Box'. This led – soon after he finished playing – to his joining the Cliff Adams Singers for a weekly television show, 'Chelsea at Nine', broadcast from the old Chelsea Palace. Their repertoire mixed light music and classical. Among the guests were Mario Lanza and Danny Kaye while his fellow singers included Anita Harris and a young Gerry Dorsey, later to be reincarnated as Engelbert Humperdinck. From this followed regular work with 'Song Parade', 'Friday Night Is Music Night' and the long-running 'Sing Something Simple'.

He had changed from Jeff Taylor the footballer to Neilson Taylor the baritone, and his musical career oscillated between opera and popular songs. One time he would be in Australia, training up a backing group for Tommy Steele; another he would be at Glyndebourne, playing Arbace in Mozart's 'Idomeneo' alongside a young Italian tenor on his first visit to England, Luciano Pavarotti.

He spent a year in Mantova in Italy, studying with Pavarotti's teacher Ettori Campogalliani, and this led to opera work in Covent Garden and Rotterdam. But one thing did not quite lead on to another. He played the part of Montfort in a radio broadcast of Verdi's 'Sicilian Vespers', but mostly he found himself back in the world of light music. He duetted with Ethel Merman on a recording of 'Annie, Get Your Gun', and he had a spell singing on cruise liners.

In 1974 he went to Scotland to become Professor of Singing at the Glasgow Academy of Music, and he stayed there for 18 years. "I've been lucky," he says. "I've always done something that I've enjoyed doing."

He is now back home in the West Riding, living south of Huddersfield, and he still sees a few select

pupils. One of them, Anthony Michael Moore, flies him out to the great opera houses of Europe to hear the final run-through whenever he sings a leading role.

He has been married twice, relationships which have not lasted. So he is left on his own to turn over the questions of his life, the might-have-beens. Could he have achieved more in the world of opera? Could he have been a more successful footballer?

'Taylor,' reads one magazine profile from his early footballing days, 'is only of medium build but he moves like quicksilver, has good ball control and is very dangerous anywhere near goal with either foot or head. He is tipped by many of the finest judges of the game to be an international of the future.' At the end of his career his manager Bill Dodgin called him 'a first-class player who might have been a great player.'

'Taylor,' reads a recent review of his reissued 'Sicilian Vespers', 'sings with such elegance of line, such a lovely sustained pianissimo, that he melts the heart. His more forceful singing is equally expressive.' Another reviewer wonders why he is not a familiar name: 'His tone is rich and secure. In all respects he is superior to the renowned Sherrill Milnes.'

"I know now that I was pretty good at the things I did, but somehow I didn't know at the time. I seemed to lack self-esteem."

Jeff's life has taken him from Primrose Hill to Craven Cottage, from Glyndebourne to Mantova to Glasgow, moving among people far beyond the horizons of his parents' world. "But I'm still a Yorkshireman," he says with warmth. "Whatever I've done, nothing has knocked that out of me."

Primrose Hill Cricket Club

From Stile Common School to Primrose Hill Cricket Club was a short walk up the hill – and a natural progression for a keen, young cricketer. The school played its matches and held its sports days there, and the club captain Frank Noble – later a senior policeman in the town – lived across the way from the Taylors' wartime home in Orchard Terrace.

Among those who had gone up the hill from Stile Common to Primrose Hill was Arnold Hamer, almost twenty years older than Ken. He had stepped up from Primrose Hill to the Bradford League and, when in 1949 he set a new league record of 1,106 runs, he was recruited by Derbyshire. He was already 33, but such was his experience in the competitive environment of Yorkshire league cricket and such was his rugged, phlegmatic temperament that he scored 1,000 runs for the county in each summer in the 1950s.

He had two brothers, both of them stalwarts of Primrose Hill, and one sold fish and chips out of a little wooden shed further up the road. "As a family we used to have fish and chips twice a week during the war," Ken remembers. "It cost five pence: twopence for chips and threepence for a fish."

Ken's cricketing prowess was spotted early and, not long after the family moved to Dalton, he started going across town twice a week in winter to attend the Shed at Marsh for coaching sessions with the old pro Horace Walker. "It was a miserable place in winter," he says. "Cold and damp, like a railway siding shed. There were six or seven of us, in the one net, and, if we turned up early, we had to stand in the bus shelter and wait. I went across there on the bus every Tuesday and Thursday."

Ken made his debut in the Primrose Hill first team in the summer of 1949, only 13 years old and on the small side for his age. In his first match, bowling off-breaks, he took two Dalton wickets for 14 runs. The following Saturday, against Shepley, he captured all the local headlines with a spell of eight for 37. 'Five were clean bowled,' the *Examiner* reported with excitement, 'one stumped, one caught and the other leg-before-wicket. With careful nursing, he is unquestionably a youngster of great possibilities.'

'He was described as almost unplayable,' wrote the *Yorkshire Evening Post*, sending a reporter to Stile Common School 'where he was putting in some bowling practice on the concrete pitch.' In the interview that followed, 'Kenneth gives credit for everything to his headmaster, Mr W.E. Heap, and to his other masters. … But he prefers batting to bowling and proudly recalls how he made 70 not out for the school in a cup final last year.'

By the next summer, his last at school, he had grown considerably, and he was a regular member of the Primrose Hill side that won promotion to the top division. He finished top of the batting averages with 337 runs at 42.12 and third in the bowling, with 35 wickets at 12.11. Among the cuttings in his mother's scrapbook are reports of his seven for 45 against

Primrose Hill Cricket Club, 1951
Ken is sitting on the right, with his captain Frank Noble in the middle. Between them is the professional Leslie Binns. "He was a quick bowler," Ken remembers. "With rather a low arm. A bit of a slinger."
Behind Binns is Gordon Holroyd: "He was a good batsman. He could have been a very good one, but he was a bit casual."

The old pavilion at Primrose Hill

Armitage Bridge and of his all-round success against Dalton: seven for 22 and 35 not out.

"If you scored a fifty or took five wickets for under 30, they'd take a cap round the ground, to hold a collection for you." With crowds of several hundred, such collections could be worth twenty or thirty pounds – but, alas for Ken, the Dalton match was away. "And it was a cold day; there were only a few people there. I got seven for 22, they went round with a cap, and I got eleven shillings and sixpence: ten shillings from our President, Norman Hopkinson, a shilling from my father and sixpence from the crowd."

The *Examiner* reporter attended the last match of the season, at home against Golcar. 'In a blaze of September sunshine', he watched Ken score 43 and take five wickets, declaring the youngster the Cricketer of the Season:

> For an hour and a half we watched young Ken Taylor playing with the ease of a veteran, making shots comfortably and with assurance. He has proved himself to be the outstanding cricketer of the season, and with luck should continue to join the list of Huddersfield players who have played for the county. His batting was a joy to behold, and later in the afternoon we saw him bowling and fielding in most impressive style.

Primrose Hill was a community club, with a core of dedicated supporters, men and ladies, and Ken recalls as a boy having to pull the roller two nights a week before being allowed in the nets. The adjoining Crimea pub had a well-kept garden at the back, and there were tennis courts as well as a bowling green next to the Liberal Club. There was none of the concrete facing

that now surrounds the field, just an open view from the hill across to the town and beyond. Everything was looked after and in good order – and even the legendary rowdiness that emanated from the beer hut in the far corner never seemed to be unpleasant.

"Very few of the team had all their own kit," Ken's school friend Tommy Lyons recalls. "As a lad I used to take the first team bag on the trolley bus to the away matches. It was five shillings for two of you to carry it, and I used to drag it there all on my own."

In the summer of 1951 Ken, still only 15, played regularly for the Yorkshire second eleven, making 386 runs at an average of 20.31 and taking 17 wickets at 19.11. He was clearly a county player in the making, but his football was also progressing and by late August, when the seasons overlapped, he was in heavy demand.

One Saturday, after he had played football for the Huddersfield Town third team in the morning, he opened the batting for Primrose Hill, putting on 164 for the first wicket with a returning Arnold Hamer. But on another Saturday there was a more bizarre turn of events.

"We were playing at Primrose Hill, and I was just walking out to bat. And Alf Young, the trainer at Huddersfield Town, appeared in his car. I saw him come through the gates. The Reserves were a man short, and he was hoping that I'd get out and go off with him. And I did. I was out for one run."

The *Examiner* continues the story: 'The white-flannelled young Ken made a 20-minute car dash to Leeds Road. A snappy change into soccer kit and Ken came out to help Town to a 4-0 win. How many did Ken get? … same as at cricket – ONE!'

"Then I came back after the soccer match and fielded."

The next summer, to advance his cricket, Ken played for Lightcliffe in the Bradford League and, though the club finished runners-up in the first division, the ground did not appeal to his artistic eye and he moved to Brighouse for the summer of 1953. Runs flowed: after six matches, he had scored 355 and only been out once. For the Yorkshire second eleven he made centuries against Notts and Staffordshire. And in June he made his first appearance in the full Yorkshire side.

In less than four years the little 13-year-old who captured the headlines with his off-breaks had become a well-built, free-scoring batsman fulfilling every Yorkshire boy's dream of playing for his county.

Art school

Ken's golden sporting career took him after school to a job on the ground staff at Leeds Road: weeding the pitch, sweeping the stands and cleaning the senior players' boots. "I soon got tired of that," he says. "It didn't last long, maybe two or three months." He decided that he could do better for himself, and he talked it over with his father. "He said to me that football and cricket wouldn't last forever and that I should learn a trade." He had been good at Art at school, and he enrolled at Huddersfield College where he studied for an Intermediate Diploma, followed by the National Diploma in Design.

"It was five days a week, nine to five, and three evenings: quarter to seven to quarter to nine. By the New Year, when I went over on the bus to Headingley on the other two evenings, I was having to fit my football training into lunch hours."

So, by the time he began studying for the National Diploma in 1954, he was playing in the Huddersfield Town first team, and he only met up with his fellow footballers on Saturdays. All week he would be studying such subjects as anatomy and perspective, then on Saturday afternoon he would be marking great centre-forwards like Nat Lofthouse and Billy Liddell.

Cricket took up more time in the summer, but he had not yet established a regular place in the Yorkshire first eleven and much of its season coincided with the college's summer break.

The footballers trained in the morning, then killed time in the snooker halls and playing golf. But Ken was away at college, his days always full.

According to Ray Wilson, who signed as a professional footballer at the same time as Ken in Autumn 1952, "he always had an excuse to be going somewhere. 'I'm at college … I'm singing today.' I hardly ever saw him."

At college he could forget the cares of professional sport. "We had one chap Ron Darlington, who was in the commercial side of the Art Department, and he was a good soccer player. He made a career as an interior designer in South Africa. He'd occasionally ask about the football, but most of the people weren't interested. It's nice that they weren't. You could leave it. You'd done that. Then on Saturday you were fresh into it."

'Taylor,' wrote Eric Stanger in the *Yorkshire Post* in February 1955, 'approaches his football more like an old-time amateur than anyone else I know today.'

"I can agree with that somewhat," Ray Wilson says. "But the guy who wrote it, he wouldn't have been tackled by Ken, I think. The big centre-forwards all fancied themselves at that time, but Ken could put them in their place. He was so strong."

'The average professional sportsman has too much leisure time on his hands,' Ken wrote in a newspaper article. 'Everyone who turns to the game for a living should use his spare time to prepare for the days when he can no longer play. Sport should only be a stepping stone.'

His wife Avril reads the words fifty years on. "That's his father talking," she says.

The Art Department was just one wing of Huddersfield College, where there were vocational courses in everything from catering to engineering, including a textiles course which attracted students from Europe to the thriving mill town.

For Avril, a student there five years after Ken, the art students stood out from the rest of the college. "We were the mucky ones. Smocks, jeans. We revelled in our difference."

For Ken there was little time for a social life in those years as a full-time student, but he does remember the youth club in the church next to the college. "We used to meet on Saturday evening and after church on Sunday. A whole gang of us. Played table tennis, drank cups of coffee. And we'd go for a walk to Castle Hill, as a group. Go to someone's house and listen to the wireless."

Some of them set up a trad jazz group, with a double bass, sax, piano and clarinet, and performed in Springwood Hall Gardens – though Ken's musical career got no further than "fiddling about at home on a clarinet."

Among those at the college at that time was the athlete Derek Ibbotson, who would go on to break the world mile record.

Also hanging about the youth club and the jazz band was Brian Jackson, a lad a year or two older than Ken from nearby Staniforth Road. He went to grammar school and on to Cambridge University, returning to write his influential study of Huddersfield schooling, 'Education and the Working Class'. Later he would become a driving force in the founding of the Open University.

With the mills and factories generating a fresh post-war prosperity, it was a happy time to be in Huddersfield, and Ken looks back fondly at the orderliness of everyday life: the patient queues that formed outside telephone boxes, the honesty boxes that bus passengers used if they got off before the conductor reached them, the respect that boys were taught to show for park-keepers and policemen.

For Brian Jackson, the working-class culture radiated from 'the close centres of family life into that whole web of ties – kinship, friendship, the shared childhood or working life, the formal groupings of club, band, choir, union, chapel – all the many strands of neighbourhood that reach out to attain community.'

At Art School the curriculum was much more structured than it became in the 1960s and 1970s. "You were taught the different mediums and their limitations. The emphasis on drawing and draughtsmanship stayed with me and will do forever. That's the foundation. You've got to be a good draughtsman before you can perform in any other direction."

Of all the staff there, he remembers most clearly his calligraphy teacher, Joe Carruthers. "He looked down when he talked to you, over the top of his glasses, with his head on one side. And he always worked in a suit, with a collar and tie. He was meticulous in everything he did. When he was decorating his own house, he used a number six sable and he'd wear cuff links and a white shirt. And not a speck of paint went anywhere. His hobby was photography. Batley Variety Club imported high-powered stars, and he took photographs of them. One time he made an appointment to see Shirley Bassey, and she turned up very, very late. 'My time,' he said, 'is as important as yours.' He really rocketed her. She came back two or three times, and she was never late again."

Joe Carruthers

"He used to go around town, criticising the sign-writers up ladders," Avril recalls. "He was a wonderful draughtsman. He did drawings of mill machinery. As perfect as a photograph."

One evening Ken and Avril were invited to his house. "He was one of the first to have a stereo system, and we went to hear it. We sat in the right places – that had to be perfect – and we listened to a train running through the room. That was the evening. We had our coffee and went."

It was another world from that of Ken's fellow footballers.

Starting at the top

It was just before three o'clock on Saturday 6 March 1954 when Ken emerged from the tunnel at Anfield. Wearing the number five shirt, he was running onto a football pitch as a Huddersfield Town first-teamer for the first time.

He was 18 years old, and he was now both a Yorkshire cricketer and a Huddersfield Town footballer. 'He must be the envy of every sport-minded Yorkshireman,' one newspaper wrote. 'No other son of the shire ever entered both First Division football and first-class cricket before he reached the age of 19.'

He could hardly have been thrown into more of a lion's den. The Liverpool crowd numbered 46,074, the largest soccer gate in England that day, and their roar was like nothing he had ever heard at Leeds Road.

> It was a tremendous experience, running out of the tunnel onto the pitch, with The Kop at one end all cheering and shouting. But there was no aggro, it was all well-mannered and, once the game got started, you hardly heard them. The build-up before a game is always worse than going out onto the field.

Ken was replacing the injured Don McEvoy, one of the set of six defenders who had been ever-present the previous winter when Huddersfield had won back at the first attempt their long-established place in Division One. Now, after 32 games, Town were third in the division, pressing for their first championship title since the legendary three-in-a-row in the 1920s. McEvoy, from Golcar, was a local hero, a reliable defender who had played every one of those 32 games, but he was struggling with a torn thigh muscle and Ken – who six months earlier had been a forward in the third team – was pulling on the number five shirt.

On Thursday he had been expecting to play as usual in the reserves but, making his way at the end of the day from College to the nets at Headingley, local reporter Bill Carter caught up with him in the street – 'in one of those tea-time drizzles which typify March' – and broke the news.

On Saturday morning there was a letter card from Jeff in Fulham: 'Go out and have a great game ... You must go on to the field tomorrow and feel just as good and important as any of the others, because you are.'

The team reached Liverpool in thick drizzle. They took a coach from the railway station but manager Andy Beattie stopped it some way before they arrived at the ground.

He always made us get out and walk the last mile. I don't think any other manager ever did it. He said it was to loosen us up before the game. So we walked to the ground in twos and threes, among all the fans. Nobody ever seemed to take any notice of us.

The fans were all cheering as the teams took up their positions, and Ken found himself marking Louis Bimpson, a bustling centre-forward. According to the *Huddersfield Examiner*, 'the young Taylor was not having an easy time against him' and 'was a little bewildered by the pace.' But the *Yorkshire Post* was much more positive: 'Refusing to be rattled by Bimpson's energetic challenges, he gradually settled down and in the second half had the upper hand.'

A further threat came from Billy Liddell, 'the flying Scotsman' whose legendary brilliance had caused many football followers to nickname the club 'Liddellpool' but, when he in turn burst through the middle, 'Taylor was on the spot to foil him.'

Liverpool scored early, but Huddersfield hit back with three goals and at 4.40 Ken ran off the field on the winning side. Meanwhile in London brother

Ken arriving at Headingley on the night of his selection

Jeff was scoring twice for Fulham against Blackburn Rovers.

The following Saturday Town entertained a Newcastle United team which included the great Jackie Milburn. 'Taylor was twice prominent in the opening exchanges' before Town went 2-0 up but in the second half, with United having pulled the score back to 2-1, 'Monkhouse avoided the attention of Ken Taylor long enough to give Milburn the opportunity of equalising.' Then, in a contest in which 'there was never a dull moment', Town's Jimmy Glazzard hit a winner. It was two wins out of two for Ken, and Town were only five points off the top of the table.

The next week they were at Old Trafford, and Ken was up against the England centre-forward Tommy Taylor.

> Tommy was the best player I marked. He was a tall man, good in the air, but he was also quick. Usually the big centre-forward would just stand in the middle and jump and head. But he was different. When there was a corner, he'd go out of the penalty box and come in on a run and head the ball. He was difficult to mark. The places he went before he came in for the run, they were unusual.
>
> He was a Barnsley lad. He used to come and watch us play cricket when we were at Old Trafford.

Matt Busby's Manchester United side, full of rising stars like Taylor and Duncan Edwards, was the talk of the football world, and that afternoon they beat Huddersfield 3-1, their forwards 'thriving on a plentiful supply of long, raking passes which often had the Town defence floundering in the mud.' The exception to this, it seemed, was the battle of the two Taylors: 'United's Taylor was worlds removed from that stylish, resourceful tactician he is now known to be. He had difficulty in controlling the ball or keeping his feet on the slippery surface, and even worse difficulty in trying to give the slip to his namesake, a young art student and Minor Counties cricketer, who stuck to him closer than a brother.'

Ken played four more matches before the return of McEvoy. The first two were won, but defeat at home to Spurs, then away to eventual champions Wolves, left them in third place at the end of the season. It was the highest that Town had finished since 1936 – and, in the half century that has followed, they have never matched it, never again finished even in the top half of the top division.

Such was Ken's promise that in the following September he replaced McEvoy in the first-choice line-up, his first three matches requiring him to mark Cardiff City's Trevor Ford, Sheffield Wednesday's Jackie Sewell, and once more Tommy Taylor. All three were among the country's most formidable goal-scorers, with Sewell holding the record transfer fee of £34,500, but none of them scored against Huddersfield. As the newspaper headline put it, 'Three £30,000 leaders couldn't master Ken'.

At Cardiff, Ford – the most prolific goal-scorer in the Welsh national team's history – tried to intimidate his young marker:

> He gave me a lot of talk early on, how he was going to kick me up in the air. He was a tall man, and I was really quite small. With men like him and Tommy Taylor, when you stood behind them, you often couldn't see anything. But I was quick in the tackle so I coped.

In the game at Old Trafford, according to reporter John Hepburn, Ken 'survived a shaky start to tame World Cup man Tommy Taylor. Tommy's namesake was a relentless, hard-tackling shadow the centre-forward couldn't shake off.'

Hepburn seemed to have an access to the players not granted to today's writers: '"I feel dead beat," Tommy told me as he lay soaking in the bath after most of his team-mates were dressed. "I could sleep for a week," said Ken in the other dressing room.'

Three winters later Tommy Taylor would die in the Munich Air Crash, but his thoughts on Ken are preserved in a cutting, written by Bill Fryer, in Ken's scrapbook:

'Tommy Taylor once told me that the hardest centre-half he had come across was a chap with his own name, Ken of Huddersfield. Ken is no more than medium height and weight but, said Tommy, "He was always with me. And he was as hard as bricks. When you felt the weight of his shoulder, it was like bumping against a lump of coal."'

It had been a baptism of fire for Ken, and he had emerged from it with distinction. But he was young, his life was full, and he did not dwell on the significance of it all.

> When you start out, you're full of enthusiasm and the fear of failing isn't there. It's only when you've been playing for a few years that the reality starts to dawn on you.

John Charles

Ken had played just two matches in the Huddersfield Town first team when he was selected to play against Leeds United in the final of the West Riding Senior Cup. It was the evening of Monday 15 March 1954 and, with 23,000 spectators in Leeds' floodlit ground, Ken was at centre-half. His job was to mark the great John Charles.

Charles – originally from Swansea – had converted from centre-half to centre-forward the previous winter and, although he was still a defender when he played for Wales, he was the leading goal-scorer in the whole Football League. In 39 league matches in that winter of 1953/54 he scored 42 goals, a total that still stands as the Leeds United record.

> He was big and strong, and he had tremendous balance. He was very quick but, like most of these big chaps, he was deceptive. He didn't appear to be moving, but he was. He would weave and sway his way through, disguising his movement and throwing his man. Henry of Arsenal is like him, but he's much more slender. He appears to be moving, whereas John would be going without appearing to be going.
>
> And, of course, John was also great in the air. He could adapt, play either forward or defender. And he was a very nice man. They called him the gentle giant, and that was quite correct. He wasn't a dirty player. He could beat you with skill, not with brawn.

"Sometimes I think I would have been a better player with a bit of devil," Charles said in his autobiography, "but it's nice to know that I've gone through a long career without hurting anyone."

The West Riding Cup Final, March 1954. It was Ken's third match as a first-teamer, and he had already played at Anfield in front of 46,000, and against the great Jackie Milburn of Newcastle. Now he had an even greater test.

Albert Nightingale, the former Town inside-left, put Leeds ahead in the 16th minute, only for Tommy Cavanagh to equalise ten minutes later. It was 1-1 at the interval and, according to the *Huddersfield Examiner*, 'Taylor's positioning kept the Welsh international out of the picture in the first half.'

With centre-forward Jimmy Glazzard limping off, Huddersfield played the whole second half with ten men, allowing Leeds to press forward repeatedly. It was a game for strong-hearted defenders, and 'Taylor not only beat Charles in the air but made three magnificent ground tackles with the Leeds man in full cry for goal.'

Alas, it was not enough. Nightingale – never a man to stay on his feet if he could gain advantage by falling – won a free kick just outside the Town penalty area, and John Charles drove home the winner.

The Cup was presented to Leeds, and fortunately there was no repeat of the pantomime some years earlier when Huddersfield Reserves had got the better of Leeds Reserves in a Junior Final, only to find that the Leeds club had not brought the trophy to the match. On that occasion John Charles had been at centre-half, marking Ken's brother Jeff.

For the first time as a Huddersfield first-teamer Ken was on the losing side – though the *Yorkshire Post* picked him out as one of Town's best players.

But strangely he never played a league match against 'the gentle giant'. Leeds would not get promoted from Division Two till the year that Huddersfield were relegated from Division One, then Charles was transferred to Italy. When he did return briefly to Leeds, Ken was wintering in New Zealand. Their paths did not cross again till the year before the Welshman died.

> I did this drawing of him, and I wanted him to sign it. So, not long before he died, Jeff and I went up to see him. He was living in a semi outside Leeds. He was suffering from Alzheimer's but he seemed very happy, and he remembered the game when they didn't bring the Cup with them.
>
> He told us that, when he went to Italy, he wasn't earning any more than he had at Leeds, but he got a big signing-on fee. And, of course, they idolised him over there. He was a god to them.

Juventus had narrowly escaped relegation the previous winter. Now, with Charles at centre-forward, they won the Italian League. In five winters with them, playing in a country renowned for the dominance of defensive systems, he scored 93 goals in 150 games. He was 'Il Re', The King.

> John Charles was the best. In all the years I've played and watched football, I've not seen anybody better.

Contracted

Ken still has all the contracts from his career as a professional footballer.

Until the dispute of 1960/61, all footballers were restricted to a maximum wage and they could not transfer to another club if their own club wished to retain them.

Ken's pay year by year at Huddersfield Town		
	Weekly pay (£)	
	Winter	Summer
1952/53	7	6
1953/54	9	8
1954/55	11.10s	10
1955/56	15	12
1956/57	15	12
1957/58	15	14
1958/59	20	17
1959/60	20	17
1960/61	20	17
1961/62	20	20
1962/63	20	20
1963/64	*Ken in New Zealand*	
1964/65	30	30

Extra payments first appear in the contract for 1961/62, as follows:
£5 per match extra when playing in first team.
£2 per week extra when first team is in top five of League table.
£2 per match extra when attendance is 20,000 or over.

In the event, only three matches in 1961/62 attracted attendances greater than 20,000 and Huddersfield finished 7th in the League table. So Ken has no memory of these extras. "But then I never did read the contract properly," he says. "There didn't seem any point reading it as you were tied hand and foot. You just signed and smiled."

In the year between 1 July 1954 and 30 June 1955, Ken played 36 first team matches in Division One, as well as six FA Cup ties. For this, he received a total income of £550.

Linking this to the rise in the Average Earnings Index in the last fifty years, this would be the equivalent to his earning about £25,000 a year in today's economy. Or, put another way, Ken earned in a year less than half what the top footballers today earn in a week.

However, in the past fifty years, earnings have risen much faster than prices and, if you link his pay to the Retail Price Index, his pre-tax income in 1954/55 would only have been sufficient to buy him about £10,000 worth of goods at today's prices. Or, to pursue the comparison with today's top footballers,

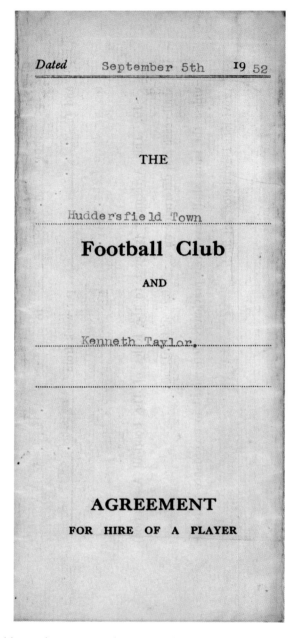

Dated September 5th **19** 52

THE

Huddersfield Town

Football Club

AND

Kenneth Taylor.

AGREEMENT
FOR HIRE OF A PLAYER

Ken in a year could earn the same spending power that some of them can earn in a day.

Ken's career was drawing to a close by the time the maximum wage was abolished. His annual income in 1962/63, with bonuses, rose to just under £1,300 and if, when he returned to Huddersfield for the winter of 1964/65, he had played most of the matches, he would have earned £1,700 – though even this, as a pre-tax income, would only have bought him about £23,000 worth of goods at today's prices.

An Agreement made the 5th

day of September 19 52 between Harry

Beever of Leeds Road,

Huddersfield. in the COUNTY OF Yorkshire

the Secretary of and acting pursuant to Resolution and Authority for and on

behalf of the Huddersfield Town FOOTBALL CLUB

of Huddersfield. (hereinafter referred to as the Club)

of the one part and Kenneth Taylor

of 30 Ingfield Avenue,Dalton,Huddersfield.

in the County of Yorkshire. Professional Football Player

(hereinafter referred to as the Player) of the other part **Whereby** it is

agreed as follows :—

    1. The Player hereby agrees to play in an efficient manner and to the best of his ability for the Club.

    2. The Player shall attend the Club's ground or any other place decided upon by the Club for the purposes of or in connection with his training as a Player pursuant to the instructions of the Secretary, Manager, or Trainer of the Club, or of such other person, or persons, as the Club may appoint. [This provision shall not apply if the Player is engaged by the Club at a weekly wage of less than One Pound, or at a wage per match.]

    3. The Player shall do everything necessary to get and keep himself in the best possible condition so as to render the most efficient service to the Club, and will carry out all the training and other instructions of the Club through its representative officials.

    4. The Player shall observe and be subject to all the Rules, Regulations and Bye-Laws of The Football Association, and any other Association, League, or Combination of which the Club shall be a member. And this Agreement shall be subject to any action which shall be taken by The Football Association under their Rules for the suspension or termination of the Football Season, and if any such suspension or termination shall be decided upon the payment of wages shall likewise be suspended or terminated, as the case may be.

    5. The Player shall not engage in any business or live in any place which the Directors (or Committee) of the Club may deem unsuitable.

    6. If the Player shall prove palpably inefficient, or shall be guilty of serious misconduct or breach of the disciplinary Rules of the Club, the Club may, on giving 14 days' notice to the said Player, or the Club may, on giving 28 days' notice to the said Player, on any reasonable grounds, terminate this Agreement and dispense with the services of the Player (without prejudice to the Club's right for transfer fees) in pursuance of the Rules of all such Associations, Leagues, and Combinations of which the Club may be a member. Such notice or notices shall be in writing, and shall specify the reason for the same being given, and shall also set forth the rights of appeal to which the Player is entitled under the Rules of The Football Association.

As Witness the hands of the said parties the day and year first aforesaid

Signed by the said Harry

Beever and Kenneth

Taylor.

Kenneth Taylor

(Player).

In the presence of

(Signature) *A. Galvin*

(Occupation) Asst Secretary.

(Address) 87 Crosland Street,

Crosland Moor,HUDDERSFIELD.

Harry Beever

(Secretary).

These are the first six clauses of Ken's first contract.

The following year the contract dropped from clause 6 the right of the Club to terminate the Agreement on grounds of the Player's being palpably inefficient.

The 1956/57 contract, in outlining the Rights of Appeal of the Player, added the following:
The Player may apply to The Football Association for a personal hearing to answer a charge of misconduct under F.A. Rule 45. He may also be represented at the hearing by the Players' Union provided that such a representative is not a member of the legal profession.

The 1960/61 contract contained a new clause:
The Player agrees that he will not without written permission of the Club grant interviews to nor write articles for or disseminate any information (acquired in the course of his employment by the Club) to newspapers or other publications nor take part in television or radio programmes.

Following the threat of strike action in January 1961, the 1961/62 contract included the following:
6. Unless this Agreement has previously been determined as hereinafter provided the Player shall not before the 28th April 1962 approach or entertain approaches from any other Club or person with a view to changing his Club, unless otherwise agreed by the Club and Player. Under no circumstances shall the Player make any payment to agents or persons other than Clubs and persons regularly employed by Clubs and concerned in the engagement of Players with a view to obtaining employment.

7. The Player shall not directly or indirectly induce or attempt to induce a Player employed by another Club to leave that employment for any purpose or reason whatsoever.

With rumblings about match-fixing, a further new clause appeared:
8. The Player shall not offer to or receive from another Club or the Players of another Club a bonus or any inducement to win lose or draw a match.

And for the first time:
11. This Agreement may be terminated at any time by mutual consent of both Club and Player.

Yorkshire cricketer

"The first county match I saw was the first one I played in," Ken says, though probably – if he could disentangle the threads of memory – he will have acted by then as twelfth man, running errands and getting the drinks in for close of play. So he will have known what to expect when he found himself selected. "Everybody had their places in the dressing room," he says. "If you were a young player, you just waited."

It was Wednesday 24 June 1953, three weeks after the crowning of the Queen. Yorkshire were playing Northamptonshire at Headingley, and Ken was in the team because the Lord's Test had taken away Len Hutton, Willie Watson and Johnny Wardle. With captain Norman Yardley on Test selection duty, Harry Halliday and Brian Close unfit and Bob Appleyard recovering from TB, it was a makeshift side, and they were 99 for six when Ken walked to the wicket. 'He made it 100 with a placed single off his second ball,' the *Yorkshire Post* reported, 'but he had only scored four more – with a late cut off Tribe – when the cunning Australian floated a slow ball and bowled him.' Apparently it was 'a batsman's paradise', and Yorkshire's loss by ten wickets was the first time that they had ever been beaten on home soil by the Cinderella county from the Midlands. It got worse in the next match at Cardiff when they lost for the first time – home or away – to Glamorgan.

Ken was scoring abundantly in club and second eleven cricket, but for the first eleven he managed just 21 runs in four innings. When he returned for a third game later in the summer, they lost at Trent Bridge for the first time since 1906, and he added only ten more runs. It was a hard summer for Yorkshire, and their final record – winning only six of their 28 matches – left them in an unprecedented twelfth place. 'A general depression seemed to overtake the side,' was *Wisden*'s verdict.

But Ken was too young to know much about any of this. He was only seventeen, he had not yet played First Division football, and not all the older players were keen to pass on to him their knowledge of the first-class game. "The more they told you, the sooner you'd be pushing to take their place."

His hero, as with so many young Yorkshiremen, was Len Hutton, though he played only once with him: in July 1954, against Combined Services at Harrogate. Hutton was making a comeback after a month out with back problems, and he scored a masterly 163.

"It was the only time I saw him play, but it made me realise how far I had to go to be like him. I remember asking him what he thought about when the bowler

Len Hutton

was running in, and he said, 'I try to think of nothing at all. I do my thinking in the nets.'"

It took Ken 15 attempts to reach his first fifty, and that was a hard-fought 56 at Neath against a Glamorgan side captained by the intimidating Wilf Wooller. "He was the first of the sledgers, chuntering away all the time, particularly against Stotty and myself. At one point their spinner Jim McConnon came up. 'Take no notice of him,' he said. 'Get on with your own game.'" Ken's was the only fifty of a low-scoring match and, by the second innings, when Yorkshire wanted 68 for victory, there was little left of the pitch. "Wooller took the new ball, and he rubbed it on the concrete steps. Billy Sutcliffe, our captain, complained to the umpires, but they did nothing about it. Wooller was an amateur so he could get away with murder. And the umpires were terrified of him." Ken was out for a duck and, after 42.3 overs, Yorkshire had struggled to just 49 for seven. Then rain brought an end to the grim contest.

"We got our own back at Swansea a couple of years later. Johnny Wardle was bowling, and Wilf hit it straight back at him. Johnny could be a bit of a comic, and he quickly put it in his pocket, pretending to look where it had gone. And Wilf stood there, thinking it had gone for four. Then Johnny took it out of his pocket and showed it to him, and he had to go. And of course it made him look a bit of an idiot."

Wardle was another of the outsize characters in the Yorkshire side, a combative slow left-armer who had little tolerance for fielding lapses when he was bowling – though, on one occasion, Ken found himself told off for fielding too well.

"We were down at Hove. Ten and eleven were in, and I was fielding at mid-wicket. They pushed one just to me, nice and slow, and set off for a run. I picked the ball up and looked at the running end for Johnny to be there. I just had to throw it gently to him, but he wasn't there. So I had to aim at the wicket and I missed. 'Christ, Johnny,' I said, 'you should have been behind the wickets.' And he said to me, 'You don't run nine, ten, jack out.' And he got him out next over."

This was another world from the playground at Stile Common or the league matches at Primrose Hill, and it took some acclimatisation. And behind the scenes there was always the presence of the Chairman of Cricket Brian Sellers, the autocratic captain of the great Yorkshire side of the 1930s. Nothing that Ken's generation did could ever match the achievements of that team and, if he came to think a player was not giving his all, there was no hope for him.

Some people reckon that Sellers stood in the way of Hutton ever becoming Yorkshire captain – because he reckoned that he was 'swinging the lead' with his back problems. And he was certainly behind the downfall of Frank Lowson, an opening bat good enough to play seven times for England.

"Nothing flustered Frank. He was a quiet, gentle fellow. But he looked a casual player. And he wasn't a good runner between the wickets. We played at Bradford, and I was waiting to go in, sitting on the balcony next to Sellers. Frank hit a ball straight from the pavilion end down to the football stand and ambled the first run. He looked, turned and was ambling the second. The fielder, Arthur Jepson, picked it up, threw it over his head and hit the wicket, and he was run out. 'He'll never play for Yorkshire again,' Sellers said."

A week later, despite being high in the national averages, Lowson was out of the team.

It was a hard environment, not one that Ken – nurtured on encouragement – appreciated. But he was young, he was happy to be playing for Yorkshire, and he had no thought of failure.

Pre-season training at Headingley: Fred Trueman, Jimmy Binks, Ken Taylor, Bob Appleyard, Vic Wilson, Mike Cowan

Huddersfield scenes

Golcar cottages
"These are stone-built weaving houses in a very old part of Huddersfield. Strong, solid buildings. The moors are just beyond, with the Huddersfield Narrow Canal running out towards them. They've cleaned it out so that there's a nice ride into Lancashire – if anybody wants to go into Lancashire."

King's Mill
"After we'd moved to Dalton, I used to pass this every day on my way to Stile Common School. It was a thriving mill at that time, with all its weaving sheds."

Minutes from glory

Ken had long and eventful careers in both cricket and football, but there is one single moment from those days that he revisits more often in his conversation than any other. And that is the goal that was scored in extra time at St James' Park, Newcastle in front of 52,380 spectators, on the afternoon of Wednesday 16 March 1955.

It was the sixth round of the FA Cup, and Huddersfield had reached that stage by knocking out Coventry City and Torquay United, both of the Third Division, then Liverpool – now in the Second Division – away from home.

The match at Anfield had been a highlight for Ken. The Kop's idol Billy Liddell had been moved to centre-forward that season, and in icy conditions Ken – suffering from reaction to an inoculation and a doubtful starter at one point – snuffed him out of the game. It was a performance which brought a glowing tribute from the former England goalkeeper Frank Swift in his report.

Billy Liddell
"He was a great all-round player, very skilful. Good in the air, good on the floor. A great mover. He had that instinctive ability to be in the right place at the right time. Jimmy Greaves had it, too. People like that, they don't always know why they are where they are. But then, if they had to think about what they were doing, it would be too late."

Ken Taylor Is Town Star

LIVERPOOL 0, HUDDERSFIELD TOWN 2

THE MATCH I SAW by FRANK SWIFT

LOOK at the score chart and you will see that Huddersfield knocked Liverpool out of the Cup with two second-half goals. Don't you believe it

Huddersfield won this match in the first 20 minutes, and the man who won it for them was centre-half Ken Taylor.

Perhaps it is a bit too early to call Ken a man, but if he can play like that at 19 years of age, heaven help the centre-forwards who happen to be knocking around in five years' time.

Taylor hasn't the elegance and the grooming yet. He's still a bit coltish. But at the rate he's going, he'll be quite a player when he grows up.

After all, an afternoon's football against Billy Liddell on ice-hard, snow-dusted Anfield is as awkward a proposition as you could find.

But young Taylor dug into the tackle with strength and accuracy, he beat his man in the air, he never gave him room to work the ball, and —even on a pitch like that—he somehow found the time and the balance to be constructive.

Billy Liddell probably realised even more astutely than Taylor that everything depended on those first 20 minutes. So the Liverpool centre-forward put all his fierce strength into his bursts for goal. Again and again he flung himself through the middle, trying desperately to force that early break which could have beaten Huddersfield.

But it was no use. All he could get past Taylor was a couple of neat flicks and one power shot which boomed off Huddersfield goalkeeper Jack Wheeler's chest. Nothing more.

Taylor kept coming at him, and slowly the clamps on the lifeblood of Liddellpool screwed tighter and tighter. More and more attacks broke down and, as Huddersfield gradually won control of the midfield, the Liverpool defence began to come apart and they began to overkick their forwards

It was the old Andy Beattie plan of drawing the half-backs in close and playing the opposing inside-forwards out of the game—though yesterday it was helped by Liverpool's weakness on the wings

No matter. Once that tense, first-half struggle had dipped Taylor's way, Huddersfield slipped into some of the football of which tehy are acpable.

Right-back Ron Staniforth directed his team with some neat positional play and the Huddersfield forwards were cleverly covered and fed with ground passes by their wing-halves, Len Quested and Bill McGarry.

The first goal came after five minutes of the second half. Two Liverpool defenders—Geoff Twentyman and Laurie Hughes—missed a clearance and Huddersfield inside-left Brian Frear slicked a ball through to centre-forward Jimmy Glazzard.

Glazzard turned it wide to Albert Hobson on the right-wing, and he pivoted on the ice before scoring with a low cross-shot.

Seven minutes from the end Frear again rolled a lovely pass through the middle to Glazzard, and this time the centre-forward was able to run on calmly and take an unhurried shot which hit goalkeeper Charlie Ashcroft before it hit the back of the net.

The draw for the sixth round was:
    Birmingham City v Manchester City
    Huddersfield Town v Newcastle United
    Notts County v York City
    Sunderland v Wolverhampton Wanderers

As well as five teams from the First Division, there were Birmingham City and Notts County from the Second Division promotion race and little York City of Division Three North.

When the four games were played on Saturday 12 March, they drew in a combined attendance of more than 214,000 spectators, with 54,000 at Leeds Road. Town had not reached an FA Cup semi-final since the war and now – at home to a fellow mid-table side – they had a golden opportunity.

Ken's task was to mark the Newcastle centre-forward Vic Keeble, a tall man who looked to get on the end of crosses from the wingers Len White and Bobby Mitchell. In the report in *The Times*, 'White's marksmanship was hard and accurate, and Mitchell's precise centres would have created trouble for a less compact defence.' But 'Taylor mastered Keeble on the ground and timed his jumps so well that his taller opponent was usually beaten.' Or, as Eric Stanger in the *Yorkshire Post* put it with more colour, 'Young Taylor, giving away several inches in height and pounds in weight, tackled Keeble so hard that the Newcastle centre-forward was often toppled like a tree under the woodman's axe.'

Town went ahead in the 63rd minute with a goal from close range by Jimmy Glazzard and, despite missing several chances to make it 2-0, they were still heading for the semi-final two minutes from time. The ball was down Newcastle's end when the Town forwards appealed for a penalty and, in the moments while they looked across at the referee, Mitchell picked up the ball and broke away on the left wing towards the other end.

> Bobby Mitchell beat Ronnie Staniforth. I looked down the field, and nobody was coming back. So I went across towards him, leaving Laurie Kelly to pick up Keeble behind me. That's what we had to do.
> But Mitchell got the cross in, Jack Wheeler stayed on his line, and there was nobody left to mark their right-winger Len White.

'Mitchell put over a perfect cross, which White met near the far post to head past Wheeler.' It was a 1-1 draw, and the replay was set for 2.15 on Wednesday afternoon. Despite being a working day, a crowd of 52,000 filled the banks around St James' Park – and, years later, Ken met one of them, a Huddersfield man with a story to tell.

"At the first match I was standing with the Newcastle supporters and we had a really good time. At the end they said, 'Are you coming to watch the replay? … We'll look after you.' They met me off the bus, we had a few pints and a sandwich, and they took me to the ground. We were cheering and clapping; we had a real good day. Then they bought me a couple more pints and put me on a bus back to Huddersfield."

The semi-final draw pitted Manchester City against Sunderland while the winners at St James' Park would face York City of the Third Division. Victory in the replay would almost certainly lead to a Wembley Final, the first for Huddersfield since the war. They set off from Huddersfield on Wednesday morning, wearing sprigs of white heather given to them by the Mayor.

With the Huddersfield Town defence at its uncompromising best, 'the game was as hard as granite and as colourless', and there were no goals at the end of ninety minutes, still no goals as the half-time whistle approached in extra time.

'Just when it seemed that both sides had given up all hope of scoring', Newcastle's right-wing Len White floated across a corner and Jack Wheeler the Town keeper came forward to punch it away.

> When we went away on a coach, Jack used to bring his ukelele and sing George Formby songs. He was really very good on it.

But his punch only went some fifteen yards out to Mitchell, whose right-footed lob cleared the keeper and was on course to dip just under the crossbar.

> Both Ron Staniforth and I had got back onto the line, ready to head it away, and Jack staggered back and knocked us both into the back of the net.

'Wheeler, retreating hard, Staniforth and Taylor all finished up in the back of the net. With them was the ball.'

I'd rather have his job than mine
When I'm cleaning windows.

> Jack was such a nice fellow. He always had a smile. He was a great team man.

Ken was young. He was not to know then what he knows now: that Town would never again come so close to an FA Cup Final at Wembley, that the following year they would be relegated and that he would spend the rest of his time with them in Division Two.

> I can still see that ball coming down. All three of us were lying on the ground, watching it coming down.

Ray Wilson

Ray Wilson signed for Huddersfield Town in the summer of 1952, at the same time as Ken.

He had been working nights repairing wagons for the railway at Shirebrook Pit near Mansfield, and he only stumbled into football when a local schoolmaster persuaded him to make up numbers for a youth team. "We got beat 6-3, but I scored all three goals. He was an ex-professional player at Derby, and he knew Roy Goodall the Huddersfield trainer. So he wrote to him."

It was a sudden change in fortune in his life. "My mother had died," he says, "and I was working with these two men who were on piece work. They had you running everywhere for them, fetching and carrying so that they could earn more money. And if you did anything that wasn't right, you got an absolute bollocking or a clip round the earhole. I was really miserable at that time."

From Shirebrook to Huddersfield. The journey took him most of the day: a bus to Chesterfield, then after a long wait he went on to Sheffield. "And from Sheffield I took this bus that went up to Penistone, and suddenly there were all these hills ahead of me. It was all very flat where I'd come from, and it was the first time I'd been beyond Nottingham and Derby. But when I saw the hills and the open moors, I was feeling as if my whole life had changed on that one bus journey. And I was thinking, 'This is where I want to be.'"

He was signed on as an inside-left, spending his week sweeping the terraces and on Saturday playing in the third team. "We used to play teams of miners. They'd come up from the pit at one o'clock and, when we played them at two, they were still covered in coal. Ken played in that team, too – but I don't remember him sweeping up the terraces with me. He always seemed to have something else to do."

The following spring, while Ken was busy at Huddersfield College, Ray was called up for National Service. "I did my training for the Royal Artillery at Oswestry. All the professional footballers used to get sent to Preston, but boxing was the big sport at Oswestry and, as it was summer, we didn't play football. So I got posted out to Egypt. The only football I played for two years was on sand."

Meanwhile Ken's football had leapt forward. By the time Ray's two years were up and he returned to Leeds Road in Spring 1955, Ken had played most of a season in the first team, and Huddersfield were comfortably placed in mid-table in Division One.

As Ken remembers it, Ray was nowhere near the first team. He had been tried in the forward line and at left-half, and he had not made much impression. "He was not showing any signs of being the great player he turned out to be. And towards the end of the season the retained list was coming out. And he wasn't going to be retained. Then on one of the Tuesday mornings, when we played the practice matches, we were short of a full-back. And Bill McGarry said, 'Play Wilson at full-back.' And Ray never looked back."

"They had to keep you on for six months after National Service," Ray says, "but I was getting to the stage when I was seriously thinking about going in and asking to move on. There must have been at least twenty of us on the staff who had never played in the first team, and I hadn't even settled to a position."

His own memory is that it was Roy Goodall who suggested his playing at left-back. "There was a chappie called Lawrie Kelly who had joined from Wolverhampton Wanderers, and he still lived down there. He only came up on Fridays so, when the first team played the second team in training, there was a gap at left-back. Roy Goodall had been a full-back himself, and he thought I ought to have a go. And I didn't really fancy it. I still thought of myself as an inside-forward. In those days the full-backs were all six foot, 12 to 15 stone. It was silly really. They were supposed to stop these wingers who were little chaps, steaming along like whippets, and they could never turn and move to keep up with them. I've seen milk turn quicker."

The change of position was an immediate success. "You need a lot of luck in all walks of life," Ken says, "but particularly, I think, in sport. If Ray hadn't played that day at left-back, he might never have had the chance to become the absolutely great player that he became."

Ray puts it slightly differently. "Football had to happen for me," he says, "because it was the only thing I had. Ken had other things. He didn't have to push to get himself that little bit further. I'm pretty sure he'd have had no problem at international level. A lot of people thought that he was a bit small for a centre-half, but he was a massive build and he was quick. He could tackle as good as anybody, straight on, and he was exceptional in the air for a small man. He had a real spring in him. As a centre-half he was very secure. If he hadn't had the cricket, if there'd only been soccer, there would have been a hell of a chance that he'd have been a good international player. But then I don't think the soccer or the cricket really affected him. They were just a sideline. He'd have got on all right with just the teaching."

"Ray was a big smoker," Ken remembers. "Before we went out onto the pitch at the start of play, he always got his cigarette out of the box. And he put it on top of the box, and a match and a matchbox. Ready for half-time." "No, not half time," Ray says. "At the end of play. Everybody smoked in those days. When I was in the England side, there were more smokers than non-smokers. That was before the proof that smoking was bad for you. As soon as I knew it caused cancer, I stopped straightaway. I've never touched one since."

"Ken was a dreamer," he says. "I remember a year when we were sitting near to the danger zone in Division Two. And one Friday we all had to go into the boardroom for a talk. We were all sat around the table, and we had this talk about the game the next day. I can't remember who we were playing. It might have been Leyton Orient. 'It's imperative that we win this game. … A great club like Huddersfield … If we can't beat Leyton Orient … If we go down to the Third Division and Leyton stay up …' On and on it went, and I looked across at Ken. It was obvious his mind was wandering. 'You've got to do this to Leyton Orient and that to Leyton Orient.' I think Ken was looking out of the window at one point. Then eventually, when it ended and we all got up and left the room, I was walking along and Ken caught up with me. 'Who do we play tomorrow?' he said."

In October 1955, only months after he had become a full-back in the practice match, Ray played five times for the first team. But the club's fortunes had slumped, they were heading for relegation from the First Division, and all five matches ended in defeat, with 21 goals conceded. Then Bill Shankly arrived as second team coach, Ray blossomed under him, and by September of the following year he was ready to make the number three shirt his own for a long spell.

The club was now in Division Two, but it did not stop Ray from being called up to the full England team three winters later, to play against Scotland at Hampden Park. It was a grim game: "I now know why the entertainment tax was taken off football," one spectator told *The Times*. But among the few bright sparks in the drab 1-1 draw were a 'gallant' performance by Ray Wilson, playing with a nose broken after only two minutes, and a display of great skill and energy by Scotland's inside-right Denis Law, who only a month earlier had been playing alongside Ray at Huddersfield. 'His stamina was boundless,' *The Times* reckoned, 'his fire unquenched to the end.'

With no more pay in the First Division than in the Second, Ray stayed four more winters at Leeds Road. By the time he moved to Everton in the summer of 1964, he had won 30 England caps – and he had only ever played five games in the First Division.

"There was very little difference between Division One and Division Two, and everybody was getting the same wages. So you might as well live somewhere nice. A place like Blackpool would have a good side. Now it's different; it's 'I don't care how lovely it is; what are you going to pay me?'"

The move to Everton allowed him to taste the glory of an FA Cup victory at Wembley and to play alongside such greats as Alan Ball and Howard Kendall. But, as Ray points out, "It was much easier playing for them than for Huddersfield. The ball hardly ever came over the halfway line."

The quiet man of the 1966 World Cup winning team, he finished with 63 England caps, the same number as the more lionised Kevin Keegan and Alan Shearer, more than Johnny Haynes or Stanley Matthews. His style of play at full-back, with its emphasis on ball skill and speed as well as defensive tackling, belonged perfectly to Alf Ramsey's set-up, even if it alarmed the traditionally-minded Roy Goodall, who had spotted his potential in the first place.

Goodall had been a member of Herbert Chapman's great Huddersfield side in the 1920s. He was an old school full-back, big and strong, but such was his effectiveness that he played 21 times for England, captaining them on 12 occasions.

"He used to say to me after a game, 'You frighten me to death the way you keep the ball and knock these ten-yard passes and get the ball back again. If I'd have played like that, I'd have got dropped.' He told me he'd only passed the ball once in his life. He was on the halfway line, and it got intercepted, and the other team went on and scored. And Herbert Chapman dropped him for two or three games. 'After that,' he said, 'I never passed the ball again. I just woofed it upfield. Every time I hit it, it went so high that it came down with snow on it.'"

In one sense Ken was not so lucky. At the point in the 1950s when he might have been considered for an England cap, Huddersfield's defence was still marking man-to-man in contrast to the England set-up where Walter Winterbottom had introduced a zonal system.

But Ray Wilson, the inside-forward who found his forte at left-back, was in the right place at the right time. "I was fortunate," he admits. "Instead of knocking somebody over flat and whacking it upfield, I was encouraged to play a bit – and for me that was easier. I probably had some influence on the change. After that, the full-back started to have a brain."

For Ray, it is a story of determination and self-belief, a contrast with Ken who had so much talent and was happy to think about other things.

But to Ken, it is also a story of good fortune. For all his great talent, Ken says, Ray would never have won his World Cup medal if Lawrie Kelly had done his training in Huddersfield, not Wolverhampton.

Huddersfield Town in the autumn of 1958

Sitting on ground (left to right): Harry Aston (groundsman), Tony Conwell, R. Castle, Gerry Smith, Mike O'Grady, K. Ogden, John Milner, Stewart Holden, Kevin McHale, J.B. Robshaw (painter)

Sitting: Eddie Brennan (Assistant Secretary), Bill Shankly, Mr F.R. Webster, Mr N. Cleal, Mr J. Woodhead, Mr J.W. Newman, Mr H. Battye, Mr D. Parker, Mr S.D. Lister, Mr J. Chadwick, Mrs E. Connally (laundry lady)

Standing, front row: Eddie Boot, Stan Hepton, Terry Caldwell, Ray Wilson, Dennis Atkins, John Battye, Bill McGarry, Brian Tickell, Ken Taylor, Les Massie, Denis Law, Anthony Galvin (Secretary)

Standing, back row: Tony France, Brian Gibson, Bobby Ledger, F. Briggs (assistant groundsman), B. Taylor, J. Anderson (assistant trainer), Derek Hawksworth, Roy Goodall, Gordon Low, Harry Fearnley, Jack Connor, John Coddington, Sandy Kennon, Stan Howard, Fred Elms (joiner), Peter Dinsdale, Alex Bain

"We had so many on the staff," Ray Wilson says, "that I'm sure they had to take more than one photograph and stick them together. There were people who had been there five or six years, and they were still playing in the third team."

Hard and honest

What a different game football was fifty years ago – with its heavy ball, heavy boots, heavy pitches and a style of play that matched the conditions: hard and heavy, a tough physical contest in which the players expected to make robust contact with each other.

"Football was a working man's game," Ken's brother Jeff says, "and the people who played were working men. It was a tough game, but it was honest."

According to the 1951 Census, 78% of Huddersfield's men were doing manual jobs, and they came to Leeds Road expecting the football to express the values of their own working lives.

They liked Jeff; he was a big, strong centre-forward, quick on his feet and able to defend himself. Then they liked Ken, whose tackling could snuff out many an opposing centre-forward's threat.

"I've never seen anybody tackle as well as him, face on with somebody," Ray Wilson says. "The big centre-forwards at that time all fancied themselves, and it was Ken's job to put them in their place. Every team had two or three players like Ken, with a reputation for hard tackling. It was a part and parcel of professional soccer at that time."

"The way Ken tackled," his Huddersfield team-mate Les Massie says, "he'd be sent off every match now."

"I was never once warned," Ken says. "I can't even remember a player sent off in a match I played."

"In a way," Jeff says, "the fouls were clean. They weren't cynical. Now, if somebody goes past a player, the player will bring him down. There's no way he'll let him go. It seems like part of the art of football now is to get away with things."

"I remember centre-halves chasing me from the half-way line," Les says. "They got very close, but they never thought of bringing me down."

"It wouldn't cross my mind to do that," Ken says. "We just didn't think like that."

"Now there's so much pushing and pulling," Jeff says, "it's hard to know if they're playing football or rugby."

Perhaps it was, as they all say, a more honest game – but it was certainly not pure. There were occasional rumours during Ken's career of club directors trying to bribe their opponents. "I do remember Andy Beattie, our manager, coming into the dressing room one game and saying, 'Their chairman's been on about our fixing for a draw. I've told him we're not interested.'"

And not every centre-forward was a true Corinthian. "There were one or two nasty players, people who would have a go at you off the ball, but they were rare. The great players like Tommy Taylor and Nat Lofthouse never stooped to that."

There were even one or two forwards – Albert Nightingale of Huddersfield and Leeds, for one – who would dive theatrically into the penalty box, as if they had been unfairly tripped. "They reckon he was worth six penalties a season," Ken says.

"He'd knock the ball past the last man," Ray says, "and do a double somersault. I used to say, 'I'm surprised they don't come out with boards. That's 9.6, Albert.' But it was frowned on more in those days."

There were even sendings off. "One time, when I was still a boy, I was watching Town," Jeff says. "Alan Brown, our centre-half, was a big, strong chap and one of the opposition had a go at him. He turned round, knocked him out and walked off the pitch."

Match fixing, nastiness off the ball, diving in the penalty area, a knock-out punch. It would be easy to argue that the game was just as corrupted then as now. But the point of all these stories is that they stand out in the memory as exceptional.

"The game hasn't improved in terms of the spirit in which it's played," Ken says. "But it has improved in other ways. It's a faster game, and the skills are much greater. We weren't as lucky playing on beautiful turf as they are today. But good players of any generation adapt to conditions. It is a better game to watch now. But put today's players on the same field we played on, and it would all be completely different."

"When I started, we played with those lace-up balls. At school we used to have to stitch them up the day before the match. They were heavy and, if it was muddy or wet, they got heavier as the game went on. If you were lucky, you missed heading the lace. If you were unlucky, you headed it every time."

Some romantics on the terraces reckoned that winger Vic Metcalfe could send in his crosses with the ball's laces facing away from the expectant heads, but Ken doubts that.

"Alf Young said to me one time, 'Don't head that heavy ball so much. It'll damage your eyes, and that will affect your batting.' He told me to be careful. Bill McGarry was the same height as me, but he seemed to hang in the air better than I did. So we worked out a system that, if a high ball came over, he would go for the ball and I would take the man coming through."

Ken was a professional footballer from 1952 to 1967, and in those years the game was changing.

"Gradually the lighter balls came in. They began to have this coating on that rejected water. So the ball didn't hold the water and wasn't so heavy. When you hit it, it went further."

"The pitches have improved," Les says. "In our day every pitch was different. Huddersfield was never that great. It was a diamond shape. The diamond was bare earth. All the grass was just in the corners."

"The bounce is much more true than when we played," Ken says. "So the ball control is better. In our day there were more mistakes made."

"I think the game's improved," Ray says. "There's more finesse. The equipment's better. The pitches are better. Everything's improved."

"We played in all weather," Jeff says. "Sometimes it was a quagmire, and the football wouldn't be very pretty. Now they weave in artificial grass so the pitches don't get heavy and muddy. And the ball is light. To me, it looks like they're playing beach ball in plimsolls. It's like circus tricks. Ronaldo would have had his legs broken in our day. We played a harder game."

"We used to wear the heavy Co-op boots," Ken says. "They were advertised by Stanley Matthews. You'd put them on and sit with your feet in a bowl of hot water for five minutes, then sit in a bowl of cold water, to mould them to your feet. Because the leather was so hard. Or you'd let the ground staff have

" *Compliments and Best Wishes for a successful season to all wearers of C.W.S Football Boots*"— STANLEY MATTHEWS

them for the first month or two, to break them in. You had leather studs that were nailed in. If you were playing on a muddy ground, you'd have the studs higher – or, if it was firm, you could take the top section of them off with a pair of pliers. Roy Goodall would have a hammer and nails and a last, and he'd do it before the match."

Such decisions could alter the course of a match.

"We went down to West Ham for a Cup game," Ray says. "They were a bit of a fairy side, who could play on a good pitch, an excellent

football team, but it was icy and slippery."

Eddie Boot was the acting Huddersfield manager after the departure of Bill Shankly, and his shrewdness before kick-off won him not only the game but a permanent appointment in charge.

"Rubbers had just come in," Ray says. "It might have been the season that people were trying them out. And Eddie Boot was cleverer than the other managers about things like that."

"He said to us, 'Get your rubbers on,'" Les recalls. "They were 13-studded boots, as against the six studs you had before, four in front and two at the back. The West Ham players were sliding around and couldn't catch us."

"We beat them 5-1," Ken says. "They could hardly stand up in the ice."

"They were a bit like ladies bobbling about on high heels," Ray says. "Their feet had got almost no contact with the ground at all."

Tactics were evolving. The game that Jeff played in 1950 was not the game that Ken was playing by 1965.

"Huddersfield played man-to-man marking," Ken says. "You had a man that you had to mark, and you stayed with him. Eddie Boot played at full-back for Huddersfield when Jeff was in the team and, if they were playing Blackpool and he was marking Stanley Matthews, he wouldn't let him go more than half a yard away from him all the match. So they played ten against ten. If Matthews had gone and sat in the stand, Eddie Boot would have gone and sat with him."

"It was an easier way to play," Ray says. "Everybody played with this one system, with the W formation in the forward line. You marked the people from the other side, and it just came down to a battle of what was going to happen. The difficulty began when the likes of Don Revie came into the game, centre-forwards who'd go back over the halfway line. They'd drag the centre-half with them and leave room for somebody else to come through. A lot of the managers started to do it. So it killed the man-to-man thing."

"Walter Winterbottom started a zonal system with the England team," Ken says. "The centre-half stayed in his place and, whoever came in, you took that player. And if he went out, somebody else would take him. You stayed as a solid unit."

Ray played for England under Alf Ramsay, and he continued this approach. "He'd say, 'You've got thirty square yards, and whoever comes into it is yours.' It was so bloody simple. And all the simple things are best."

"The sweeper started coming in when I was finishing," Ken says. "He was behind everybody. He used to run across the field wherever the ball was coming down. Now they're playing all sorts of systems."

"Football has become almost like a chess match between the two managers," Jeff says. "Instead of eleven against eleven, it's changed into a manager's tactical game. They've got all these systems, 3-4-5-6-2-4, and they're forever bringing on substitutes. I cannot remember at any club ever going to a tactical talk. We were picked because of what we could do, and we were told to go out and do it. 'Go out and play your game, and enjoy it.'"

"The first time I practised a set piece," Les Massie says, "was at Halifax when I was 35 or 36. That would have been about 1970."

"There was one winter when we missed about five penalties," Ken says. "And there was a great debate every week in training whether you should run up and hit it or whether you could place it. I remember Tommy Cavanagh taking one. He tried to stroke it in, and he was so confused that the ball bounced a couple of times before it reached the keeper."

Training was mornings only, and little of it involved ball work. "When I started," Ray says, "they had this absolutely stupid idea where they used to say, 'Don't give them the ball during the week. Because at the weekend they'll be hungry for it.'"

"When I was at college, up to February when I had to go over to Headingley, I used to do two evenings of training at Leeds Road," Ken says. "There were no floodlights so I couldn't go on the field. So you're running up and down the corridors of the stands, then in the gym. You're not actually seeing the ball at all. But as a youngster you don't need the amount of training that you do when you're over 25. You are fit anyway. The danger is to make players over-fit – so that they're so fit that they break down all the time. They might be fit, but they're not strong."

"The game was a lot slower in our day," Les says. "And there weren't so many injuries. I played twenty years, and I only pulled one muscle. I'm not sure they're really fit enough to play at the speed they're trying to play at now."

"There's fitness and fitness," Ken says. "I used to go training with Derek Ibbotson round Armitage Bridge Cricket Club. 20 laps, with 30 yard striders between each one. And that killed me. But I took him down to Leeds Road and, when he played a five-a-side in the car park and he was doing quick sprints for three yards, five yards and moving off the ball, he was jiggered in a quarter of an hour. They're completely different things. You do train for a specific job. That's

Ken, on holiday from The Slade, draws his training partner Derek Ibbotson, who is home after winning bronze in the 5000 metres at the Melbourne Olympics. Ken's mother looks on.

why all the players are injured all the time these days. They're trained for everything. At Huddersfield Town the year before I was in the side, they went the whole season with the same five defenders."

If there were aches and pains to sort out, they reported to Roy Goodall, the former trainer who had taken over as physio. What was his equipment? "A red heat lamp," Ken says, "and fingers. Very rigid fingers. You didn't stay on the table very long with his fingers."

Knocks and cuts during the match were dealt with quickly, with a minimum of fuss. "I broke my nose against Preston," Ken says. "I stopped it bleeding and carried on. I had lots of cuts in my eyebrows and head. But you waited till after the game to get them stitched up. The club's doctor was James Mason's brother. You had to go up to his surgery."

During the week, though, it was up to Roy Goodall to sort out the little niggles in his treatment room.

"Roy was ever such a nice chap, but he was very forgetful. Denis had been having a lot of treatment for a leg injury, and he had him underneath the lamp one Friday morning. And he forgot he was there. He locked up and went home. I think Denis finished up having to climb over the wall."

They often trained on the playing fields out by the gas works. Huddersfield was a town noted for the poor quality of its air, as the mill chimneys belched out their fumes.

"The fogs from the pollution were unbelievable," Ken says. "At the training ground we had two chemical companies, ICI and LB Holliday, and goodness knows what we were breathing in from them. I had a little white MG later in my career there, and it would get spotted with all kinds of colour you couldn't get off. Bright yellow one day, pink the next, purple the day after."

"You could see little yellow and green things floating in the air," Ray says.

"They used to pour all the dyes in the River Colne," Ken says. "Then, if the wind blew the other way, you got the smell of the gas works."

"I'd come from Aberdeen," Les says. "That was nice and clean. And, when I first saw Huddersfield, it seemed so black and dirty. It was a wet day and, somewhere between Leeds and Huddersfield, I was thinking, 'What the hell have I come to?' I nearly turned back."

Except in the time that Ken was studying at The

Slade in London, he lived at home with his parents till he married. But Ray Wilson and Les Massie, coming to Huddersfield as young, unattached men, were put into digs, Pond House in Mold Green, where they lived along with Gordon Low, Jack Connor and – not long afterwards – Denis Law. The five of them still hold an annual reunion.

"The landlady used to take in theatricals from the Palace Theatre," Les recalls. "Hylda Baker was there one time, and I remember a lady who did a fan dance."

"I came to Huddersfield for £5 a week," Ray says, "and the lodgings were £2 – 15s. So we never had much money. We had a couple of hours' training in the morning, and what do you do for the rest of the day? We played golf, we played snooker. But we didn't go drinking. We couldn't have afforded it. Ken was different. He was in his home town. He always had other things to do."

"The clubs used to take you away the week before Christmas for special training," Jeff says. "At Huddersfield we went to Blackpool; at Fulham it was Torquay. They kept you in a hotel and took you training on the beach. It was to keep the players away from their wives so that they'd be fresh for the Christmas games. They didn't say it, but everybody knew that was the purpose of it. We were being policed."

"We were at Blackpool one time," Ken remembers. "We'd been training hard all week, and we were all sitting round in the hotel foyer, waiting to go off for the match. Then one of our older players walked in with this blonde on his arm. We all sat there, looking astonished, and we watched them as they walked across to the lift. He pressed the button, down came the lift and the doors opened. And out stepped Roy Goodall.

"The player signalled the blonde into the lift. 'In you go,' he said. 'Room 54.' And away she went. Then Roy and he stood there, looking at each other. There was this deathly silence for what seemed like an absolute age. It couldn't have been more than two or three hours till kick-off.

"Eventually Roy spoke. He could be quite slow. 'What are you doing with that?' he said, and back came the reply, 'I'm going to shag it.' We were all sitting there, waiting to hear what Roy would say to that. Finally his face lit up. 'Well, all right,' he said, 'but just once.'"

It was not the response that Bill Shankly would have given.

White rose against red

Ken played his first Roses match at the end of July 1955. At Bramall Lane, Sheffield. He was 19 years old and he had been called into the team at the last minute, having scored 177 for the Second XI against Cheshire and 57 and 32 for the Minor Counties against the touring South Africans.

He was in a rich vein of form and, with Hutton, Lowson and Sutcliffe all injured, he found himself opening the batting with Brian Close. At 11.30 on Saturday morning, in front of a packed house, they walked out together. Nothing so far in his cricketing career had been at this level of intensity.

"Bramall Lane was a good batting wicket," Ken says, and Jim Kilburn's report in the *Yorkshire Post* confirms that it was at its best that morning: 'Yorkshire won the toss and went to bat first on a pitch not even green and the air shimmering with summer heat.'

Close took first strike, taking a single off the last ball of Statham's first over. Ken had still not faced a ball when, off the final delivery of the next over, Close hit the ball into space at mid-wicket and again set off. 'He hoped for two runs, but Marner moved quickly from mid-on and the batsman's hasty change of mind left Taylor far from home.'

With Lancashire following on and rain ruining the third day, there would be no second innings for Ken. And it was June 1957, the Whitsun Bank Holiday, before he again appeared in a Roses contest.

This time the match was at Old Trafford. On a cold, damp Saturday play did not start till 2.15 and Ken came out to bat at 24 for two. He played his shots and quickly reached 15, then he was bowled by Brian Statham. 'Taylor threatened prosperity,' wrote Kilburn, 'and departed before he reached it.' By close, Yorkshire were all out for 153.

Bank Holiday Monday was a much brighter day. The sun shone, and the roads filled with motor cars. All around Old Trafford the streets were jammed.

> The players weren't allowed to park in the ground. We had to get there early, unload our bags and find somewhere to park in the streets.
> It was a full house that day. There were boys sitting several deep on the grass around the boundary, and my girl friend at the time came over to watch me.

Lancashire made watchful progress, with Washbrook and the young Pullar taking the score to 109 for four. Then suddenly they were 113 all out, and Yorkshire were batting again. Statham bowled

Close for nought and, when the tall off-spinner Roy Tattersall removed Frank Lowson, it was 12 for two and Ken was stepping out to bat once more.

He was 21 years old, not yet a regular in the Yorkshire side, and he was playing in front of the largest cricket crowd he had ever experienced – as well as the many more who were sitting at home, watching BBC Television's live coverage.

> It's a long way from the changing room down to the middle. You have a lot of time to think. There was a gate onto the field with a man to open it. 'Don't be long now, son,' he said as I went past him. Tattersall was bowling. A great off-spinner. He had three men close in on the leg-side for the catch. I tried to sum up in my mind how I was going to play him, and I told myself not to play anything which set off on the leg stick or outside.
> Well, the first ball he sent down was on the leg stick, so I brandished arms.
> It was his floater. Off and middle went over. First ball – with twenty-three and a half thousand people in the ground.

Jim Kilburn was not impressed. 'Taylor made such furious misjudgement of direction and spin that he was bowled first ball without offering a shot.'

> I could have died on the spot. I dragged myself off the pitch and, as I passed the gateman, he touched his cap and said, 'Thanks very much, son.'

Things did not improve greatly in his next four Roses matches, with Statham claiming his wicket five times in seven innings.

> Brian never gave you a bad ball to hit. You had to make a half-bad ball into a bad one and, of course, that was when you got out.
> He could hit the seam consistently, and you never knew which way it would move. I don't think he did, either. And he never wasted his energy bowling a bouncer.
> He had a double-jointed action. When he peeled off his sweater, he could take his arm down behind the back of his head, catch hold of the bottom of the sweater and pull it up over his head, all in one movement.
> He never got frustrated, never argued with a decision. His temperament was quite opposite to Fred's, but they made a wonderful partnership together.

Then, when Ken did survive Brian Statham's new ball burst at Headingley in June 1960, he was

Brian Statham

But I was always pleased when I was put on. It's not as tense as batting. If you bowl a bad ball, you've got another chance.

That match at Old Trafford was the only time in my whole career that I bowled for any length of time.

According to A.A. Thomson, he 'bowled his harmless-looking deliveries to destructive effect', and he came off with figures of six for 75. It was the only five-wicket haul of his career, and in another 22 overs in the second innings, he took one for 19. In a fixture that so often ended in an unyielding stalemate, Yorkshire beat Lancashire for only the third time in 31 championship matches since the war.

Unlike Geoff Boycott, whose appetite for the big occasion saw him make centuries in each of his first three Roses matches, Ken did not make a hundred against Lancashire till May 1964 when he hit 153 at Old Trafford, putting on 236 for the first wicket with Geoff Boycott. "I always enjoyed playing at Old Trafford," he says. "It was a very good ground to play cricket. Much better than Headingley."

When he stepped out to bat in his last Roses match – at Headingley in June 1968 – he had still not made a hundred against the old enemy on his home soil. And what better occasion would there be to do it! Yorkshire – with a generosity not even accorded to Len Hutton, let alone to Trueman, Close or Illingworth – had granted him the match for his benefit.

Whit Monday. The collection buckets were on their way round the large crowd during the afternoon as – in the words of Peter West in *The Times* – 'he delighted the home supporters with a debonair innings.' He had reached 85 when he 'wafted' at a short ball from Ken Higgs.

I got a thin bottom edge. I don't think anybody appealed hardly. If they did, it was very half-hearted.

He was 15 short of his hundred. In his benefit match. In front of a large Bank Holiday crowd. The thought of it was enough to make him hesitate.

I could have got away with it. I think I knew that the umpire wasn't going to give me out.

Almost forty years have passed and he tells the story with a chuckle, happy with the decision he made.

It did cross my mind to stay. But honour won the day.

dismissed in both innings by the leg-spinner Tommy Greenhough.

Tommy bowled mainly googlies. You had to play him as an off-spinner. I think he'd fallen down a lift shaft when he was younger and broken a lot of bones. So he had this very peculiar action.

It was not till Whitsun 1961, at Old Trafford, that Ken made a match-winning impact on a Roses match – and that, amazingly, was with the ball. With Trueman and Platt both unfit, he found himself bowling 44 overs on the first day.

I was very medium pace. Little wobblers. They moved a bit both ways. Normally I'd come on when the batsmen were well set and, if I took a wicket, I'd get taken off and they'd bring back one of the main bowlers.

The most wanted young man in Britain

When Ken became a professional footballer with Huddersfield Town, he was given a letter, signed by Andy Beattie the manager and Harry Beever the Secretary.

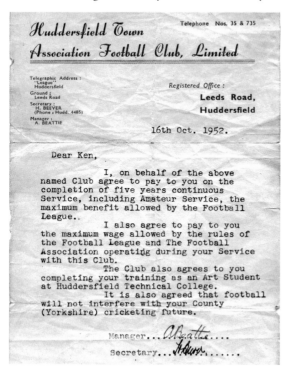

Huddersfield Town
Association Football Club, Limited

Telephone Nos. 35 & 735

Telegraphic Address :
"League
Huddersfield
Ground :
Leeds Road
Secretary :
H. BEEVER
(Phone : Hudd. 4485)
Manager :
A. BEATTIE

Registered Office :
Leeds Road,
Huddersfield

16th Oct. 1952.

Dear Ken,

        I, on behalf of the above named Club agree to pay to you on the completion of five years continuous Service, including Amateur Service, the maximum benefit allowed by the Football League..

        I also agree to pay to you the maximum wage allowed by the rules of the Football League and The Football Association operating during your Service with this Club.

        The Club also agrees to you completing your training as an Art Student at Huddersfield Technical College.

        It is also agreed that football will not interfere with your County (Yorkshire) cricketing future.

Manager...Beattie....

Secretary...Beever.......

"In my father's eyes," Ken says, "the club hadn't done right by Jeff when he was studying. So he came down with me when I signed, and he insisted on their making this agreement and putting it in writing."

It was a letter which saved him from many of the problems experienced by other cricketing footballers. At Bristol Rovers, for instance, Ron Nicholls and Barrie Meyer were transfer-listed one August when they continued to play cricket for Gloucestershire rather than report back on the first day of pre-season training. Bill Shankly, when he was Huddersfield manager, grumbled whenever Ken returned late, but his hands were tied. If Yorkshire were in the running for the championship, Ken would not arrive till the beginning of September.

In the autumn of 1956 Ken's schedule reached its most demanding. Throughout June and July he had played in the Yorkshire first team, scoring his first century in first-class cricket, and in August he began his third winter as a regular in the Huddersfield side, having already been selected the previous September as a substitute for the England Under-23s. He was just 21 years old and, in addition to so much sporting success, he had won a place at The Slade School of Fine Art in London. For three years he had had his National Service deferred while he completed his Diploma at Huddersfield; now it was deferred for a further two years.

In the words of one newspaper feature, he was 'the most wanted young man in Britain':

> The lavishly gifted mill-worker's son is a flashing batsman, the best out-fielder in England and a tough tigerish footballer with a flair for the delicate art of painting. At the moment he is walking arm-in-arm with his three loves.
> Some people say that Ken, with three targets to aim at, will miss the lot. Perhaps he will. But he says football is a wonderful game, cricket is better and he loves painting. He's really living. Good luck to him.

The Slade, situated in Bloomsbury and part of the University of London, was one of the top institutions in England for art students, as it still is. In the 1950s Professor of Art there was Sir William Coldstream, a man of such influence that he was sometimes called 'the Prime Minister of British painting'.

Coldstream was a member of the Euston Road school, which – setting itself to avoid the influence of the abstract – encouraged pupils to draw and paint directly what they saw, especially the subtleties of light and mood that the urban environment offered.

"He was a very dapper man," Ken remembers. "He always wore a trilby and a suit, with a collar and tie. You'd never imagine that he was a painter. If you'd passed him in the street, you'd think that he was a stockbroker. He was very keen on cricket. I think he was a member of MCC. He came to see me at Lord's."

Ken's plan to fund himself through The Slade by playing professional sport had a recent precedent. David Storey, the Leeds rugby league footballer and later the author of 'This Sporting Life', had done the same, starting three years earlier, though his Slade education did not end in glory. A troublesome President of the Students' Union, he was involved in some rowdy scenes and was eventually asked to leave because he was spending more time writing than painting.

Ken was a calmer figure. He appealed to Coldstream not only because of his cricket but because his portfolio displayed both talent and an approach that resonated with Euston Road values. "I get plenty of inspiration from the industrial West Riding," Ken said in a newspaper interview. "The usual colourful country landscape leaves me cold. But if there's a mill and a canal in the picture, I can't stop till I've got it down on canvas."

Life Study
Painted by Ken at The Slade

When he had been at Huddersfield College Ken had had classes in different subjects all through each day, so most of his football training had been done on his own, in lunch hours and at the end of the day. But at The Slade the time was less structured. "You'd just go in and work on a painting at your own pace. People would come round and make suggestions, and you'd go to see your tutor every couple of weeks to talk about your work."

Now he was able to train two mornings a week, joining his brother Jeff at Brentford. Then on Friday afternoon he took the train to wherever Huddersfield were playing. In the spring term he also fitted in an evening with the Middlesex cricketers at their indoor school in Finchley. "Bob Gale used to pick me up. Then on the way back we'd eat bangers and mash in Swiss Cottage."

It was too busy a life, however, to fit in everything. "I was away at the weekends when all the parties were taking place. So my social life at The Slade didn't really get going."

On a Wednesday in October he travelled down to Bristol, again to sit on the bench in an England Under-23 international, this time against France. Substitutes were only allowed onto the field up till half-time, and then only if an injury had occurred. There was an injury that night, in the tenth minute, but it brought on the substitute forward, not Ken. And it deprived the English game of one of its brightest young stars, the 17-year-old Alick Jeffrey of Doncaster Rovers, already in mid-October with 16 league goals to his name. 'Going into a hard tackle, his right leg was fractured,' *The Times* reported, 'and the crack of it could be heard all over the ground like a pistol shot. As he was carried mournfully away, something went with him out of the struggle, and a hush fell on the crowd.'

It took Jeffrey seven years to return to league football, and he never became the player he had promised to be. "He was a bit like Rooney or Jimmy Greaves," Ken says. "He could pop the goals in. I can still hear the crack. It was awful."

Ken himself was injured two months later, when the Swansea winger Cliff Jones buried his aluminium studs into his leg. "I cleared the ball over the touchline, and he came sliding in, very late. It was the only season they allowed aluminium studs; they banned them after that."

Ken found himself out of the Huddersfield Town team across Christmas and into the New Year, finding time to compose an article for the Huddersfield Examiner about his extraordinary triple life, an article that passed on the values and advice of his father.

Everyone who turns to the game for a living should be prepared to use his spare time to prepare himself for the days when he can no longer play.

Jeff and I are both proud that we have been self-supporting throughout all our studies, but we know that what we can do is within the scope of many other professional sportsmen if they would only have a go.

Before returning to London for the spring term, he drew a portrait of his Huddersfield Town team-mate Ronnie Simpson.

Also studying at The Slade at that time was John Nash, son of the Yorkshire County Cricket Club Secretary. "The emphasis at The Slade was on drawing," he says. "Life drawing. Still life. Not that much serious painting."

Nash's father – also John – had left school at 14, working as an office boy at the Yorkshire Club's Old Bank Chambers office under Sir Frederick Toone. Then, after a spell working for an organ company, he was called back in the summer of 1930 when Toone fell ill and they needed somebody to organise the Test match against Australia that summer. "He did it almost single-handed, and on the strength of that they offered him the post of Secretary."

Young John was a sickly child at school, excused games, so he was further away from the world of sport than his father, as Bryan Stott, a builder's son, discovered when he visited Ken in London. "We went for dinner with John Nash. It was a typical student set-up. There was I in my suit and tie, and John and his girl friend were in this flat in Belsize Park. I can't remember the furniture. There can't have been much. To me, it was Bohemia. They were talking art, and I was sitting there, listening."

Ken's best friend at The Slade was Harry Riley from Salford. Starting at The Slade before Ken, he too had set out to play football while studying, though in his case only as an amateur.

"I was training with Chelsea," he says, "and travelling each Saturday to play for the Manchester United junior team. But it didn't work out. I was painting a still life one day, a pear and apple that were decaying, and I had to leave them for the weekend to go off to football. And I realised that they'd be gone by the time I came back. So I rang Matt Busby, and I told him that I was giving up football, it was interfering with my art. For me, it was the art that was the obsession, not the sport. It was with the art that I was going to say something."

Eventually Ken also had to make a choice. The summer term arrived, and he did not want to put his Yorkshire place on hold while he was at The Slade. "If I'd not played, there would have been one or two others who might have nipped in ahead of me," he says.

Wrongly he was advised that he could spread his six-term course over three years, missing the summer terms. So he left at Easter, expecting to return in the autumn. Then during the summer he was informed that university regulations did not allow this. "I was disappointed," he says, "but I felt that I could go back to the art when the sport had finished."

"I've always respected Ken's art hugely," Harry Riley says. "He's got a fine eye, and he'd got everything technically. I know William Coldstream admired him greatly as an artist. He had the ability to say a lot of things. But his obsession was with the sport. That's how he wanted to prove himself."

Ken agrees. "I know that I was technically good but, to be an artist, not just an artisan, you've got to have something new. You've got to get to that stage where something else is happening. And I didn't feel I'd got to that. In any case, the sport was already providing me with success, there and then, and it was providing the money."

When he had finished at The Slade, Harry Riley returned north. He became a pupil of L.S. Lowry and set out on the road to a successful career as an artist. He recorded the everyday scenes of the North-West,

and he became a painter of portraits of the wealthy and famous. Always a good talker, he was for several years a regular contributor to Brian Redhead's Saturday night radio programme, 'A Word in Edgeways'.

"We stayed in touch," Ken says, "and there was a time when he was very poor, living on the top floor of a converted coach house in Salford, with no electricity and the loo downstairs. In many ways I think I was probably as technically competent as he was, but I didn't have his drive to succeed with it. I had other things in my life."

"What matters in the end," Harry says, "is how much you want to do something. And Ken's motivation was to be a first-class sportsman."

Though he had not realised it when he left at the end of the Easter term in 1957, Ken's time at The Slade had ended, and in June he received a letter from William Coldstream. The National Recruiting Board had withdrawn his deferment from National Service, and he could expect to be called up within a couple of months. 'If you ever want to come back here in any way after National Service,' Colstream added, 'we should of course be very pleased to have you.'

His call-up papers arrived after the end of the cricket season, and he attended his medical on Tuesday 17 September 1957, having played all seven of Huddersfield Town's matches up to that point.

The doctor in charge of the medical was attached to Town, and he looked at the after-effects of Ken's injury the previous winter. "He didn't think that my leg would stand up to all the square bashing so he signed me off as Grade 3. Unfit for service.'

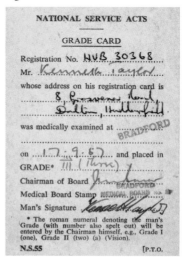

Till he returned to cricket the next April, Ken did not miss one match for Town that winter.

Twin peaks

Before the summer of 1956 Ken's appearances in the Yorkshire side were largely limited to filling gaps when more senior players were injured or away on Test duty. He had played 24 innings and made just one fifty, that 56 at Neath when Wilf Wooller had tried to talk him out of his game. His greatest claim to fame, recorded in the cricket annuals, was his football – and his three wickets with consecutive balls in 1954. The first two, against the Pakistani tourists, were on June 29, but the third did not come till his next appearance on July 10 against Surrey. It was not considered a proper hat-trick, but at least he did not suffer the fate of Joe Johnson, the Yorkshire slow left-armer who took two wickets in two balls against Leicestershire in August 1939, went off to war and never bowled again for the county.

Len Hutton and Norman Yardley had both retired before the summer of 1956 and, under Billy Sutcliffe's captaincy, there were more opportunities for the next generation. Ken was brought into the side in late May, now approaching his 21st birthday, and he stayed in it till he returned to football at the end of July. There were three fifties in his first five matches, raising his top score to 74, but his great breakthrough came in early July at Trent Bridge.

Nottinghamshire had been lucky opponents for Ken. He had made his first hundreds for both the Federation Under-18 and the Yorkshire second team against them.

Notts had been all out for 167 on Saturday, and he went out to bat on Monday morning to find the Trent Bridge pitch at its most benign. His start was slow. He survived two chances – a catch and a stumping – on 26 and 37. But the hours passed and 'as Arthur Jepson peppered his left pad with in-swingers and kept calling on the heavens to witness what awful luck he was having, he carried on regardless.'

After tea he reached 99, and he found himself facing 'a teasing over' of leg-breaks and googlies from the Australian Bruce Dooland. At the other end stood the imperturbable Willie Watson and, when Ken 'cracked his 100 with a sizzling off-drive off Dooland', he was congratulated by his fellow Huddersfielder.

"I'd never felt under any pressure for my place in the team," he says. "I suppose I'd always thought, 'If this doesn't come off, I've got the football.' But it was a wonderful moment, like a coming of age. And the telegrams poured in afterwards."

He still possesses them all: from Mum and Dad, from Wally Heap, from the Huddersfield League, from Primrose Hill and many more.

With all care released, he cut loose, racing from 100 to 168 in an hour. By the end, one reporter – full of artistic metaphors – wrote that 'the whole of Trent Bridge was his canvas, and he was painting it red.'

Even after six hours in the middle, when 'some Notts fielders had sunken into sudden middle age', he was 'sprinting short singles.'

'We'll have to send for the bailiffs,' one spectator shouted, 'to get you out.'

Later that week, on a fiery Taunton pitch, Yorkshire bowled out Somerset for 71. With dark clouds rolling down from the Quantocks, Ken went out to bat in the evening. Enduring the barracking of Somerset supporters, he grittily survived for the morning when he and Frank Lowson took their partnership to 176. A fortnight later he was off to football, and stuck in his mother's scrapbook were the Yorkshire averages, with Ken second to Willie Watson. He was 21 in August, off to The Slade in London, and his cricketing future was bright.

Ken's injury at Swansea brought a break to his football season for five weeks from December 8, missing the busy Christmas period and finding that his replacement at centre-half, Ronnie Cockerill, had made such an impressive start that Bill Shankly decided to fit Ken into the team in a different position.

As a youngster Ken had been a winger before moving to inside-forward. There is even a cutting in his mother's scrapbook of a game for Huddersfield Town Juniors when he played in goal and gave such 'a polished display that he hardly looked new to the position. His crowning glory came towards the end of the game when he saved a penalty.'

The *Examiner* welcomed the idea of his moving out of defence: 'One school of thought has held that playing at centre-half has been foreign to his temperament. He has a strong shot and a fine turn of speed.'

So on Saturday 12 January, in a home match against relegation-threatened Bury, he wore the number nine shirt that brother Jeff had worn five years earlier. It was not a success; he was not fully recovered, he had a poor game, and the visitors won 2-1.

Back at The Slade, he was not picked for the next three games. But he travelled up to Nottingham on Thursday 21 February for a 0-0 draw with Forest, then on Saturday turned out at Leeds Road, still at centre-forward, for the visit of a West Ham side pressing for promotion after a winning run of seven matches.

It was a bitterly cold day. Sleet and snow fell during the morning, and among the many matches called off or abandoned was the one at Bradford City. But at Leeds Road, forty minutes before kick-off, the referee decided to play, ordering the lines to be swept and coloured blue. Only 5,878 hardy spectators gathered, barely one-tenth of the number who had attended the Cup game the previous week, and those who stayed away missed what the *Yorkshire Evening Post* called 'the most dazzling display of football Town have given at Leeds Road for years and years!'

The slippery pitch was not at all suited to the sophisticated West Ham team's 'tip-tapping' game. 'They kept the ball too close,' one reporter reckoned, 'and their forwards, clever enough in midfield, constantly tried one pass too many.'

The first chance fell to Ken straightaway, but he 'lost sight of the ball at the crucial moment.' However, within fifteen minutes, Town were 3-0 up, with a fourth goal declared off-side. The second of the three had been scored by Ken, breaking clear of his marker Malcolm Allison to 'head a picture goal'. It was his first goal in 103 appearances for Town – but not his last of the afternoon.

In the 52nd minute a shot from Les Massie was parried by the West Ham keeper, only for Ken – 'dashing in for the kill' – to score the easiest of goals. The score was 4-1, and after an hour a freak West Ham goal made it 4-2.

But this was a day for goal-scorers to cause

mayhem in the mud. Straight from the restart 'Taylor ploughed his way forward, bulldozed through three tackles and shot through a ruck of players to complete his hat-trick.'

Ten minutes later he made it four with 'the best of the lot': 'When Les Massie centred, he pitched himself into an astonishing diving header, flicked the ball into the net and finished on the cinder track.'

"I do remember that goal," he says. "I nearly hit the upright."

It was a rugged display, tough and courageous in the sleet and snow. He was in another world from that of The Slade, where one of his fellow students Margaret Evans had just won first prize in a 'Young Contemporaries' exhibition in a London gallery. 'One can note with satisfaction,' read the review in *The Times*, 'the general standard of painterly execution, though its incidence is markedly higher in the products of the larger London schools than elsewhere.'

The cuttings of Ken's triumph fill two pages of the scrapbook, but the headlines of the day were captured elsewhere in the Second Division. In a mudbath at Stoke the home team's outside-right Tim Coleman had eight shots in his club's game against Lincoln City and scored with seven of them.

Were Ken's goals 'a mere flash in the pan', or could he – as Robert Arnott in the *Examiner* thought – 'make of the centre-forward position the success he has made at centre-half'? Could he follow the path of John Charles and turn from a dependable and solid centre-half to a match-winning centre-forward?

"John Charles said to me, 'They don't remember the goals you stopped, only the ones you scored.'"

Ken scored four more times in the last nine matches that winter, but the following August Shankly moved him to right-half, and he was back out of the limelight.

"I wasn't worried where I played," he says now. "I enjoyed all the positions."

Ken, 'a strong centre-forward of the worrying type', scores the winner against Rotherham.

Bill Shankly

In December 1955 Ken was in his second full season in the Huddersfield Town first team. A run of seven successive defeats had taken the club to the foot of the First Division table, and the manager Andy Beattie – looking for support – turned to his fellow Scot and former Preston North End team-mate Bill Shankly to become his assistant.

In the six years since he had retired as a Preston player, Shankly had already managed three lower division clubs – Carlisle, Grimsby and Workington – but in each case, after reviving their fortunes, he had become frustrated by the directors' lack of ambition and resigned.

"Bill was a man of great principles," Ken says. "I remember talking to him about jobs. 'If I was employed to clean Huddersfield market place and toilets,' he said, 'they'd be the cleanest in the whole country. You've got to have pride in whatever you do.'"

Shankly was put in charge of the reserve team, among them Ray Wilson. "Roy Goodall was the first-team trainer," Ray says, "and his sessions were so boring. All you did was lap and lap and lap. And when you did have a game, first team against second, there were to be no serious challenges. Then Bill came along, and he was so full of enthusiasm. He was absolutely bonkers about soccer. You'd go round the pitch with a ball each, doing little things with it. Then you'd be playing five-a-sides."

"He always played in the five-a-side matches himself," Ken says. "And at half past twelve, when we should be finished, if he was on the losing side, you played on and played on. So in the end we used to let him score, just to get the game over with. He was a real competitor."

Training was mornings only – but not with Shankly. "We'd come back in the dressing room," Ray Wilson recalls, "and he'd point to some of us. 'You … you … you, come back this afternoon.' He used to have us playing outside on the car park. The pitch would be marked out, and you'd look round. And there'd always be five Englishmen, four Scotsmen and him. 'And here we are,' he'd say, 'going out at Hampden Park now.' And we'd walk out onto the car park. We could never score a goal. If there was ever any doubt he'd say, 'Not in.' We used to play till it was nearly dark. So we'd nod to each other and we'd say, 'Let him score the winner.' And as soon as he did, he'd blow for time.' 'Here they come in now,'

he'd say. 'And yes, Scotland have won again.' He was childish about it, to be honest. But he had so much enthusiasm. In the end all the first-team players went in and complained. They wanted to be trained by him."

Huddersfield were relegated that winter and, when they made a poor start in Division Two the next autumn, the club sacked Andy Beattie and appointed Shankly to replace him.

"Andy Beattie used to try to work out the opposition, which system they were playing," Ken says. "But Bill wasn't worried about the opposition. His idea was to collect good players and to let them play.

"We never had a proper pre-match talk. He would just go round building up our confidence, telling us how good we were, how the other side 'weren't fit to be on the same park.' He'd walk around the table. 'The police are going to be upset,' he'd say. 'There'll be eleven murders out there this afternoon.' He was a great motivator. That was his greatest quality.

"He told us never to look at the programme before the match. 'Always play the player on the pitch,' he'd say. 'Not the name in the programme.' It's the same in cricket. If you're not careful, you finish up batting against their reputation, rather than the ball that's being bowled to you. With Bill, it was never about the opposition; it was always about how good you were."

"I wouldn't say he was doing it just to wind us up," Ray Wilson says. "I think sometimes he really believed it. When he watched the game, he just watched his own side. 'He's the best,' he'd say. Then, when the player had gone, a year later he'd be saying he couldn't play at all, he was bloody useless. You'd say, 'But you were talking about him being an international.' 'No, no, he's not. He's absolutely rubbish.'"

So what did he make of Ken? "You had to be 150% into soccer for Shankly," Ray Wilson says. "You had to dream about it. In many ways Ken wasn't his sort of person, with all his cricket and his art. And, when Ken came out on the field in his shorts, he always had this handkerchief tucked inside them, and he used to pull it out and wipe his nose. You can imagine what Shankly thought of that. I said to Ken, 'Do you use that to upset Bill?' But, of course, Ken could tackle as well as anybody. Face on, with the side of his foot. Like Shankly did."

Is that how Ken remembers it?

"We were talking one day about motor cars and how flashy some were, and he said, 'It's what's underneath the body that counts.' As a footballer, I was reasonable in the air, I was fast on the ground and I'd tackle hard. So Bill liked me. There was always a place in the side for me somewhere. But he didn't like it when I was off playing cricket. He called it 'a lassie's game'."

Shankly was a tough man. He had started his working life down a pit in Ayrshire, and he made his reputation at Preston as an uncompromising wing-half.

"I think he played for Preston 350-odd times without ever reporting an injury. If you were unfit, he didn't want to know you. He wouldn't even speak to you."

"We went special training to Blackpool once," Ken's team-mate Les Massie remembers. "I'd got an ankle injury, and on Thursday he asked me if I was going to be fit for Saturday. 'I shouldn't think so, Bill,' I said. 'Well,' he said, 'it was a waste of bloody time bringing you.'"

"He never believed anyone was injured," Denis Law says. "I was coming out of the treatment room once. Shankly's office was only just down the corridor, and he was walking towards me. The corridor was only about six feet wide, but he didn't even so much as glance at me as he went by. He had no time for you at all if you had your tracksuit bottoms on."

Ken confirms this. "They say that, when he was a player at Preston, during the playing season, he never slept with his wife. That was the rumour, anyway.

"One day he told us that it was his wedding anniversary and he was taking his wife out. So the next morning we asked him if they'd had a good time. 'Very nice, thank you,' he said. So we asked him, 'Where did you take her, Bill?' And he said, 'I took her to watch Accrington Stanley Reserves.'

"Ronnie Cockerill went to see him in the middle of one season, said he wanted to get married. 'If you get married,' Bill said, 'you're on the list.' He got married, and he was transferred to Grimsby the next week."

Les Massie wanted to marry in the winter of 1958/59 and got the same response: "He'd banned me from marrying. 'Wait till next summer,' he said. Then in March he came up to me and said, 'I'll see you in the office.' I went along, and he said, 'You can

get married. If you do, there'll be a bit of tax coming back to you.' He even gave me a fiver."

Alas, Shankly's generosity had its limits. "I had to go off and marry in a great hurry. Everybody thought Shirley was pregnant. But the day I got married, it was a Monday, there was a game in the evening at Leeds, and Bill said I had to play. It was only the West Riding Cup, but he wouldn't let me have the night off. Shirley and I caught the milk train from Leeds and got into King's Cross at six o'clock in the morning. I remember knocking on the door of this hotel and nobody answering. We had a two-day honeymoon in London, and I had to be back at training on Thursday. That was Shanks for you."

"He was absolutely besotted with soccer," Ray Wilson says. "Right from the first game of the season he'd be able to tell you who you were playing on the Saturday and Wednesday, right through the season.

Almost like going through the alphabet. 'And in October we've got …' As though he couldn't wait for all the games."

But unfortunately Shankly's time at Leeds Road came to an end. He was building a good, young side – with Denis Law, Ray Wilson and Les Massie – but, as at his other clubs, he could not get the directors to support his ambition.

"Bill wanted success," Ken says, "and he could see that Huddersfield weren't a club that were striving to make a great impression. The directors weren't prepared to spend any money."

On Saturday 28 November 1959 Huddersfield beat Liverpool 1-0 at Leeds Road. The Merseysiders had drawn two and lost three of their last five encounters, and they were four places below Town in the Second Division table. But, unlike at Huddersfield, the Liverpool directors had a vision for their club, and by Tuesday they were announcing that Shankly had signed as their new manager.

The following winter, having brought both Ian St John and Ron Yeats from Scotland, Liverpool were pushing for promotion. By 1964 they were First Division champions, in 1965 they won the FA Cup and in 1966 they were champions again. Meanwhile, Huddersfield meandered along in Division Two, one year only escaping relegation on the last day of the season.

"Shankly had got everybody playing for him," Ray Wilson says. "After he went, people were just doing their job and going home. Denis Law was sold, and it all went downhill. It was very sad. Huddersfield had Bill in their hands, and they let him go. If they'd given him some money to buy a couple of players, he could have turned us into a good First Division side. What he did at Liverpool, he might not have done all that at Huddersfield. They had the advantage of 30 or 40 thousand every game at Anfield. But the people of Huddersfield could have had a really good team."

Instead, struggling through the 1960s in the Second Division, Town rarely attracted a gate much greater than 15,000.

"Football supporters in Yorkshire are more fickle than in Lancashire," Ken thinks. "If their club gets relegated, they'll go and watch another club. Whereas at Manchester United and Liverpool, they'll stay loyal.

"Bill went to Liverpool. He spent some money, got in the players that he wanted and of course he had a lot of success."

Shankly and Liverpool. "If ever there was a perfect marriage," Ray Wilson says, "that was it. Because the people up there are as bonkers about football as he was. He got them all behind the goal, singing and kissing his arse. And of course that's what he wanted. He became their god."

Walk on through the wind,
Walk on through the rain,
Though your dreams be tossed and blown,
Walk on, walk on, with hope in your heart,
And you'll never walk alone.

Shankly and Huddersfield. Was it possible that, if he had stayed and the directors had given him money for players, he could have created that fervour at Leeds Road?

"He had this idea that we should have a club song at Huddersfield," Ken recalls. "I can't remember what it was. It might even have been 'You'll Never Walk Alone'. He wanted to get the supporters singing. But it didn't catch on. I remember thinking that it was a silly idea. I think most people did."

"The Huddersfield crowd," Ray says, "I don't think they've changed that much over the years. I think they like a good moan."

Through the 1960s they had plenty to moan about, especially when they looked across to Merseyside. "I should have left when he left," Ray Wilson says.

But Ray was now an England international, where Ken was less ambitious. His cricket was taking him to greater success, and now he was married. He was happy to play for his home town side, though he – like all the others – missed their mad Scots manager.

"Bill was always busy, doing things. There was a fussiness about him. He knew what he wanted, and he had this great ability to inspire people and to create enthusiasm. He was by far the best manager I played under."

Denis Law

Denis Law arrived at Huddersfield in 1955. A frail-looking fifteen-year-old, he came down from Aberdeen with his two older brothers.

"They stayed in our digs," Ray Wilson recalls. "They sat around the table, and we were taking bets which of them it was, which of the two who'd brought the little lad along."

Ken recalls the surprise when he arrived for his trial.

He was a skinny, little lad, and he had these horn-rimmed spectacles and a squint. He really didn't look as if he was going to be any kind of player. There was talk that the club phoned back to Scotland to check that we'd got the right one.
But as soon as you saw him on the field, you realised that he was absolutely magic. Even at that stage, when he was only fifteen.

"Shankly fed him up," Ray Wilson says. "Put some weight on him. And he turned into the best player Town had ever seen. And he was only just twenty when he left."

Ken agrees:

He had balance, and he had speed off the mark. The main thing you try to do as a defender is to slow the forward down as he approaches you, then you can get your tackle in. But Denis would come up to you, he would show you the ball and ffffsshhh, he was away.
His acceleration was like Stanley Matthews or George Best. It was obvious from the start that he had that ability. It's something you're born with. You've either got it or you haven't. You can't teach it. And it's a very special gift, because it breaks down the other team's defence.

Denis Law was playing at inside-right in the Huddersfield first team before his 17th birthday, and at 18 he became Scotland's youngest ever international.

He was a sparkly, little fellow. He was full of life, and his football reflected that. He always played with that spirit, and that was his greatest asset.
To me he was never overpowered by the limelight he got. He took recognition and praise very well, and he kept his feet on the ground.
I can see a little of Denis in Michael Owen. He's the nearest to him in the present day game. But Owen isn't as good in the air as Denis was.
I'd rate Denis ahead of Matthews and Best. Matthews wasn't as direct a player. He wasn't a goal-scorer; his job was just to get the ball across to the forwards. And

I think that George Best was probably difficult to play with, because his team-mates would never have known when he was going to release the ball. His job was to do the unusual, but the unusual thing can confuse your own players as much as the opposition.
Denis was easier to play with. He was great in front of goals; he could put the ball away. And he was a good team player, aware of everybody else.

It was Bill Shankly who nurtured Law, promoting him to the first team and encouraging his talent. Then, soon after Shankly left for Liverpool, Law was transferred to Manchester City.

He might have gone to Arsenal. They were a grander club, and their Highbury ground – with its marble halls and underfloor heating – oozed class. But Law, having agreed terms with their manager George Swindin, had a childish fit of pique when Swindin sent his deputy Ron Greenwood to Huddersfield with the paperwork, and he signed for Manchester City instead. "I'm embarrassed to think about it now," he says, "because I'm not big-headed."

The proposed move to Arsenal came only months after Swindin had enquired about Ken's availability for a move down to London, raising the intriguing possibility that the two of them might have ended up playing together at Highbury.

There was no point in my leaving Huddersfield. I had my family, and I had the cricket in summer. And anyway, with the maximum wage, I wouldn't have been earning any more money. But Denis was still single, and he didn't want to be playing in the Second Division. It was the right thing for him to do.

The season after Denis Law's departure, Huddersfield struggled to avoid relegation from Division Two.

It went very flat after he'd gone. We bought new players, but it was impossible to replace him.

While Huddersfield limped on in the Second Division, Law moved to Torino in Italy, then to Manchester United where – with George Best and Bobby Charlton – he became part of one of the great forward lines of English club football, winning the European Cup in 1968.

He was a great player. If I were picking a team from all the footballers of my time, John Charles would be the first name I would write down, and Denis Law would be the second.

The valley of tears

Saturday 21 December 1957

It was the last Saturday before Christmas. The Queen was preparing for her first televised broadcast to the nation, the government had come out against a proposal to legalise homosexual acts, and the new rock'n'roll sensation Elvis Presley received news of his call-up to the US Army.

Ken was now a full-time footballer in winter, his art education over, and he was at number four, right-half, in the Huddersfield Town team that Bill Shankly took on the train to London, to play Charlton Athletic at The Valley.

For the first time since 1936, Charlton were down in the Second Division and, with a persistent drizzle in the cold air, the vast and mostly unroofed ground – with a capacity of about 80,000 – contained only 12,535 spectators.

Denis Law was suffering from a thigh injury, and Bill Shankly – faced with a Christmas schedule of four games in eight days and a Charlton pitch on the heavy side – decided that he would not risk the young Scot.

After only 15 minutes Law's replacement Stan Howard challenged for a loose ball on the edge of the Charlton penalty area, causing the home team's centre-half and captain Derek Ufton to be carried off with a dislocated shoulder. With no substitutes, his Charlton team-mates were left to play 75 minutes with only ten men and, by half-time, they were two goals down – though, according to the *Huddersfield Examiner*, they were lucky that it was not four or five 'as Taylor and McGarry, the Town wing-halves, took advantage of the weakness of the opposition.'

During the interval the Charlton manager Jimmy Trotter exhorted his team to attack. He switched his out-of-form left-winger Johnny Summers to centre-forward and sent his team back out with a formation that looked to the *Examiner* as 'four forwards and five half-backs.' Summers, who had been playing in old boots held together by sticking plaster, put on a new pair, not fully broken in, and, after three minutes, he mis-hit from close range with his weaker right foot to close the gap to 2-1. Inevitably, however, there were spaces appearing at the back and, after an hour, Huddersfield's lead had increased to 5-1.

According to Denis Law, sitting beside his manager, "Shanks was full of what a bad side they were and how we were going to rub it in."

In the first match of the season, back at Leeds Road, Charlton had gone three up against Huddersfield and, thanks to a late goal by Ken, Town had forced a 3-3

draw. Surely, 5-1 down after an hour and with only ten men, Charlton could not match their recovery.

Two minutes later it was 5-3 as first Johnny Ryan, then Summers – again with his weaker foot, this time the ball bouncing in off the post – brought the damp crowd alive with hope. Then in the 74th minute Summers completed a remarkable, right-footed hat-trick, driving the ball in 'with a tremendous shot' that beat the diving effort of Sandy Kennon, Town's young Rhodesian keeper.

"Sandy was a showman," Ken says. "A great lad, but he liked to turn easy saves into slightly more difficult ones, by moving to one side and diving at the ball. And that day he kept missing them."

A fortnight earlier, Summers' place in the Charlton team had been under threat. "Things weren't coming off for him," his manager said afterwards. Yet here he was with a second-half hat-trick, and in the 80th minute the story of his afternoon grew even more fanciful. 'Charlton's ten men kept up the pressure and, as the Town defence slithered in the mud, pandemonium broke loose when Summers drove in the equaliser.' It was only his fourth shot of the match, and they had all gone into the net.

"Later, when I moved to Everton," left-back Ray Wilson reflects, "if we were ever two or three in front, especially if we were away from home, the other side might as well have gone off the field, because we just used to keep the ball. But at Charlton we were 5-1 up, and we were still having a go. That was Shankly for you."

It was 5-5, with ten minutes left – but the drama was not over. 'Three minutes later, Summers ploughed through the mud and shot again.' Kennon had the ball covered, but it deflected off centre-half Jack Connor's leg and went into the net through Kennon's outstretched legs.' *Charlton 6 Huddersfield 5.*

"I'll keep these boots for the rest of my life," the bewildered Summers told reporters later, displaying the boots that he had only worn for 45 minutes. "I never dreamed they would bring me five goals – all with my right foot, and I'm a natural left-footer."

He was also presented with the ball, signed by all his colleagues, but sadly the souvenirs of his fairy tale day would not be with him for long. Within five years he would be dead from leukaemia.

"If you wrote a book about that match," Ray Wilson reckons, "you'd get halfway through and you'd say, 'What a load of bollocks!' It was incredible."

That afternoon at Leeds Road Barry Garthwaite was watching Huddersfield Reserves, and he recalls the disbelieving gasps of the crowd as the electronic scoreboard changed Charlton's goal tally five times in 22 minutes: 5-1, 5-2, 5-3, 5-4, 5-5, now 5-6.

But it was not yet over. With just three minutes remaining, Stan Howard bustled in an equaliser. 6-6. And, in the words of the *Examiner*'s reporter, 'everybody, it seemed, was content with the draw.' As the match entered its last seconds, a Charlton player lingered over a throw-in forty yards from the Huddersfield goal, picking up and putting down the ball, and 'a spectator, breathing down the back of my neck, said in agonised tones, "For pity's sake, referee, blow the whistle!"'

The throw-in, however, was taken. 'The ball travelled across the field. There was no apparent danger. Conwell was moving for an interception. Then – disaster! He lost his foothold in the mud, and Ryan was left to race on his own towards goal.'

"I can still remember that," Ken sighs. "Our full back had it all nicely covered, and he just slipped. He fell. BANG! And that was it."

'Kennon came out.' the *Examiner* reported. 'It was all he could do. Ryan shot. It was not a hard drive, and Kennon's attempt to divert it merely sent it up in the air. It had not enough velocity to go up over the crossbar, and it fell into the net.'

Charlton 7 Huddersfield 6.

The final whistle went, and 'the crowd gathered in front of the stand, chanting "We want Summers!" They refused to move until the whole Charlton team made an appearance. One might have thought that Charlton had just won the FA Cup.'

In the visitors' dressing room, Denis Law remembers, Shankly was not best pleased. "He tore into everyone, even the reserves for not being good enough to get in the team in the first place."

The train journey home was a subdued one. "Shankly was pacing up and down," Ray Wilson recalls. "He was muttering to himself: 'It's just one of those things … It's history …' He was trying to sort it out in his mind, how it had happened." But Ken can only remember him sitting in a stony silence. "He didn't speak to anybody for days afterwards."

On Christmas and Boxing Days, Town played home and away against Middlesbrough, with Ken moved back to centre-half to mark their dangerous centre-forward Brian Clough. "Brian was an excellent player," Ken says. "He wasn't tall, but he was quick. He moved well, and he could put the goals away." Town won both games 1-0, and the *Examiner* reckoned that he 'kept their dangerous centre-forward Clough under control.'

Next came the FA Cup, and Town were drawn at home to Charlton. They drew 2-2 in Yorkshire. Then, on a sunny Wednesday afternoon, 26,637 spectators arrived at The Valley, expecting yet another feast of goals. The two teams had produced 23 in three meetings, but this time a match of little distinction was settled by a single goal from Charlton's Johnny Ryan that even his team-mates assumed was off-side.

Charlton 7 Huddersfield 6. Nearly fifty years have passed, and the match still stands as a record. No other team in the history of the Football League has scored as many as six goals and lost.

"It was a weird game," Ray Wilson says. "It took me ages to come to terms with it."

Ken is more philosophical. "We had a good side at that time. It's just one of those things that happen. When you played in muddy conditions like that, all sorts of things could happen. In many ways football wasn't as skilful a game as it is now, but it could be more exciting."

Teams
Charlton Athletic: Duff; Edwards, Townsend; Hewie, Ufton, Kiernan; White, Lucas, Ryan, Leary, Summers.
Huddersfield Town: Kennon; Conwell, Wilson; Taylor, Connor, McGarry; Ledger, Howard, Bain, Massie, Simpson.

Bryan Stott

"Opening the innings is special," Bryan Stott thinks. "You start to get your nerves, the adrenalin starts to flow when the other team is nine wickets down, and you're waiting to get off and gather your thoughts. And it makes such a difference who your partner is. Opening the innings with Ken was a wonderful experience for me; I wouldn't swap it. We were good friends, we roomed together, and in the middle we were working together, not in competition. Batting is so much more enjoyable when you're on a wavelength with your partner."

"We were both good runners between the wickets," Ken says, "and we could put pressure on the other team with our running. I think there was a Roses match once when we ran six singles in the first over, and that was unheard of in Yorkshire."

"When you bat a lot with someone," Bryan explains, "you get to know when they're moving into position what's going to happen next. And often we'd be running without saying anything, and the other team would be saying, 'How's that happened?' Ken had tremendously strong legs; he had that power to burst from a standing start. We had some hairy escapes at times and Dougie Padgett, if he was next in, would be a nervous wreck by the time he got in. But it was a great joy. Very exhilarating."

"Bryan was like me," Ken says. "He liked to play his shots. He was a left-hander, and he'd flash away outside the off stick. Arthur Mitchell the coach virtually crucified him in the nets when he was a youngster. It was only Maurice Leyland who saved him. He took him aside. 'Come into my net,' he said."

Stott and Taylor. They were a new generation, reaching adulthood at a time of post-war optimism and they played with a greater freedom than was customary in Yorkshire.

"I remember one net with Arthur Mitchell," Ken says. "I'd batted for ten or fifteen minutes, hitting the ball everywhere, and I said to him as I came out, 'You know, Arthur, if you get your feet in the right position, you can hit every ball for four.' He looked at me. 'Eeh, you don't want to do that,' he said. 'You'll get the bowler taken off.'"

"Ken had some beautiful shots," Bryan says, "especially against left-arm slow bowlers and leg-spinners. He used to paste them. He'd get to the pitch and let the bat go straight through. It was wonderful to watch."

The two of them had known each other from their early teens. Bryan was a year older than Ken, a grammar school boy at Aireborough who played for Airedale and Wharfedale Schools against Huddersfield Schools, and they were soon playing together for Yorkshire Schoolboys, the North of England, the Federation side and then the county second eleven.

Together in second eleven days

"We seemed to get on right from the beginning," Ken says. "In some ways we were in competition, two young batsmen trying to get into the Yorkshire team, but it never felt like that. Even when we played away matches for Yorkshire Schools and we were billeted with the parents of one of the other side, we always seemed to be put together."

Bryan had had two summers away from Yorkshire, doing National Service in the RAF, and in the second of those years, 1956, Ken had made his mark with 168 at Trent Bridge. But Bryan took his chance the next year, hitting two big hundreds in a week in July, and the following week they were paired together at the top of the order.

It was not a happy time for Yorkshire cricket. Surrey were in the sixth year of their seven-year reign as county champions, and Yorkshire – under the captaincy of Billy Sutcliffe – had lost their way. Between 1900 and 1946 they had won the championship 19 times in 37 summers. Yet they had only the shared title of 1949 to show for their efforts in the next eleven summers. The team was full of outsized personalities, and Billy Sutcliffe – appointed because he was an amateur and because he was son of the great Herbert – could not make a cohesive group of them.

"He had a hard time," Bryan says, "from the spectators and from his own players. And his father interfered too much. Even when we were away, Herbert kept appearing, taking Billy to one side. The spirit in the team was terrible. I think, when Ken and I got in the side, it was a breath of fresh air for Billy."

One who provided quiet encouragement to the young Bryan was fellow left-hander Willie Watson. "A beautifully balanced batsman," Bryan calls him, "and as nice a chap as you could meet. I was always having to bat with Freddie's rough outside my off stump, and one day at Sheffield he took me and Ken to the nets. 'Come on, Bryan,' he said. 'I'll show you what to do.' He roughed up a patch and got Ken bowling leg-spinners. And he showed me how he used to sweep the ball from an upright position, with his bat almost vertical. Here was I, a new player threatening to take his position, and he was prepared to show me how to play. There were others in the team who wouldn't have done that."

In only their second match together, at Trent Bridge, Bryan and Ken shared a partnership of 122 (Bryan 50, Ken 79) in the first innings and one of 230 (Bryan 114, Ken not out 140) in the second. 'They were undisturbed by the new ball,' Jim Kilburn wrote in the *Yorkshire Post*, 'undisturbed by the leg breaks of Dooland and Goonesena and, to all appearances, undisturbed by the stentorian instruction (mostly contradictory) from the corner of the ground nearest to the Trent Bridge Inn.'

For Bill Bowes in the *Yorkshire Evening News* it promised to be the turning point in a dismal summer: 'Both youngsters used their feet, they hit powerfully to the covers and they ran well between the sticks.' Eric Stanger in the *Post* even speculated that they 'could become the modern counterpart of Brown and Tunnicliffe, or Sutcliffe and Holmes.'

A third century stand followed the next week at Hove; then Ken went back to football. His only visit to cricket came when he was summoned to Headingley to be presented, along with Bryan Stott, with his county cap.

One old pro at Leicester remarked to the *Yorkshire Post* that, if they had been playing for the Midland county, they would not have had to wait so long. "They wouldn't only have had their caps. They could have had the pavilion and half the bar takings as well."

Yorkshire were not a county to build up their young players too quickly. It was either that summer or the next that there was a rumour that the England selectors wanted to catapult Bryan and Ken into the England side while they were still young and brimming with confidence. "But Brian Sellers scotched the idea," Ken says. "He said we weren't ready."

There is a tide in the affairs of men
Which, taken at the flood, leads on to fortune.

So much of one's fate comes with the flow of events, and we can only wonder what might have happened had Sellers reacted more positively.

Bryan topped the Yorkshire averages in 1958 and 1960, scoring more than 2,000 runs in the year between. But he never came into serious Test contention again. And Ken's brief England career in 1959 ended in failure.

They were vital members of a side that won four championships in five years, and in Ken's view that affected their chances of a Test place. "There were batsmen at other counties, who weren't running for the championship, who could play for themselves. They could play every innings at the pace that suited them, and at the end of the season they would have a better average. Nobody ever looks at the averages and thinks, 'A third of his knocks were on account of the position in the match.' To a certain extent, figures spoil the game. The object of playing a team game is for your team to win. That's how we played it at that time at Yorkshire. And Bryan was a great team man."

Despite all their success, the players at Yorkshire were never allowed to feel secure. Players were only ever offered one summer's work at a time, and the closest that anybody came to a feeling of security was the award of a county cap. At the start of 1962 even this was not a great reassurance.

"We had 14 capped players at the start of the season," Bryan remembers. "On the first day of outdoor practices in April, we had our players' meeting with Brian Sellers. We were all sitting in the old dressing room with a fire going, waiting, and Brian Sellers comes clomping along the corridor. And he closes the door behind him and leans back against it. 'There's fourteen of you here now,' he says. 'But there won't be at the end of the season.' That was our pre-season pep talk."

Vic Wilson was captain, and there were obviously places in the team for Fred Trueman, Brian Close, Ray Illingworth and Jimmy Binks. "But the rest of us started the season under a cloud. One of the papers, the *Express* or the *Mail*, even had all our pictures printed on the top of the back page, with an axe hanging above each of us. It was a terrible situation."

The bowlers were Mike Cowan, Mel Ryan, Bob Platt and Don Wilson. The batsmen under threat, apart from Ken and Bryan, were Doug Padgett, Phil Sharpe and Brian Bolus. The assumption was that one of each would go – and this was further complicated when Geoff Boycott, John Hampshire and Tony Nicholson all forced their way up from the second team during the summer.

"Knowing Ken," Bryan says, "the whole thing would have passed him by. He wouldn't have been bothered about it."

"That's right," Ken says. "I never gave it a thought that I would be one that ought to go. I was bowling as well at that time, and I was saving runs as a fielder."

Perhaps Bryan did not feel threatened when Sellers spoke his words, but he soon had a rude awakening. With his bags already packed for the opening three-match tour of Lord's, Cambridge and Oxford, he was taken aside and told that he was not going with the team. "It was like a bombshell. Everything in my world had collapsed."

The next day he went to see John Nash the secretary at his offices in Park Row. "I didn't know what to do. The second team weren't playing for nearly a month; there was no cricket for me. 'We've approached the Yorkshire leagues,' he said, 'to see if they're prepared to take players on a temporary basis, and you've been allocated to Doncaster.' Apparently, they'd put all our names in a hat and drawn them out. 'Don't worry, Bryan,' he said. 'Everybody will be given a chance.'"

At Doncaster he could not score a run. "I was trying, I really was, believe you me, but I kept getting out. There were a couple of lbws among them. So obviously Doncaster didn't really want me. I wasn't even breaking any pots when the second eleven started. The stuffing had been knocked out of me. I was convinced I was never going to play for the first team again."

Eventually, after 13 matches, Brian Close was injured, and he returned to the side to play Derbyshire at Hull. "I was as nervous as a kitten. I went in at number five at one o'clock, and I hardly touched the ball. I might have edged a couple of singles. I was totally at sea. I took my pads off at lunch, and I sat on my own in the dressing room. Then I thought, 'Bugger it, I'm going to have a lunch.' Because the catering at Hull was excellent, and I thought I might as well eat, I wasn't going to last long. And as I passed the press table Ross Jenkinson from the Sheffield paper grabbed my arm. 'What on earth are you doing, Bryan?' he said. 'How did you get into this side? … Well, go out there and play like that.' And I went out. I played my normal game. I thought, 'If I'm out, I'm out.' And I got 100. And, of course, that put the cat among the pigeons."

Six weeks later they were playing at Bristol while the Yorkshire committee and the vice-presidents – about 35 of them in all – met to make their decision. "Vic had to go off at three o'clock to take the call. We were in the field, and we could see him through the window of the secretary's office, waiting by the phone. Eventually we saw him talking. Then he came back out. 'It's Mike Cowan and Brian Bolus,' he said."

There was a sequel in the bar at Sheffield in the next match. "One of the senior vice-presidents, a chap called Furniss, he walked with a limp and had a moustache, came up to me. 'Congratulations, Stott,' he said, 'on still being a Yorkshire player – by one vote.' 'Thank you very much, Mr Furniss,' I said."

That winter Bryan sat down and re-assessed his life. He decided to play just one more season, then go into the family building business. He hit 143 in the Roses match at Sheffield, putting on 249 with the young Geoff Boycott, but Ken missed much of the season injured and they played only four times together. Their golden days were over.

"It wasn't the same for me after Bryan retired," Ken says.

"We had a great friendship," says Bryan. "We seem to be on a wavelength even now. The other week I rang him. I'd been thinking about him, how I hadn't rung for a bit. And he answered. 'I've just been thinking about you while I've been washing the car.' That's always been there between us."

Frederick Sewards Trueman

Fred Trueman was the spearhead of the bowling attack throughout Ken's years as a Yorkshire cricketer. Born into a mining family near Maltby, he had the great ability to swing the ball late at high pace, and his fitness was such that, in a 20-year career which took in four major overseas tours, he never broke down. Each year he would play in more than 30 matches and at his peak, in the four summers from 1959 to 1962, he bowled 4,464 overs and took 623 wickets.

He was the first bowler to take 300 Test wickets, a total that might have been nearer 400 if the England selectors had been less reluctant to engage with his fiery reputation. He retired at the end of 1968, at the same time as Ken. Their last match together brought the championship to Yorkshire for the seventh time in ten years.

Fred was the greatest fast bowler I've ever seen. He had everything: a beautiful action, speed, control, stamina. And he had the will-power to bowl as quick at half past five as he did at half past eleven. He was a tremendous trier. He'd bowl 1,000 to 1,200 overs in a summer and never give up. He expected a wicket every ball, and he'd look disappointed if he didn't get it.

We were paid about £20 for an away match, out of which we had to pay our own expenses, and about £12 – 10s for a home match. Well, Fred lived in Scarborough so a home match for him was an away match. He used to look at his pay after he'd taken out his expenses, and it came to about thirty bob. One pound fifty. He'd sit there: "Do they want me to bowl second innings?" But he always did. I only ever faced him in the nets, and he didn't like anybody to hit him, even there. He'd always be trying.

Occasionally the Yorkshire team would play a football match, and Fred wasn't a bad player in a rugged kind of way. He liked to play centre-forward – but then so did Closey. And neither of them had any idea of passing the ball. We needed three footballs – one for Fred, one for Closey and one for the other twenty of us.

I can see Fred now, coming in to bowl from the pavilion end at Bradford Park Avenue with the white wall behind him. He had a beautiful run-up. I would be at cover, Don Wilson at mid-wicket, and everybody else would be behind the bat. It was a wonderful sight. He came in at a slight angle to the bowling crease, his back foot would drop behind the bowling line and his front leg would go across. A typical sideways-on action. It was so good that he automatically swung the ball away.

In those days it was a back-foot law for no balls, and Fred would wear a metal plate on his toe cap. His back foot would drop behind the back line, and he would drag it forward about two feet so that, by the time he was releasing the ball, he was two foot over the front line. You can see it in the picture. Tyson did it, too. It meant that the ball was onto the batsman quicker.

He had strong shoulders and a big backside to give him power. The first three matches of the season were MCC at Lord's, then Oxford and Cambridge. And by the end of that, Fred was fit. He rarely went out more than ten minutes before a match to warm up. Not many of us did. But he was always fit to bowl.

In Test matches he bowled with Brian Statham. Brian had an unorthodox action. He was open-chested, but he dropped the ball on the seam and moved it about. He bowled straight and quick and, if you missed, he hit the wicket. He bowled a slightly shorter length than Fred, who had to bowl fuller to give the ball a chance to swing. As a pair the two of them were magnificent.

For the last few years Fred was senior pro to Brian Close but, instead of turning to Fred, Closey would consult Illy, who was a great thinker about the game. Fred had so much natural ability, he didn't have to think. But in our last season Fred was captain when we beat the Australians at Sheffield. In those days the tourist match was a hard game, not just a chance for practice like it is now, and we won by an innings. And Fred took wickets. He'd lost a bit of pace by then, but he was a crafty bowler. He knew his trade.

It's the bowlers who win matches; the batsmen only save them. It was a great ten years, and a lot of it was due to Fred and the other opening bowlers: Bob Platt, Mike Cowan, Mel Ryan, Tony Nicholson. They all struggled uphill against the wind while Fred was coming down.

If I'm ever asked to name the greatest fast bowler in my lifetime, I always say Fred Trueman.

Not the Taylor who won selection

From 1951 to 1958 England had not lost a Test series. The Ashes had been won back in 1953, held in 1954/55 and held again in 1956. It was a golden age, rich with great players, but it all fell to earth in the winter of 1958/59 when Peter May's side were beaten by four Tests to none in Australia.

The Indians were the visitors in the summer of 1959, and all talk was of blooding some younger talent. Ken was among those under consideration, and at Middlesbrough – in front of selector Herbert Sutcliffe – he reinforced his claim with an innings of 103 against Notts. The young Peter Forman, making his debut for the visitors, was helpless as in one over Ken hit the last five balls for 4, 4, 6, 6, 4, all with classical shots. "Nice little slow left-arm bowler," he says with a smile. "I kept hitting him straight."

A fortnight later Ken was at Lord's, playing for the MCC against the Indians in what was in effect a Test trial. His newspaper cuttings record that he scored a 'fluent' and 'praiseworthy' 45 runs that 'gained admiration' before 'being bowled off a stroke which looked a bit careless.'

Back in Bradford, Ken's Yorkshire place was filled by a nervous Dickie Bird. 'Whenever he was next man in, you knew where he'd be. He'd be on the loo. If a wicket dropped, you'd have to go and knock on the door. 'You're in, Dickie.' But he wasn't so nervous once he got out to the middle.' And that day at Bradford, though Ken did not see it, he played the innings of a lifetime: 181 not out. His previous highest score was 62, and he was in seventh heaven as he walked off to great applause. But, Ken says, repeating the much-told story, "Brian Sellers met him as he came off the

field. 'Well batted, Dickie,' he said. 'You're back in the seconds tomorrow.'"

The following Sunday, while Ken was playing golf at Woodsome Hall, the team was announced for the first Test at Trent Bridge, and somebody came up to him with the news he had been hoping for: "You're in."

The letters and telegrams poured in, including one from his former painting tutor William Townsend: 'You never know what may come out of the Slade. I am sure you can claim to be the first England Test player we have produced.'

It was a new England team: no Lock or Laker, no Bailey, Graveney or Watson, not even the younger Peter Richardson who was out of county cricket, re-qualifying for Kent. It gave Ken a golden opportunity to establish himself in one of the opening slots.

> Trent Bridge was my favourite ground. I'd got my first hundred for the second team there – and my first two hundreds for Yorkshire. So I was looking forward to playing.

The toss was won, and at 11.30 on a bright June morning he and Arthur Milton walked out to the middle. Two footballing cricketers brimming with ability, could they realise their potential at Test level?

> I didn't know Arthur very well. He was a really nice chap, but he was a bit older than me and I'd never played against him at football.
> You're in a bit of a haze. You just go through the motions to a certain extent. You're not too conscious of what's happening.

'The sky was blue,' John Bapty wrote in the *Yorkshire Evening Post*, 'the sun was bright and hot, and the wicket was reckoned to be a beauty, despite the touch of early green. It gave Taylor a wonderful chance.'

Arthur Milton and Colin Cowdrey fell cheaply, and at 29 for two Peter May was coming out in a minor crisis. Ken was playing the new ball with care, but he was not wholly in command. 'He was not the Taylor who won selection,' John Arlott wrote sympathetically. But he was still there at 12.40 when the seamer Desai took his sweater, and his score of 24 had been made out of a healthier-looking 60 for two. In the words of John Bapty, 'the promised land seemed in sight.'

'He saw the new ball away,' Len Hutton wrote. 'He did nothing spectacular; on the other hand, he never

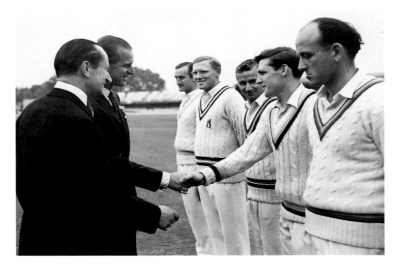

Prince Philip meeting the MCC team at Lord's. *From left to right:* Ted Dexter, Mike Smith, Arthur Milton, Ken and Frank Tyson

looked to be troubled.'

Gupte the leg-spinner took the ball, and Ken's upbringing in the Stile Common yard – his confidence against the ball spinning away from him – now offered him the chance of quicker runs. The first ball came down. He reached out to it, as he knew to do, and it spun to leg, a googly that hit his pad.

> I played as far forward as you can get. It hit the outside of my left leg and went down for leg byes. Peter May and I crossed. And I was almost at the other end when Gupte appealed.

The umpire was Eddie Phillipson. If only it had been Hugo Yarnold or even Syd Buller, the man at square leg. But Phillipson, the former Lancashire bowler, was one who was inclined to give the lbws. The Sussex seamer Ian Thomson always used to say that he checked the direction of the wind when deciding which end to bowl – "except when Eddie Phillipson was umpiring, when I always went to his end."

> Eddie Phillipson – he liked to give everybody out – he raised his finger. And that was it.
> We won by an innings so I didn't get in again. Peter May was very upset for me when I was given out. And I believe Johnny Wardle, who'd seen it on telly, he even phoned with his anger. I don't know who he phoned. He thought it was disgraceful.

Batting conditions grew easier. After surviving a dropped catch Ken Barrington, another of the selectors' experimental choices, made a 'workmanlike' fifty, though *The Times* thought that he was 'not a born Test match cricketer' and that 'Taylor had more natural class' than him.

Under pressure to produce runs in the second Test at Lord's, Ken made only 6 and 3, and both he and Arthur Milton – along with Martin Horton and the veteran Godfrey Evans – found themselves discarded for Headingley. By contrast Ken Barrington, with another 'competent' fifty, established himself as a fixture in the England side.

Nearly half a century has passed, but Ken still thinks from time to time about that lbw decision. He had not batted well, but he had played himself in and who knows what might have followed if fortune had looked more kindly on him?

John Arlott, perhaps intuiting some deeper insecurity in Ken's make-up, put it differently. 'He is a far better player than this: but until he himself is convinced of his own merits, he might be happier establishing himself as a genuinely big fish in the lesser, but still exacting, waters of county cricket.'

After the Lord's Test, Arlott wrote to Ken:

From:
John Arlott.   69, George Street,
                                                London, W 1
22nd June 1959   Welbeck 8766

My dear Ken,

My *associate* membership of M.C.C. does not take me into the Lord's pavilion, alas. That meant I could not see you during the game, and at the end we were tied up trying to maintain some sort of service and doing recordings after the game was over until half-past-six.

So sorry not to have seen you – but do let's meet up again during the season. I am sorry, too, that things did not go well for you at Lord's. It is becoming an old story now, with men getting their first break on a first morning green'un, and then on a quick bowlers wicket at Lord's, then giving way to someone who gets an easy ride at Headingley, but I hope that opportunity may come your way. Meanwhile, don't fret a scrap. It has to work out right and I know the selectors have had very much in mind that the three men who did not succeed at Lord's – Arthur, Martin and yourself – looked the three best fieldsmen in the side.

Now to the other game. This, of course, very confidentially. I have talked to George Swindin, and he thinks you would be just the right sort of player for Highbury. Although he did not say it, I imagine that he thinks to make a straight approach to Huddersfield might well push the price up, so I wonder if you could let me know if Huddersfield have a mind to sell you? What they might want? and to what extent cricket would limite your soccer availability? – and anything else that might be relevant.

See you about the country – until then, kindest wishes.

Yours
Jon.

Ken Taylor, Esq.,
c/o Yorkshire County Cricket Club,

Alas for Ken, it was just as Arlott predicted. On an easy-paced Headingley pitch the new England openers, Geoff Pullar and Gilbert Parkhouse, put on 146 for the first wicket.

Neither Ken nor Arthur would open for England again. Instead, they returned to their counties and to the most thrilling championship for years. For Arthur, not quite feeling at home in the England side, there was an element of relief about his return home. But not for Ken.

> It was awful. I really enjoyed being in the England team.

The golden summer of 1959

It was a glorious summer, with day after day of warm sunshine, the best summer for many years. And Britain, finally emerging from the years of austerity, was in the mood to enjoy it. Three-quarters of homes now had television sets, there was a Mini car on sale for only £500, and new inventions – from the transistor radio to the hovercraft – were filling the country with a sense of hope and progress. The young Queen was expecting her third child, and the Prime Minister Harold Macmillan was happy to be associated with the catch-phrase of 'You've never had it so good.'

After a gloomy and wet decade, cricket basked in the sunshine, with crowds everywhere flocking back to the grounds. Gate receipts for Yorkshire's home matches were up by more than 50%, and – with the Test series against India disappointingly one-sided – the county championship took centre stage with as thrilling a

contest as there had ever been. Never had so many of the counties stayed in contention for so long.

Yorkshire were turning to a new generation of cricketers. The previous year it had appointed the 40-year-old Ronnie Burnet, a chemical engineer with no experience of first-class cricket, to take over the captaincy, and in a spectacular showdown at the end of July he had brought about the sacking of his great slow left-arm bowler Johnny Wardle. With Willie Watson already gone to Leicester and Bob Appleyard and Frank Lowson forced out by poor health, he started the summer of 1959 with the most inexperienced team Yorkshire had ever fielded in the modern era. His senior professional Vic Wilson was 38; the others ranged from 28 to 18.

All through the 1950s, when Surrey had dominated year after year, Yorkshire supporters had grown ever more

The Yorkshire team early in the summer of 1959
back (left to right): Ken Taylor, Don Wilson, David Pickles, Bob Platt. Jimmy Binks, Doug Padgett, Bryan Stott
front: Ray Illingworth, Vic Wilson, Ronnie Burnet, Brian Close, Fred Trueman

frustrated at the county's failure to win the title. But in 1959 summer began with a greater acceptance that there would be no immediate glory. "We are in the process of rebuilding," chairman Brian Sellers said at the pre-season lunch. "We cannot expect to win the championship in the next three or four years." Or, as Jim Kilburn put it, looking back to the dissent that characterised the years of Billy Sutcliffe's captaincy, 'An inadequate team trying hard all the time is more acceptable than a team of better technicians showing indifference.'

The instructions were out from Lord's to provide hard, true surfaces and, with so much sunshine and with some covering of the pitch now allowed after the hours of play, the runs flowed. More than twice as many centuries were hit as in the previous year, and a record 23 batsmen completed 2,000 runs. It was certainly not a year to be a bowler, and Fred Trueman – whose 1,072 overs came on the back of a hard winter in Australia – took his wickets at 19.50 each where in 1958 he had averaged 13.33.

For Ken it was a summer that promised so much. He hit a century in the first championship match at Middlesbrough, and he impressed when summoned to Lord's to play for the MCC against the Indian tourists. But his two Test appearances were not a success, and by late June he was on the reject pile, sent back to play for a Yorkshire side that was mixing good days with bad in a way that did not suggest any rapid change to the county's recent fortunes. On 20 June, with more than a third of the programme completed, they lay in eighth place in a table headed by Essex, Glamorgan and Derbyshire.

But something was starting to click. Vic Wilson had lost his place, leaving the team even younger and less experienced, and Ronnie Burnet contributed very few runs, averaging barely ten – but, in Ken's view, "he created such a great atmosphere in the team. He didn't bowl, he hardly scored any runs and he only caught the ball when it came straight to him at mid-off, but he got an extra ten per cent out of everybody else. So it was worth having him in the side."

The sacking of Johnny Wardle the previous summer had sent shock waves through the side, and now the message was clear to anybody else with an awkward streak. There was no alternative but to step into line and accept the charismatic mix of discipline, encouragement and sheer fun that their amateur captain brought with him.

"A journey in his Jaguar from one game to the next

was a nerve-jangling experience," Bryan Stott recalls. "We'd be in the back with all the cricket bags, and in the passenger seat would be our scorer Herbert Walker. There were no motorways in those days and, when Ronnie got up to 100 miles an hour, Herbert used to pull his hat down over his eyes and pretend to be asleep."

"Sometimes he'd be driving at nearly 140," Ken reckons. "It had two petrol tanks so he wouldn't have to stop. We used to have a steak meal at this hotel in St Neots, the owner always made us very welcome, and sometimes it would be after twelve when we set off again. He was a great character. As long as you tried your best, he was happy."

"You always had to keep an eye on him in the field for instructions," Bryan says, "but you kept your other eye on Closey. That was the unwritten rule. He'd be the one who would be moving people about. Ronnie didn't read the game like Closey, but he was the one who changed the focus back from the individuals to the team itself. It was a very happy team that summer."

Then on the afternoon of Tuesday 7 July, surrounded by the limes and horse chestnuts of the attractive Queen's Park ground at Chesterfield, they produced a performance that leap-frogged them over Warwickshire to the top of the championship table.

It had been a game with plenty of runs, and Donald Carr the Derbyshire captain was reluctant to set too easy a target. So, to the annoyance of his Yorkshire visitors, he batted on for one ball after lunch so that the final target of 301 would have to be made in only three hours nine minutes. A victory for Derbyshire would have put them – not Yorkshire – top of the table, but Ken rose to the challenge with as important an innings as he played in his career. For Derek Hodgson it was 'an innings that would not have disgraced Len Hutton' as he raced to 144 and, with lively support from Sharpe, Padgett and Illingworth, the target was reduced to just 28 in 35 minutes. His dismissal was the cue for a pantomime in which Ronnie Burnet – breaking an accepted convention in county cricket – sent out Bryan Stott to bat ahead of the last recognised batsman. Bryan had not fielded since Saturday, and the normally mild-mannered Donald Carr waved him back into the pavilion. "Every time I've seen him since," Bryan says, "he's apologised to me."

For both sides it was a vital match, and – thanks to Ken's spectacular innings – Yorkshire won it with time to spare.

Taylor sets pace in Tykes' 95 r.p.h. dash to the top

By STEVE RICHARDS

CROUCHING, dynamic Ken Taylor, dropped by England after scratching failures against the Indians, yesterday led young Yorkshire to the top again and their greatest win this summer with a merciless 144 in 155 minutes that electrified Queen's Park, Chesterfield.

THIS magnificent Taylor, back to form at last, WILL do for England. He made the point with 22 fours and three crowd-frightening sixes.

"We didn't think we had a cat in hell's chance," gasped skipper Ronnie Burnet after Yorkshire (12 points), set to get 301 at 95 an hour, had beaten—or should it be slaughtered ?—Derbyshire (4 points) by six wickets with 15 minutes of extra time left.

THIS Yorkshire CAN win the county championship.

Amid dressing-room cries of "Get the beer out," Burnet said: "This win, without Trueman and Close, and with Stott not batting in the second innings, gives us tremendous confidence."

● KEN TAYLOR
. . . hit 144.

Ken looks at the cutting now and wonders. "I seemed to play all my best innings in games when I had to go for it. Against the clock. Perhaps I should have played a bit more positively all the time."

Yorkshire were top of the table, and they stayed there for a fortnight. Then at Bradford they took on Surrey in a contest that pitted the young pretenders against the long-time champions.

Monday was a normal working day, but the gates were closed and 'in a Test match atmosphere' Ken came on to bowl in the Surrey second innings. The reporter for *The Times* had last seen him bowling at Cambridge in May, when he had been experimenting with leg-breaks and googlies; now he was delivering 'innocuous-looking slow-medium in-swingers'. Yet, in a thrilling half hour, he broke the Surrey innings taking four good wickets for ten runs, including that of Peter May. Then in the evening and on the next morning he completed 'an eye-catching all-round performance' with 'a fine innings of 78. He played some lovely strokes, and he was watchful and selective, too.'

Alas, it was not enough to prevent Surrey completing a double of victories over their Northern rivals and, for the disappointed West Riding crowd who made their journeys home, the season seemed

to have reached a vital turning point. For those who had followed county cricket through the 1950s, the championship table now had a familiar look to it.

	Played	Won	Points
Surrey	16	8	126
Warwickshire	19	9	126
Yorkshire	18	8	124
Gloucestershire	18	7	112

May, caught Platt bowled Taylor, 22. It was an entry in the scorebook for Ken the part-time bowler to be proud of, but little could anyone there that day have realised that it would be the Surrey captain's last innings in England for nearly two years. He left the field on the Tuesday morning debilitated by internal pains and was diagnosed before the week was out with a deep-set abscess. With Jim Laker and Alec Bedser past their best years and Tony Lock remodelling his action, the loss of Peter May was a blow too many for the champions. It was indeed a turning point, and three weeks later Yorkshire were again top of the table.

Then began Yorkshire's traditional Southern tour: Lord's, Bath, Bristol, Worcester and Hove. Seventeen days away from home, travelling and playing in the heat of the long, hot summer.

Victory at Lord's, while their rivals faltered, gave them a significant advantage in the race – but there followed a disastrous week, losing for the first time for 56 years to Somerset and thus conceding first place to Warwickshire, then being skittled out for 35 by Gloucestershire who themselves went to the top.

It did not help that game after game Ronnie Burnet was losing the toss and that they were forever chasing runs on the final afternoon. Nor that, as Ken likes to point out, opposition captains treated the Yorkshire game as different from those against Gloucestershire and Warwickshire and would tend to set stiffer declarations. At Bath, on a turning pitch, they had to score 255 in two sessions, and – despite an attacking 70 by Ken – they collapsed as the lower order were persuaded by Brian Close to adopt his trademark lap shot in countering the off-spin of Brian Langford.

"I told you we should play normally," the captain protested when he got back to the pavilion after his own attempt to play the lap shot had ended up in Langford bowling him.

"No," Brian Close insisted, never one to leave the last word to others, "I told you to get your foot across when you played it."

Quite what went wrong at Bristol has never been agreed. The Saturday night drinking session that had

86

several of the more high-spirited members of the team facing a late night showdown in the hotel foyer cannot have helped, nor did the fog that came up the Bristol Channel and not only reduced visibility but created a damp pitch. The game barely lasted into the final morning, and the championship was suddenly looking a distant prospect.

	Played	Won	Points
Gloucestershire	26	12	186
Warwickshire	27	13	184
Yorkshire	26	12	178
Surrey	25	11	174

"Everybody was tired," Bryan Stott remembers. "Losing so badly at Bristol was actually the best thing for us. We finished early, and on the way to Worcester we stopped at Droitwich and we had a brine bath. It was a heavy, heavy season, and it gave us time to freshen up for the last two matches."

On Wednesday the bowlers all took wickets to dismiss Worcestershire for 120, then Bryan Stott – his legs no longer weary – carried his bat for an exhilarating 144. Don Kenyon fought back with a century for the home team, and Yorkshire's victory eventually came with only minutes to spare, to be followed by a long cross-country drive to Hove.

Gloucestershire's prospects took a grievous blow when they unaccountably prepared a spinners' wicket for the visit of Laker and Lock to their Wagon Works ground in Gloucester, and now the mathematics were getting clearer. If Yorkshire won at Hove, only Surrey could stop them and then only if they won their last two matches at The Oval.

	Played	Won	Points
Yorkshire	27	13	192
Surrey	26	12	186
Gloucestershire	27	12	186
Warwickshire	27	13	184

And what a game it was at Hove! Ken played his part, though only with the ball, taking four of the first five wickets to fall, and Ray Illingworth contributed a magnificent 122. "Ray really came of age that summer," Bryan says. "That hundred never gets mentioned, and it was vital. That was the time when he was really blossoming, coming into his own."

Ronnie Burnet had lost the toss again, and on the last day – when Fred Trueman was exhausted and the Yorkshire bowlers could not end the Sussex innings – it came down to another declaration. Only, with the championship at stake, the home captain Robin Marlar insisted on batting on. The innings did not end till a couple of the batsmen, fed up with their team's approach, threw away their wickets.

Yorkshire were left with the daunting task of making 215 in only 105 minutes. It was near impossible, some thought.

With news filtering through from The Oval that Surrey were almost certain not to win, the whole long summer was coming down to an hour and three quarters of batting at Hove.

Ken was lbw to Ted Dexter for one, and Brian Close – after one gigantic six over the scoreboard – soon followed. Then Bryan Stott was joined by Doug Padgett, and the whole team effort of the summer came to fruition with a stand that ran the Sussex team ragged. "I think Dougie's attitude," Ken says, "was that, if you weren't dour, you weren't playing the game properly." Yet that day he was far from dour.

"He was technically the best player in our side," Bryan Stott says. "He was polished, balanced; he just didn't have that confidence in himself to say to the bowler, 'I'm in charge.' But that was one of his most attacking innings. He played pure cricket shots, and he scored as fast as me. In a way, Ken's innings at Chesterfield set up our summer, and Dougie copied it on that last afternoon at Hove. He really did play well."

The two of them added 141 in an hour. The Sussex captain Robin Marlar tried all manner of fields; "I've never fielded so far from the bat as I did that day," his close catcher Alan Oakman says. But they still ran singles and twos at will. Such was their dominance that Ian Thomson, the steadiest of bowlers, bowled ten overs and went for 87 runs.

In the end they were both out, but there were seven minutes to spare when Brian Bolus glanced the winning boundary. The champagne corks popped, Harry Secombe appeared in the dressing room, and the next morning – between one and two o'clock – the people of Scarborough stood on the streets and cheered them into their hotel.

"The reception that night will stay with me as long as I live," Bryan says. The next morning, when they played the MCC, they took the field to even greater cheering.

It had been a wonderful summer, and Yorkshire cricket was strong again.

But Ken was not with them at Scarborough. He had gone home to Huddersfield – and to the new football season. While the team celebrated, he was left on his own to enjoy his memories of the long summer.

"It was a great side to be in," Ken says. "The spirit and the camaraderie were tremendous. Man for man we weren't as good as the previous Yorkshire side, but Ronnie Burnet created this wonderful team spirit. There was no selfishness, no jealousy. And that's what made the difference."

Marriage and family

Ken and Avril met at Huddersfield College of Art. She was a full-time student, but he had finished by this time. One of Avril's evening classes was Life Studies, with a model, and one week Ken turned up at it, wanting to keep his hand in with his drawing.

"We all had our special places," she remembers. "And there were these other people who came in. Older men, mostly, and, because we had a model, we were always rather suspicious of them. On the occasion that Ken came, he sat behind me and I thought that he was just another one of them. We had a break for the model to have a rest – they could be quite bruised at times from leaning on a hand for an hour – and I looked round at Ken's drawing. And I thought it was really very good, specially for someone coming in off the street. So I complimented him. 'It's very good,' I said. 'You ought to take it up.' And that's how it all started."

She was the daughter of a self-employed textile merchant, a middle man who bought from the mills and sold on to shops. Although she had no interest in sport, she does have a memory of her father coming home from watching football at Leeds Road one Saturday afternoon when she was only a small girl.

"He was a very keen Town supporter. If they'd won, we were all right for the rest of the day. And that day they had won. 'Jeff Taylor played a blinder,' he said. 'And they say he's got a younger brother who's even better.' It's funny. It stuck in my mind, and I don't remember anything else he said about football.'

"When we first started going out together, I asked Ken, 'What do you do for a living?' And he said, 'I play cricket.' 'Yes,' I said, 'but what do you do to earn money?' I had no idea that people were paid to play."

Early in their courtship Ken invited her to London, to watch him play cricket at Lord's. He arranged for her to catch the train down from Huddersfield and to stay with his brother Jeff and his wife Biddy.

"Ken was supposed to meet me at the station," Avril recalls. "I was quite young, and I'd never met Jeff and Biddy. I was very scared. And he wasn't there, just Biddy. He was having supper with John Arlott at the Carlton Club and, when he turned up, he was quite squiffy. They'd had wine with every course, and he was giggling. So I was really very nervous."

Next morning, as he took guard, Ken looked across to Avril in the stand. "He stuck his tongue out at me. It really was the most romantic thing."

It was the summer when Ken was trying to establish a regular place in the England team. But his relationship with Avril was a more lasting success and the following Spring, on the morning of Saturday 26 March 1960, they married at Holy Trinity Church in Huddersfield. Ken should have been at right-half in the Town team that played that day against Middlesbrough, but fortunately a knee injury – "a tongue-in-cheek injury," Ken calls it – gave him the afternoon off. His best man was Yorkshire cricketer Bob Platt, and others present included Derek Ibbotson, Bryan Stott, Ronnie Burnet, Doug Padgett and Chris Balderstone.

Ken and Avril have two children – Nicholas, born in June 1963, and Cameron, born in June 1966 – and, after several years of travelling about the world, the family settled in 1972 in Norfolk, where in time both boys attended Gresham's, the public school where Ken was by then Head of Art.

Nicholas, following his father's sporting path, was briefly a professional cricketer, playing as a fast bowler for Yorkshire, Surrey and Somerset, while Cameron, more inclined to the artistic, gained a degree in Graphic Design from Ipswich School of Art.

Nicholas now lives in California, where he experiments with abstract painting while earning his living as an interior decorator. Cameron is back in Norfolk after a spell in New Zealand, working as a graphic designer. His son Aidan is a central part of the lives of Ken and Avril.

Avril, Aidan, Ken

Top left: Nicholas
Top right: Cameron
Bottom: Cameron *(left)* and Nicholas

Travels around cricket

The summer of 1960 was not as relentlessly hot as that of 1959, but Yorkshire's schedule increased from 35 to 38 matches. And where should they start their defence of the championship but at Hove, the scene of their triumph eight months earlier?

It was a game that Ken remembers. On Monday morning, with Sussex all out for 280, he and Bryan Stott stepped out to bat, and in less than four hours on a true batting surface they had taken their partnership to 281. 'Theirs was a rare magnificence,' Jim Kilburn wrote in the *Yorkshire Post*. 'Their understanding and mutual confidence were a joy to behold and a constant source of profit. ... Boundaries came because the ball was hit firmly. ... In their innumerable swift singles they must have tired themselves joyfully, and they tired the Sussex fielding to the point of desperation and bedragglement.'

Vic Wilson, the new Yorkshire captain, declared. "The idea," Ken says, "was that Sussex would declare, then we'd have a go at whatever they set."

This part went to plan. Sussex left them 250 to win, and on Tuesday afternoon the two of them set out once more. Only this time Ken was caught at short leg for nought, and the batting collapsed. "I was the first Yorkshire wicket to fall in the match. It was nearly tea-time on the last day, and we finished up losing."

The old Fenner's pavilion 1958

Next they played on the easy-paced Fenner's pitch in Cambridge, where Phil Sharpe came into the side and made a double century. Then it was on to a low-scoring contest at Bradford, where Ken's 66 and 63 were the highest innings in a match that Yorkshire won in two days. From there they went out to Hull, where the arctic conditions are still vivid in Ken's mind.

It was absolutely freezing. Paul Gibb was umpiring, and

he was wearing three sweaters and two pairs of trousers. A wicket dropped, and he dashed off the field to go to the loo. And we waited and waited and waited for him to come back. We were all perishing and eventually, when he still hadn't reappeared, we sent Fred off to get him. They came back together. Apparently his hands had been so cold that, with his two pairs of trousers, he hadn't been able to do up his flies. Fred had had to do them for him.

"I think it was even snowing at one point," Phil Sharpe reckons. "I was twelfth man, and I had to send out every available garment onto the pitch, even my own. I was in my shirt sleeves, absolutely freezing, in the pavilion."

From Hull they drove down to Portsmouth, then to Gravesend, then back to Sheffield. And so it went on. From April 30 to September 6 they played six days every week, 37 matches in 18½ weeks. Then, with the championship won, they had a three-day break before playing against the Rest of England at The Oval.

The worst of it was that we played on so many different grounds in Yorkshire; we never really felt that we were playing at home.

The following year, 1961, they were required to play 39 games, and the 20 home ones were distributed as follows: Bradford 4, Sheffield 4, Scarborough 4, Headingley 3, Hull 2, Middlesbrough 2, Harrogate 1. Not till the final week at Scarborough did they stay for two matches in the same place.

That summer the fixture card started Lord's – Cambridge – Bradford – Oxford – Swansea – Hull. 900 miles of driving by the middle of May. In June they had Bradford – The Oval – Bristol – Middlesbrough. Then in July Taunton fell between matches at Chesterfield and Bradford.

The county paid our bed and breakfast, but we had to pay for all the travelling and if we had an evening meal. So I don't suppose they were bothered how long the journeys were.

It was a fixture list that would send the modern cricketer into a state of apoplexy. They were at the northern tip of the county circuit, and twenty times they were scheduled to pack up after a day's play and drive more than 100 miles – not on motorways but on winding 'A' roads that ran through town centres.

"We used to double up in cars," Bryan Stott says. "Sometimes three. With all the luggage it wasn't easy. We'd plan a route, with all the road numbers."

I remember going to Neath. We thought we'd take a short cut, and we got completely lost. By the time we got there, the others had had dinner and were coming out of the pictures.

Their card had 117 days squeezed into 20 weeks. By contrast, their 2004 counterparts had 93 days spread over nearly 24 weeks – with only one overnight journey of more than 100 miles.

"You just used to set off and do it," Bryan Stott says. "It was tiring, but I can't recall ever thinking, 'Oh, this is a bind.' In my early days we used to do the longer journeys by train – dashing like mad to get to the station, with the junior players having to load and unload all the bags – and going by car was better than that."

Nobody ever wanted to go with Closey; he was a bit of a hair-brained driver. And Fred wasn't much better. In the early years I was lucky because Bob Platt was in the team. He was from Huddersfield, too, and he used to enjoy driving his father's old cigar-shaped Rover. So I went with him.
Jimmy Binks was the one who did the most driving. Most of us had injuries at one time or another, but he never missed a match. He lived out in Hull and, if we were playing at Bradford or Leeds, he would drive home every night in his Triumph two-seater.

"It was a game of stamina," Bryan Stott says. "The legs did get very tired at the end of the season, especially if it was hot. But that was the routine. It was what we all expected. And it was a thrilling life."

So which of the Yorkshire grounds did Ken enjoy?

Not Headingley. It had this gravel cycle track all round, and it felt as if you were playing in a desert. You were so far removed from the spectators. And there were no sight screens. At one end they had the back of the benches behind the bowler's arm painted white, and at the other you were looking into the black seats of the rugby stand.
Not Scarborough. I didn't play there that much. I'd usually gone back to football. But I found it difficult to see there, looking into the terrace.
Definitely not Hull. There was nothing there.
There was more enthusiasm for cricket at Middlesbrough, and the wicket was sporting. But the pavilion was tiny. It looked like a flat-roofed air raid shelter.
Harrogate could be nice. You got a good crowd there. I remember one game when Peter West was commentating. He'd made himself a bit unpopular in

Yorkshire as a result of something he'd said on TV, some North-South debate. And he had to walk round the ground from his car. He was presenting *Come Dancing* at the time, and the crowd started chorusing 'one, two, three, one, two, three.' as he walked along. We were fielding at the time, and it was really very funny. He had to walk all the way from one side to the other.

Bramall Lane 1958

Sheffield was a good batting wicket, and the crowd there were good – though they were a long way away. But it was a soccer ground, and at one end the outfield was very bumpy.
Bradford was my favourite. The Bull Ring. There was a white wall at the pavilion end and white seats. When it became dark, the heads of the people sitting there could look like cricket balls. You could find yourself knocking a head off instead of the ball. But it was a good ground. A sporting wicket, 150 could be a winning total, and the crowd felt part of the game itself.

Yorkshire had so many handicaps: a longer fixture card, more punishing journeys and no regular home ground. They often provided two or three players to the England team, and other counties raised their game against them. Yet, between 1959 and 1962, they were three times champions and once runners-up.

Three from Huddersfield

In the early years after the war it was not uncommon for cricketers to play football in winter. Arsenal had at least six cricketers on their books around 1950: Denis and Leslie Compton, Arthur Milton, Brian Close, Don Bennett and Jimmy Gray. And Kent cricket in the mid-1950s boasted four Charlton Athletic footballers: Syd O'Linn, Derek Ufton, Stuart Leary and Freddie Lucas.

As each sport has come to make greater demands on its players, it has grown harder to play for long in both. Phil Neale and Ted Hemsley, both Worcestershire cricketers, played regular league football in the 1970s, and even later Andy Goram became a double international of sorts, keeping goal for Scotland and playing occasionally for their cricket team.

But it is unlikely that the list of England double internationals, which comes to an end with Willie Watson and Arthur Milton, will ever be extended. Indeed, among England's post-war Test cricketers, there are only six who have had significant footballing careers: Denis Compton, Willie Watson, Arthur Milton, Ken Taylor, Chris Balderstone and Arnold Sidebottom. And only three of these notched up more than 100 league appearances: Chris Balderstone (524), Ken Taylor (301) and Willie Watson (255). The three from Huddersfield.

Willie Watson, from the Paddock district, was a natural athlete, a graceful mover who exuded style both with his left-handed batting and with the ball at his feet at inside-forward. He missed much of the 1950 cricket season when he played in that summer's World Cup finals in Rio, then in 1953 he caught the nation's imagination by defying Australia at Lord's for nearly six hours. Up to that point, the former Yorkshire cricketer Bill Bowes reckoned, his batting had suffered from 'a quiet modesty, perhaps an inferiority complex.'

"He was a quiet man," Ken says. "When I started playing for the county, he would give me lifts to the home matches. And he never said much. He kept himself to himself. Not like some of the Yorkshire team, who could get quite aerated."

Chris Balderstone, five years younger than Ken, was also from Paddock. As a cricketer he never established himself as a first-choice Yorkshire player, and in 1971 he followed Ray Illingworth to Leicestershire. There his unruffled and steady batting was effective enough to bring him a Test call-up at the age of 35 to face the West Indian quick bowlers.

In football, he – like Ken – fell victim in 1965 to the new Huddersfield manager Tommy Johnston.

"Baldy was a very good footballer," Ken says. "He could control the ball quickly and distribute it well. He was a very good passer of the ball. He had a lot of vision. But he did look very casual, and you do get managers who want hustle and bustle."

Encouraged by Ken, he agreed to a transfer to Carlisle United. There he became an iconic figure, the creative heart of the midfield in the team that briefly reached the First Division and for a few heady days in August 1974 topped the table.

The following winter he was playing for Doncaster Rovers. On one memorable September day he came off the cricket field at Chesterfield at 6.30, with 51 runs to his name, and an hour later, 25 miles away, he was running out of the tunnel at Doncaster's Belle Vue ground to face Brentford. The next morning he completed his century, bowled 16½ overs of slow left-arm, and Leicestershire were presented with their first ever championship pennant.

Watson, Taylor, Balderstone. Three footballing cricketers who divided their loyalties over long careers. Between them they played 1,181 first-class cricket matches and 1,080 football league matches. "And we all had very similar temperaments," Ken reflects. "Quiet, placid." And perhaps not as pushy or as self-confident as others with their talents might have been. How strange that Huddersfield should produce three of them!

"It must be something in the smoke," Ken says.

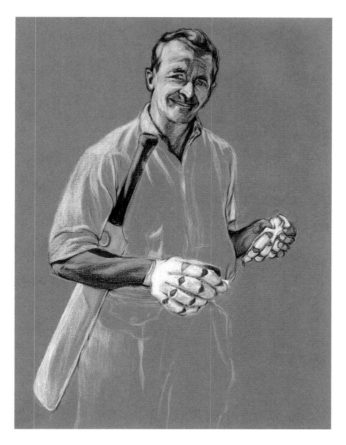

Willie Watson

Ken drawing Willie Watson when he was manager of Halifax Town and running a turkey farm. This was just before Ken's last summer as a Yorkshire cricketer. When he reported back to Headingley, he was immediately confronted by Brian Sellers, Chairman of Cricket. "Get that beard off, or you'll never play for Yorkshire again." Jimmy Binks wielded the razor.

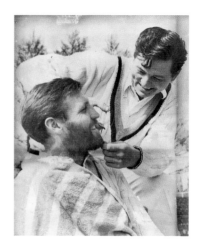

Under the lights

Wednesday 11 January 1961

By January 1961 Huddersfield Town Football Club had sunk to depths never previously experienced in its history. Bill Shankly had left for Liverpool to be replaced by the club's loyal servant Eddie Boot, Denis Law had been sold to Manchester City, and the team languished just one point off the bottom of the Second Division.

"Huddersfield weren't a club that were striving to make a great impression in football," Ken says. "The directors weren't prepared to spend any money on players."

Law's sale had brought in £55,000 but, to the disgruntlement of many, little of it was spent on new players. Eddie Boot bought the young goal-scorer Derek Stokes from Bradford City for £18,000. "A funny buy," Ken calls him. "He'd got nothing that we hadn't already got. But I suppose Eddie had to show he was doing something."

A larger sum, £23,000, was spent on floodlighting the ground. The locals nicknamed them the Denis Law lights, and they were switched on for the first time on that memorable Wednesday evening in January 1961 when the mighty Wolverhampton Wanderers came to Town for an FA Cup third round replay.

Wolverhampton Wanderers. In the last three seasons they had been league champions twice, runners-up once. "A fantastic side at that time," Ken says. "Their manager Stan Cullis had the same sort of temperament as Shankly. A hard man. Quite outspoken."

Wolves were the first English club to play in the European Cup, and Town's 1-1 survival at Molineux on Saturday had been, in the words of the *Yorkshire Post*, 'due to the defence's refusal to crack under the fiercest pounding'. In particular, keeper Harry Fearnley 'transformed himself into one of those exotic Eastern figures sprouting arms and legs.'

In the battle for survival Town's Peter Dinsdale sprained his ankle badly, and for the replay Eddie Boot was forced to move Les Massie to left-half and to give a Cup debut at inside-left to Chris Balderstone, a local lad from Paddock. With Bill McGarry also injured and Wolves reinforced by the return of Slater and Durandt, the odds were set against the Yorkshire side.

It was a cold, wet January. The United States was preparing for the inauguration of John F. Kennedy as its 35th President, the first contraceptive pill was going on sale, while Johnny Tillotson topped the Hit Parade with 'Poetry in Motion'.

Preparing for Cup task against Wolves

The Town players, who face Wolves in the third round of the FA Cup at Molineux Park on Saturday, look in happy mood as they chat to manager Eddie Boot during this week's training. The players are (left to right): Dinsdale, McHale, Coddington, Bettany, Fearnley, Parker, Wilson, Taylor, O'Grady and Massie.

Starved of top football and caught by the romance of the Cup, some 50,000 spectators approached the ground, with traffic jams reported as far away as Heckmondwike. The official attendance was 46,155, but thousands more were locked out, including scores who squatted on the roof of the 50-foot high stand.

"I was living out in Slaithwaite," Ken remembers. "The only special parking at the ground was for the directors, and I couldn't get anywhere near. I had to park under the railway arches in town and walk in the last mile and a half with the crowd."

The lights had kept the engineers at work much of the previous night, when rain had lashed down on them, but their 168 bulbs came on now to a great cheer – though, in the nearby houses, there was a groan as television screens went blank. "I wouldn't have minded so much," one resident told the *Huddersfield Examiner*, "but it was right in the middle of Coronation Street."

It was a harsh night. The ground had a bone-hard crust that had not thawed out, and the all-star visitors were slower to settle than Town. In the third minute Chris Balderstone, 'displaying intelligence and quick thinking, chipped the ball over Kirkham's shoulder to catch the Wolves defence completely on the wrong foot.' There in the penalty area was Derek Stokes leaping high and, in the words of the *Yorkshire Evening News*, 'he took his opportunity with consummate coolness.'

Huddersfield Town 1 Wolverhampton Wanderers 0

'The whole stadium erupted with cheering that was almost loud enough to bring the floodlight towers crashing down.'

So great was the excitement on the terraces that a 43-year-old civil servant collapsed and was taken off to the Huddersfield Royal Infirmary, where he died.

Town continued to dominate, with Balderstone – in the reckoning of *The Times* – 'showing a shrewdness more suited to a veteran than a novice.' "Baldy was a very good player," Ken says. "He looked casual, but he could control the ball quickly and his distribution was superb."

Stokes, on National Service and specially released from an important inter-unit match, had a chance of further glory in the 35th minute when he stepped up to take a penalty, but 'he smashed the shot into the legs of the keeper'. And, when Wolves themselves were awarded a penalty a minute before the break and Murray sent Fearnley the wrong way, 'the crowd could sense that Huddersfield's luck was running out.'

Huddersfield Town 1 Wolverhampton Wanderers 1

After the interval the game was all one way as, in the words of *The Times*, 'Huddersfield were pinned back, toiling against attacks which seemed too strong to be denied.' Or, as the *Evening News* reporter put it, playing on the visitors' name, 'With their fangs bared, Wolves tore into Town.'

"I had to mark a chap called Broadbent," Ken recalls. "He was an England international. He was a slightly built chap – but very tricky. He was the one who made their forward line tick."

The *Examiner* thought 'Wilson a stirring influence at left-back and the Taylor-Coddington-Massie formation in terrier-like form.'

Somehow Town survived and, as the Wolves continued to bear down on the Town goal, there were opportunities for Massie, Balderstone and Bettany to create counter-attacks with 'sweeping, cross-field passes'. One such occurred in the 76th minute, after 'frantic pressure in the Town goalmouth'. Bettany's pass forward found the 18-year-old left-wing Mike O'Grady running unmarked into the Wolves penalty area. Now it was a Town player who was the hound as 'in like a hungry wolf chased O'Grady to grab the winner.'

Huddersfield Town 2 Wolverhampton Wanderers 1

'The cheers of the home supporters could almost be heard in Manchester.'

Two years later O'Grady, still playing in the Second Division with Huddersfield, would join Ray Wilson in the England side. "A good, little player," Ken calls him. "He was in the style of Giggs or George Best, not frightened to take on a man and beat him."

Poetry in motion.

A wave out on the ocean
Could never move that way.

But the drama of the evening was not over. Wolves pressed for the equaliser and, when the referee blew his whistle in the dying moments, the crowd swarmed onto the pitch in celebration.

The floodlights glowed. 'And oh! – how those Town fans' faces glowed too! In that tightly packed swaying mass of terrace-siders was a hard core who had endured the agony of seeing Town losing four of their last six home league matches. Yet here were those same footballers not only taming the mighty Wolves but outsmarting them in the skills of the game.'

The whistle had gone only for an infringement. The police cleared the pitch and, when play finally resumed, Town's concentration was broken. The Wolves centre-forward Farmer broke free, beat Fearnley and, with almost the last kick of the match, crashed his shot into the woodwork.

Huddersfield Town 2 Wolverhampton Wanderers 1

At last it was over. The Town players took 20 minutes to reach the dressing room through the triumphant crowd. The pubs filled up all along the Leeds Road, the buses were packed to over-flowing and for one glorious evening 'the one-time wonder club of English football had recaptured something of its former glory.'

Even Bill Shankly was there. "A great game," he said. "And a most just result. I rate O'Grady the finest left-wing prospect in the country."

But it was not a harbinger of better times ahead. They lost 1-0 at Barnsley in the next round, they finished only one place above relegation, and the following February two of the lighting pylons were blown down in a gale, one burying itself in the playing surface.

Teams
Huddersfield Town: Fearnley; Parker, Wilson; Taylor, Coddington, Massie; McHale, Bettany, Stokes, Balderstone, O'Grady.
Wolverhampton Wanderers: Finlayson; Stuart, Showell; Clamp, Slater, Kirkham; Deeley, Murray, Farmer, Broadbent, Durandt.

Called back to cricket

Wednesday 7 – Friday 9 September 1962

The tug of war between Huddersfield Town and Yorkshire County Cricket Club was never fiercer than at the end of summer 1962 when, on the first day of the football season, Ken found himself on the team-sheets to play against both Kent at Gillingham and Derby County at Leeds Road. He had missed four weeks' cricket, with a thumb fractured after scoring 163 against Notts, and for once the football club – with its own injury crisis – managed to hold on to its man. In a 3-3 draw, the *Yorkshire Post* reported, 'Taylor gave a rugged display at centre-half.'

By the following Saturday, though, Ken was at The Oval, once more with a bat in his hands, for a match with Surrey that was billed as the championship decider. In front of 12,000 spectators, Ken – 'in the rustiest possible form', according to the *Daily Telegraph* – took 2½ hours over his first 20 runs. "It was a very dour match," says Richard Jefferson, the Surrey fast bowler, later to teach with Ken in Norfolk. "They were determined to stop us winning, and they batted till about three o'clock on the second day."

On the final evening, when Jefferson himself batted out ten maidens to save Surrey from defeat, it became clear that Yorkshire's caution had cost them a crucial ten points. A fortnight later, when they took the field for their last match, against Glamorgan at Harrogate, it looked possible that the lack of those points might cost them the championship. Worcestershire were now top of the table, only outright victory for Yorkshire would displace them, and – most worrying of all – rain clouds were racing in from the Atlantic.

St George's Road, Harrogate. Each summer Yorkshire county cricket spent three days at the pleasant, rural-feeling ground. At the end of August 1960 it staged the victory that brought a second successive championship to the county. Now they were hoping for a third in four years. "The Harrogate people are lovely," Ken says, "and it was a great cricketing area. But it was only a club ground and, when it was wet, the wicket always did a lot."

And what a lot it did on that Wednesday! Fred Trueman's opening burst was without success, even featuring a delay while he demanded that the pitch's length be checked, but the spinners Ray Illingworth and Don Wilson found straightaway that they could turn the ball sharply. By early afternoon Glamorgan – with the wind strong and storms encircling – were all out for 65, and Don Wilson was leading off the

Yorkshire side with figures of 19.3 overs, six for 24. "He bowled really well," Ken says, "and he took a caught-and-bowled that was absolutely magnificent. I can still see him flying through the air and catching it."

September 1962. Saturday evensong at the new Coventry Cathedral was attracting a weekly congregation of 3,000, BBC Television broadcast a new medical drama 'Doctor Finlay's Casebook', and Frank Ifield sang 'I Remember You'.

Soon a procession of Yorkshire batsmen were making their way back to the cramped pavilion: Hampshire 4, Sharpe 13, Close 0, Stott 5, Illingworth 0, Vic Wilson 1. Glamorgan's bowling – in the hands of medium-pacer Ossie Wheatley and the off-spinner Don Shepherd – was testing, and the playing surface made confident stroke play almost impossible. 'The pitch looks well cared for,' *The Times* thought, 'but in parts it carries little grass, and it is hard to see it ever playing really well.'

Ken, alone among the batsmen, survived. "It was hard work," he says. "Don Shepherd didn't spin the ball a lot, but his line and length were so consistent. He took thousands of wickets for Glamorgan."

For many, Ken was the greatest unfulfilled talent in English cricket. 'He is almost as thrilling to watch as Dexter when he is making runs,' Bill Bowes had just written in *The Cricketer* magazine, 'but the pleasures, as yet, do not outweigh the disappointments.'

'Showing what discipline allied to method could do', Ken mixed careful defence with 'handsomely timed and perfectly shaped drives'. When he finally edged Don Shepherd to the keeper, his innings of 67 stood as the decisive difference between the two teams.

Glamorgan 65 Yorkshire 101

It was 'his most valuable innings of the season', worth far more than the 163 he plundered against Notts, so what was his special technique? How had he scored 67 runs when his ten team-mates could manage only 32 between them?

"You just keep your fingers crossed. You've got to have things going for you. On a wicket like that, you need more than ability to survive."

Six years later, in Ken's last match at Harrogate, the young South African Barry Richards – in his first week as a Hampshire player – battled in similar vein to make 70 out of 122. "I saw him on television a year or two ago. They asked him about his greatest innings, and he talked about that one at Harrogate."

Glamorgan ended the day on 13 for no wicket. Yorkshire had one hand on the championship.

Then came the rain. Low clouds hung over the ground all Thursday and 'by lunch time,' Jim Kilburn wrote in the *Yorkshire Post*, 'the field was saturated. By mid-afternoon the pools were spreading like a picture of complete cricketing desolation.'

Tidal wave near the pitch as the Harrogate Cricket Club groundsman, Mr. Bert Wilson, attempts to keep in check the rain water during yesterday's downpour which delayed the Yorkshire-Glamorgan match.

"The next morning," Ken says, "the ground staff, with a lot of volunteers, turned up before dawn. They put the car headlights on and used squeegees to get rid of all the water."

"Some of the local residents," Yorkshire captain Vic Wilson says, "turned up with garden forks to help drain the water."

Miraculously play began on time. A brisk wind had blown away the clouds, leaving the sun to create a drying pitch that provided sharp turn for the spin bowlers. 'All strokes except to the full toss contained anxiety,' Jim Kilburn wrote. 'Some had to be hastily abandoned as the turning ball leaped towards the batsman's shoulder.'

Glamorgan crept to 43 for two, a lead of seven runs, and hopes rose in Worcester that Yorkshire would be thwarted. But, with 11,000 spectators packed into every corner of the little ground, the last 45 minutes before lunch saw Glamorgan crash to 75 for seven.

Now 'Yorkshire's main worry was the weather.'

For 40 minutes after lunch the unlikely Glamorgan pair of Ward and Evans resisted Illingworth and Wilson. 'Spinning fingers tired, and the pitch eased beneath the absorbent wind,' while 'anxious glances at the sky were not entirely reassuring.'

It was 97 for seven and, more in hope than expectation, Vic Wilson tossed the ball to Brian Close. His first delivery was a long hop that Evans cut to the boundary. His next was a half-volley that finished in the hands of Phil Sharpe at first slip.

"That was Closey all right," Ken laughs. "Somehow he made things happen. He was never frightened to try something different, and often the batsmen would lose concentration."

In seven more deliveries Brian Close took the last two wickets, and suddenly – weather permitting – there were three hours of playing time to score 66 runs.

The *Yorkshire Post* reported that their London switchboard had requests for the latest score 'coming in at the rate of one a minute from anxious men all over London and the Home Counties.'

Ken went out to face the first ball, with the left-arm fast bowler Jeff Jones, with two wickets at the end of the Yorkshire first innings, on a hat-trick. 'The clouds in the west were comfortingly high against a backcloth of blue,' Jim Kilburn wrote, 'but there was a sharp drop in spirits when Taylor was yorked first ball.'

"That's cricket, isn't it?" Ken says. "Up one minute, down the next."

Sharpe followed at 18, Close at 53 but, with two to win, 'a hook from Stott sizzled towards the boundary, and dozens of small boys immediately chased on to the pitch to cheer their heroes.' Champions once more!

On the boundary Jones pulled off 'a remarkable piece of fielding', and 'the small boys, their premature elation snatched away, ran sheepishly from the field.' One more run was wanted. 'Tension reached fever pitch. Then, with a gracious stroke from Hampshire, came the vital single.'

It was the second championship in Vic Wilson's three summers as captain, and he told the *Yorkshire Post* that 'it was a story-book ending to my career.'

Glamorgan, 65 and 101   Yorkshire, 101 and 66 for 3

"We had a few drinks," Ken recalls. "But there was no celebration dinner or anything like that. I wouldn't have seen any of them again till April."

A fortnight later Ken was at centre-half in the Huddersfield Town team that beat Preston North End 1-0.

Stanley Matthews

When Ken played against Stanley Matthews at Christmas 1955, the great Blackpool winger was already 40 years old. Yet he was still a regular on the right wing in the England team, as he had been since 1935, and at the end of the season he would be named as the first European Footballer of the Year.

He had lifted the nation's spirits in the wartime internationals, and in 1953 he had been at the heart of the greatest of Cup Finals. In front of the Queen herself, a month before her coronation, he had woven his magic so brilliantly that Blackpool came back from 3-1 down to Bolton Wanderers to snatch a last-minute victory. Such was the popularity of Matthews that every football follower outside Bolton rejoiced, with *The Times* calling it 'a rightful consummation of a great career'.

Amazingly Matthews played for Blackpool in football's top division till he was nearly 47, then he was transferred back to his home town Stoke where he completed his career with a fairy-tale ending that saw the club rise from near-relegation one year to the Second Division Championship the next. In 1963, in his 49th year, he was named Footballer of the Year, and he only hung up his boots five days after his 50th birthday.

> He was a one-off. Great players like him don't come along very often. He kept himself fit by training on the sands at Blackpool and watching his diet. I think he had a day of the week when he fasted.
> He had a very low centre of gravity, which gave him great balance. And he had this great ability to manipulate his feet round and over the ball. He could sway from side to side and throw you off your balance. His feet were all over the place and, if you weren't careful as a defender, he'd send you right up the creek.
> You had to watch the ball, not the feet. You had to forget who the guy was and play the ball. If you moved with his feet, he'd put the ball in the opposite direction.

Ken was not in the Huddersfield side that played at Stoke on the day in October 1961 when Stanley Matthews made his emotional homecoming. A regular crowd of 8,000 swelled to 35,974, including his mother who had not seen him play since that golden Cup Final day at Wembley. The boy who thirty years earlier had been cleaning boots at the Victoria Ground for a pound a week now brought the whole town alive, lifting his side to a 3-0 victory that kept them hovering just above the relegation zone.

Ray Wilson, by this time England's first-choice left-back, was the man with the spoilsport task of having to mark Matthews. "I really did worry about it the week before. I didn't know how to play the game. So I just stood in his way and let him knock it to somebody else. I never tackled him all game, and he never went past me. At the end the referee congratulated me. 'You treated that excellent,' he said."

The *Huddersfield Examiner* confirms this, calling Wilson 'the one man in Town's defence who refused to be flurried by the old man's tricks.' But *The Times*, caught up with the romance of a 'very gay and electric' occasion, described the England full-back as 'twice sprawled on his back as Matthews' fluttering footwork brought a swelling roar of enjoyment.'

> You could never get near him, because he'd have his elbows out. He wouldn't be tugging onto you, like they do today, but he did get a little bit protected by the refs.
> This chap Ronaldo's a bit like him. It's very difficult for the rest of the forward line. They never know when they're going to get the ball. Not like Tom Finney. He was a much more direct winger.

The following winter, when Stoke were pushing for promotion, Ken was in the side that travelled to Stoke on a wet Saturday in December. In a division where 15,000 was a good gate, almost twice that number roared with Matthews' every touch of the ball.

> Our ground at Leeds Road was a good pitch to play on; the rain ran off it. But Stoke was the muddiest of all the grounds. If it got water on it, it was like treacle. And it had this awful smell when you went down.

Stoke City 2 Huddersfield Town 1

> I do remember that match. There was a big crowd, a fantastic atmosphere. The winning goal came over from Matthews on the right, and Dennis Violet – the old Manchester United forward – knocked it in.

Two years later he was Sir Stanley Matthews, professional football's first knight.

Brian Close

Throughout Ken's years as a professional cricketer Brian Close was a prominent member of the Yorkshire side: an attacking left-handed batsman, an effective off-spinner and a close catcher whose fearlessness was legendary. He took over the Yorkshire captaincy in 1963 and, in the six years that Ken played under him, they won the championship four times and the new Gillette Cup once.

Brian Close had made his debut as far back as 1949 at the age of 18, and such was his natural ability that in that first summer he performed the double with 1,089 runs and 113 wickets and became England's youngest ever Test cricketer.

> Brian was a great leader. You admired him so much because he had so much natural ability. Anything that he asked you to do, you always felt that he could do it better.
> You always knew that something was going to happen when Brian went in to bat – or came on to bowl. When he was captain, there was never a time when we went into the field and just went through the motions for two hours.
> As a batsman he could give it a slog or he could play defensively, whatever the situation required. His technique was excellent. If he'd played for himself and not the team, his average could have been far higher. He'd sometimes have these pre-conceived ideas of what he was going to do: coming down the wicket to a quick bowler, or pretending to move before the bowler released the ball, to put him off. He'd get an idea, and he'd have to try it. Sometimes his ideas would come off, but they'd be his downfall on a few occasions each season.

In the limelight of Test cricket, such an approach was not always appreciated. At Lord's in 1963, against the West Indian pacemen Hall and Griffith, he was a national hero, advancing with breathtaking courage down the track and hitting a spectacular 70 that left him covered in purple bruises. But two years earlier at Old Trafford, when the Australian leg-spinner Benaud was turning the ball awkwardly out of the rough, his pre-meditated plan to whack him out of the attack only resulted in his being caught on the boundary and becoming the scapegoat for a disastrous England collapse. Jim Laker called it 'the most extraordinary innings I've ever seen by an accredited Test batsman', and the former Yorkshire captain Norman Yardley on *Test Match Special*

expressed the hope that he would never play for England again.

Life with Brian Close was never a dull affair, and his captaincy was in the same spirit.

> With Closey, you played to win. There was always something happening. His theory was that you declared on how long it was going to take you to get the other side out, not on how long they needed to get the runs. It was a different approach from most counties. He sent Phil Sharpe and me out one time to score some quick runs before a declaration. 'I want 100 runs in 40 minutes,' he told us. 'Don't get out, and don't make it look easy.' Well, we got the 100 runs in 40 minutes, but I think we lost six wickets. He'd get frustrated if people started to play for themselves. He'd strut up and down in front of the window, making his presence felt. 'Get on with it, or get out.' That sort of thing. And of course it affected all our averages. But we won the championship with that system.
> It was an unselfish side. Everybody was happy for everybody else to do well, and Closey was the most unselfish of players. The feeling started to fall away towards the end; people came in who had a different attitude. But I could name one or two counties who would have been pushing us for the championship if their star players had played more for their teams. But they played to get a nice average at the end of the season and to be picked for England.

Recognition of such dynamic captaincy came finally in August 1966. Sobers' West Indies had gone 3-0 up against an England side led first by Mike Smith, then by Colin Cowdrey, and the selectors decided that, for the final Test at The Oval, there was nothing to be lost by giving a chance to the Yorkshireman. In the event England pulled off a comprehensive innings victory, with their captain's finest moment coming on the final morning when he stood at forward short leg as Sobers took guard and caught him first ball via a bottom edge that bounced off the batsman's box. It was a typical moment of Close inspiration, and the following summer, against India and Pakistan, he conjured up a further five wins and a draw. At this point, as he prepared to lead England in the Caribbean, his record of results made him the most successful England captain of all time.

Then, as if to confirm the worst prejudices of some in the MCC establishment, he became embroiled in controversy and, refusing to offer a full apology, was stripped of the England captaincy. The accusation was

Brian Close
"He loved his cigarettes.
They kept him calm before going out to bat."

that at Edgbaston, in the dying minutes of a county match, he had unfairly slowed down play and that, on returning to the pavilion, he had assaulted a spectator.

It was raining, and he did take his time, but Mike Smith the Warwickshire captain said afterwards that he'd have done the same.
I was twelfth man, sitting right in the aisle when they came off, and there was this Warwickshire supporter who stood up in front of Closey and became very abusive. Closey just pushed him aside. He didn't hit him or push him more than to get him out of the way. He'd never hurt anybody.
He didn't have the right image to be an MCC captain, and they used every excuse to get him out. They wouldn't have done it if he'd been a Southern County player. He didn't talk about it – not to me, anyway – but we all felt very upset for him.
He was the best captain I ever played under. Without doubt.

Alas, two years after Ken retired, Brian Close's Yorkshire captaincy also ended in dismissal. In November 1970, he was summoned to Headingley where Brian Sellers, Chairman of the Cricket Committee, gave him a ten-minute ultimatum: resign now or be sacked. 'You've had a good innings, Brian,' he was told and, after 22 years as a Yorkshire cricketer, he departed, only to play out seven more summers with Somerset.

The move was the best thing that happened to him. When he went to Somerset, he realised that he had to produce the goods again, and he did. He brought on Botham, and they became a good team.

In an improbable finale to a long and entertaining career, he was recalled to Test cricket in 1976 at the age of 45. It was thought that his courage against fast bowling was England's best hope against a rampant West Indian attack, and at Lord's he top-scored with 60 and 46. Thus England's youngest Test cricketer became its oldest of modern times.

The great thing about Closey is that he loved a physical challenge. He always liked facing the quick bowlers, and of course he was fearless when he fielded at short leg. He stood closer than anybody does today and without a helmet. There was a game at Bristol when the batsman lapped the ball, and it hit Closey so hard on the forehead that it flew all the way to Phil Sharpe

at slip. And he hardly flinched. It was as though it had hit a lump of wood.

Phil Sharpe confirms the story: "It came like a rocket off him. And, after we'd persuaded him to go off, he came back on with this minute bit of sticking plaster in the middle of his forehead."

Closey was a tough cricketer, but he had this childish, giggling side to him as well. He would act the fool. I remember him batting at Bristol with about a quarter of an hour to lunch. I was next in, on a pair, and I was quite anxious. It was a dusty wicket, and the wind was blowing the dust into the eyes of short leg. And Closey thought this was a great challenge. He kept rubbing his feet into the ground and laughing, 'Ha ha ha' as the dust got up. And I was waiting there, on a pair, getting more and more agitated. I could see he wasn't concentrating, wasn't thinking about me. 'Ha ha ha,' he was going. He got out. I had to go out to bat just before lunch, and I think I did bag them.

Bristol, June 1961
K. Taylor,   bowled Brown, 0   lbw Mortimore, 0

Closey was always up for a challenge. If you said, 'Brian, I bet you can't ...', he'd say 'What?' And off he'd go. We were in the bar at the Diglis Hotel at Worcester. We'd had an evening meal, and the river was very full. Somebody said, 'Jesus, Closey, I bet you can't swim that river.' 'What?' And straightaway he was throwing his coat and his shirt off and running down the lawn. We looked at each other. It was a silly thing to do, the river was running quite fast, but he swam there and back. Of course they collected up his clothes and took them into the bar. I can still see him, knocking on the french window, trying to get back in, dripping wet, just in his underpants.
Another time we were playing Hampshire at Portsmouth, and we were invited to a cocktail party on the HMS Victory. Closey was having a few and someone said, 'I bet you daren't go up to the crow's nest, Brian.' 'What?' So again everybody put their glasses down and went up on deck to watch him climb this rigging. And, instead of going through the trap door in the middle, as you're supposed to do, he clambered up the outside of the rigging and over the top. It was really very dangerous, but he always managed these things. He was so strong. He did this walking on beer bottles in the bar. You had to stand with your feet behind a line and walk the bottles with your hands, without touching the floor in front of the line, see how far forward you could walk

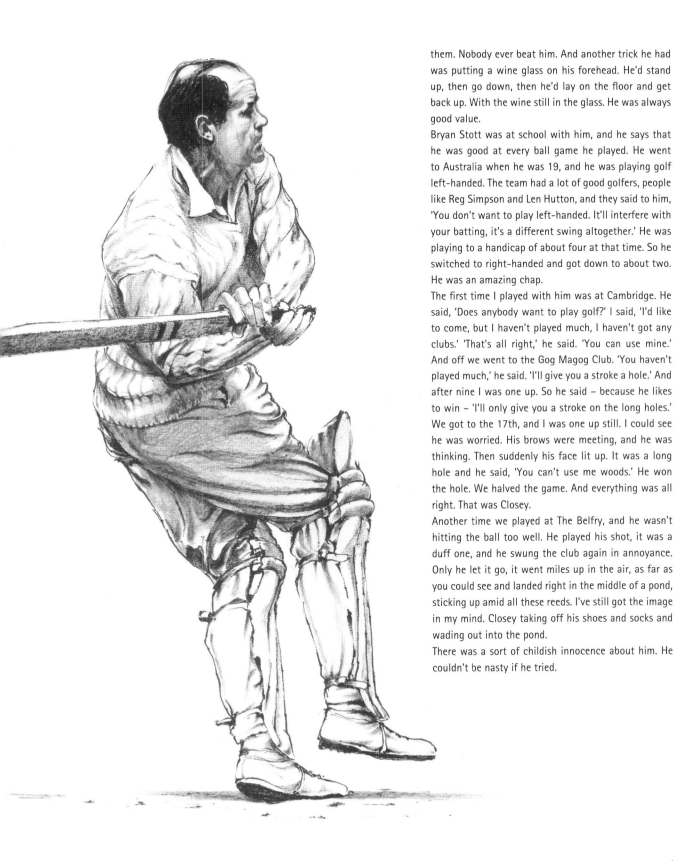

them. Nobody ever beat him. And another trick he had was putting a wine glass on his forehead. He'd stand up, then go down, then he'd lay on the floor and get back up. With the wine still in the glass. He was always good value.

Bryan Stott was at school with him, and he says that he was good at every ball game he played. He went to Australia when he was 19, and he was playing golf left-handed. The team had a lot of good golfers, people like Reg Simpson and Len Hutton, and they said to him, 'You don't want to play left-handed. It'll interfere with your batting, it's a different swing altogether.' He was playing to a handicap of about four at that time. So he switched to right-handed and got down to about two. He was an amazing chap.

The first time I played with him was at Cambridge. He said, 'Does anybody want to play golf?' I said, 'I'd like to come, but I haven't played much, I haven't got any clubs.' 'That's all right,' he said. 'You can use mine.' And off we went to the Gog Magog Club. 'You haven't played much,' he said. 'I'll give you a stroke a hole.' And after nine I was one up. So he said – because he likes to win – 'I'll only give you a stroke on the long holes.' We got to the 17th, and I was one up still. I could see he was worried. His brows were meeting, and he was thinking. Then suddenly his face lit up. It was a long hole and he said, 'You can't use me woods.' He won the hole. We halved the game. And everything was all right. That was Closey.

Another time we played at The Belfry, and he wasn't hitting the ball too well. He played his shot, it was a duff one, and he swung the club again in annoyance. Only he let it go, it went miles up in the air, as far as you could see and landed right in the middle of a pond, sticking up amid all these reeds. I've still got the image in my mind. Closey taking off his shoes and socks and wading out into the pond.

There was a sort of childish innocence about him. He couldn't be nasty if he tried.

Football winds down

The wear and tear of playing sport twelve months a year gradually caught up with Ken.

> Up to the age of 24 or 25 it was all right. But after that the football, in particular, got quite hard. You had to train harder to keep fit, and the knocks and bumps didn't go away as quickly. Ten or twelve years, it does take its toll.
>
> Every year Yorkshire were in the running for the championship so I was missing the start of the football and, when I did come back, I was fitting in anywhere. So I didn't feel as involved as I had done.
>
> It became less important than the cricket, and my enthusiasm faded, especially after Bill Shankly had gone.

The winter of 1962/63 provided an unexpected break. Huddersfield Town had started the season well, in contention for promotion back into the First Division, but their match on the Saturday before Christmas fell victim to fog.

Then even worse weather conditions arrived. Ken was living on a hill, high above Slaithwaite, up a little-used lane, and he remembers getting up on Boxing Day.

> I looked out of the window, and I thought, 'We're going to get some snow.' So I took my car down to the pub on the Manchester Road, a mile and a half away. The snow blew across our lane, making it impassable, but the Manchester Road stayed open. The M62 hadn't been built at that time so there were always lorries on it.

The Boxing Day match at Leeds Road was postponed. They managed to play at Grimsby three days later, but after that the snow and ice took a grip. There was no more football till March.

> We were near Blackmoorfoot Reservoir, and that was the coldest place in the country. For a month, day and night, it was freezing. Our house had spring water so we kept the tap running so it didn't freeze over. Avril was pregnant at the time. She had to trudge up and down the hill, pulling a sledge with the groceries.

For a while the Halifax Town ground was opened to the public for skating sessions. By the time the fifth round of the FA Cup was drawn at the beginning of March, there were ties like 'Walsall or Manchester City or Birmingham City or Bury versus Norwich City or Blackpool or Bradford City or Newcastle United'.

Huddersfield finally played their third round tie on a cold Monday evening in March, losing 5-0 at Old Trafford where Denis Law, not long back from Italy, renewed old friendships with a hat-trick.

Huddersfield's league programme had been worse affected than most and, when Ken returned to cricket at the start of April, there were still 14 matches to be played.

The following year Ken did not play at all, wintering in New Zealand. When he returned for the 1964/65 season, he soon found himself under a new manager. Eddie Boot was replaced by the former Notts County left-half Tommy Johnston.

> The Chairman said, "We've done really well to get him. He played for Blackpool for many years." He thought we'd signed a different Johnston, a centre-half who'd played for England.

That was in October. Ken soon found that he was not a part of the new manager's plans, and he was approached by the masseur at Bradford Park Avenue, Colin Kay, who had been at Huddersfield. In February he signed for the Fourth Division side as a part-timer.

> It was a nice, little club, and I felt at home there because I'd played cricket so often for Yorkshire on the other side of the stand. It had a tremendous slope, twelve foot down from the top corner flag to the one diagonally opposite, but it was a nicer place to play than Bradford City. I'm sorry that it's gone.
> When I was there, they had a reasonable side, and they were keen to do well.

A young Kevin Hector was established as their leading goal-scorer, scoring 113 goals in 176 league games before moving on to greater things at Derby County.

> He was great in front of goal. He put the ball away, which a lot of players are frightened to do. They get in good positions, but they're timid about finishing off.
> He went to Derby when he should have gone to Liverpool – which would have been a better move for him. Shankly wanted him at Liverpool, but he wasn't prepared to offer him the same terms – as you might say – as Cloughie was.

So did Ken find it easier playing at this level?

> Oh no, it was more difficult – because you were used to the ball being released from players when you expected it.
> You move into a good position and expect the ball to come to you, and it doesn't. Then three or four seconds later, when somebody's marking you again, it arrives. And they say, 'Look at him. He's not as good as we thought he was.' The quality of negotiating between players is a lot less good in the lower divisions.

Ken started teaching part-time at local secondary schools, at Rastrick and at Slaithwaite, and he did his football training from home. Then, after he had finished at Park Avenue, he had one last winter of football when each Sunday morning he flew from Manchester Airport to Dublin and played for Sligo Rovers in the Irish League.

> The ground didn't have many facilities; it was a bit like the third team ground at Huddersfield Town. But Sligo was a lovely place, with a river running through it. The last bit of land before you get to America is the Sligo golf course.

With him in the Sligo team was Len White, the former Newcastle forward who had moved to Huddersfield late in his career and had played with Ken in that winter of snow.

Back on that never-forgotten afternoon at Leeds Road, when Ken was only 19 years old and Town were two minutes from an FA Cup semi-final against little York City, it was White who had shot in the heart-breaking equaliser for Newcastle. He had gone on to Wembley to collect a winners' medal, a highlight greater than any in Ken's career, and now they were playing out their last days together on the West coast of Ireland.

Ken was 32 years old. He had a calling to be a teacher. It was time to hang up his boots.

New Zealand and the Far East

Holidays had not been a part of Ken's life. With football in winter, cricket in summer and an art education to fit in, there was never a break. By the summer of 1963, he had been married for three years and he had never been on holiday with Avril.

His only two overseas trips had been with Huddersfield Town: to Denmark and Sweden in May 1954 and to North America in May and June 1955.

> The trip to North America was wonderful. We sailed from Liverpool on the Empress of Scotland via Montreal, down the St Lawrence River, past Quebec. Two of the team had been in the Navy during the war – Lawrie Kelly and Len Quested – and they'd had such a bad time that, as soon as we set sail, they went down to their bunks and stayed there for seven days.
>
> The quality of the opposition wasn't what it would be now. The teams were all local amateurs, a lot of them immigrants from Europe. But it was a nice, friendly tour. We always let them score.

As far as cricket was concerned, Ken just missed out on selection for the tour of the West Indies in 1959/60. 'More is the pity,' wrote the editor of *The Cricketer* magazine, preferring him to the young Ted Dexter. 'Taylor is a beautiful player whose fielding and throwing have to be seen to be believed.' He also came close to touring Australia in 1962/63 when, considered as an all-rounder, he lost out to Essex's Barry Knight.

Jim Swanton was one who longed for Ken to establish himself in the England team, and he recruited him for his private tour of the West Indies in Spring 1961. He wrote to Ken to say that he thought that Ken had a good chance of being in the England team that would play Australia the following summer: 'It would certainly help you to make runs in the West Indies. When my last side came home all the batsmen made bags of runs in May.'

Huddersfield Town only agreed to release Ken on condition that they were safe in mid-table by that stage of the season and, as luck would have it, that was the winter when they only avoided relegation on the last day. Ken was unable to go.

Ken's first winter break from football did not occur till 1963/64 when he took a coaching appointment with the Auckland Cricket Association in New Zealand. It would be his first proper break with Avril, and they now had a three-month-old baby with them.

> We flew via Amsterdam and Vancouver, with Nicholas swinging about in a cot that was fastened above our seats.

> We stopped off in Honolulu. Everybody had to get off the beach because of a tidal wave warning. There'd been an earthquake in Japan, and we had to stay up till they gave the all-clear at about two or three in the morning.
>
> We landed on the north shore of Auckland, on a grass runway, and were met by the President of the Eden-Roskill Cricket Club. He told me that he wanted me to play the next day.

He calmed the nerves caused by the strange new world and made a century on debut. "Once I got to 20 I felt much better," he told the local paper. "It would have been terrible to make a blodger first up."

He won a trophy as the league's best batsman, and his coaching was a great success. 'We have struck pure gold,' the Auckland Association's Deputy Chairman said. 'His handling of schoolboys has been a masterpiece of tact. We have our share of difficult young characters, and they are now the most ardent of a not inconsiderable host of Taylor hero-worshippers.'

Alas, Ken did not carry his success into the Plunket Shield. Auckland won the trophy, but Ken made only 56 runs in ten innings. Such was Ken's failure that, when Worcestershire's Martin Horton arrived the following winter, he was told to forget the state matches and concentrate on coaching.

In March Avril and Nicholas returned to England while Ken joined Jim Swanton's side in Penang. From there they travelled to Singapore, Kuala Lumpur, Hong Kong, Bangkok and Calcutta.

It was an international party, with Sonny Ramadhin, Seymour Nurse and Gary Sobers from the West Indies, Richie Benaud and Ian McLachlan from Australia and the Nawab of Pataudi from India. And it took the manager back to a part of the world he had not visited since he had been a prisoner of the Japanese in the war, working on the Bridge over the River Kwai.

> We played at the Singapore Cricket Club, and he told us that the last time he had seen the pavilion was when he was being marched past it at bayonet point.

Ken had a good tour with the bat, but the stars were the West Indians. Seymour Nurse was the leading run-scorer, Sonny Ramadhin the leading wicket-taker – "We used to hold him back till after tea. Then, when we wanted to get finished, we'd throw him the ball." – and Gary Sobers had an extraordinary all-round tour. At Kuala Lumpur he took five wickets in five balls, then two days later – after beginning the day with eighteen holes of golf – he hit a hundred in an hour and a quarter. 'I've never known anyone with quite so much compulsive energy,' Swanton later wrote.

For Ken the tour offered much more than cricket. He took a cine camera, and the forty minutes of film is mostly shots of the people and places that he visited, most notably a trip that he and Jim Swanton took while they were in Thailand.

> Jim asked if anybody wanted to go with him up to the Bridge. And I was the only one who volunteered. We set off in a chauffeur-driven, air-conditioned limousine – Jim didn't do anything by halves – and, when we reached the river, we travelled on a long canoe, with an outboard motor and driver.
>
> When we got to the cemeteries, Jim didn't talk much. We walked round the headstones, and he stood in front of a few, of men he'd known and helped to bury. It was quite a couple of days.

Ken Taylor had a bond with Jim Swanton and, when the *Daily Telegraph* correspondent contributed to Ken's benefit brochure in 1968, he wrote: 'I have taken four sides overseas, numbering in all the best part of fifty players. If ever I were to take another, Ken is just about the first man I should invite. He is a quiet, modest fellow, among Yorkshire cricketers very much in the tradition of such as Hedley Verity, Maurice Leyland, Ted Lester and Bill Bowes.'

Ken's eye for a picture is clear in his film footage, but his memory also retains images that still trouble him.

> People were wandering about in squalor outside the ground in Bangkok, and we went through a guarded gate in a wall to go into this sports club with cricket, golf and polo. The contrast was unbelievable. They had women on their hands and knees picking out the weeds on the golf course and others who would tee up the ball for people driving off. And they were thankful for their jobs. It really upset me.
>
> But it was far worse in Calcutta. Outside the ground there were all these invalids, with limbs missing, with their begging bowls, and they sat there making moaning noises. You gave at first, but it was never ending. As soon as you did, hordes more surrounded you. It was a real shock to me.

In Calcutta they played a four-day match and, thanks to a century in each innings by Nurse and another all-round performance by Sobers, they beat a full Indian side who were fresh from a drawn series with England.

> We were playing in 120 degrees of heat. Seymour Nurse and Sobers said they'd never played in anything like it. We had drinks every ten overs, I think.

Then it was back home and, as Jim Swanton predicted, Ken was making 'bags of runs in May.'

E.W. Swanton's Commonwealth Tour, 1964
Standing (left to right): Sonny Ramadhin, Nick Pretzlik, Ken Taylor, Mike Griffith, Dan Piachaud, Tim Coghlan, Richard Hutton, Seymour Nurse
Sitting: E.W. Swanton, Nawab of Pataudi, Richie Benaud, Colin Ingleby-Mackenzie, Gary Sobers, Ian McLachlan, John Haslewood (treasurer)

Geoffrey Boycott

Geoffrey Boycott was a 21-year-old civil servant, working for the Ministry of Pensions in Barnsley, when he broke into the Yorkshire first team in June 1962. The county already had 14 capped players, several of them wondering anxiously whether they would be retained at the end of the summer, so the arrival of a newcomer – on the back of a rich vein of run-scoring in the second team – was not universally welcome.

He played without success against the Pakistani tourists. Then in his first championship match, at Northampton, he sent back Phil Sharpe when – according to the *Yorkshire Post* – 'there looked a comfortable single.' He was roundly told off in the dressing room, but there was a repeat performance in the next match at Chesterfield. He opened with Ken, the first time the two of them had batted together, and, when the score reached 67, Ken 'played a ball to mid-on's left hand and came up the wicket for a run. Boycott had failed to back up because he was too intent on following the ball. He refused to run, and the wicket was broken with Taylor down at his end.'

For Ken, who 'was batting soundly at the time' and whose running between the wickets was a vital part of his game, it was an event to puncture his usual placidity. According to Don Mosey, 'he retreated to the rear of the pavilion, there to give his Volkswagen the most vigorous polishing it was ever to experience.'

> Running between the wickets is about trust. There are rules about who calls, and the other person has to trust that call and do as he's told. If you don't do that, if you start looking after yourself, you're bound to get run-outs. Perhaps he was thinking about his position in the side and was playing safe, but he shouldn't be thinking at all if it's my call.
> Once the trust is broken, it's very difficult to mend.

In the case of Geoff Boycott and Ken, the trust was never mended. With Boycott returning to the second team and Ken missing much of the following season with injury, the two of them did not open together again till August 1963 when at Scarborough the scorecard read:

| G. Boycott | not out | 165 |
| K. Taylor | run out | 37 |

By now Geoff Boycott was an established member of the side, winning the Young Cricketer of the Year award, and their pairing at the top of the order did not always end in disaster. From Scarborough they travelled down to Leicester for the final match of the championship programme, wanting one more victory to bring them the title, and Geoff Boycott and Ken found themselves batting first on a pitch made treacherous by storm waters that had swept under the covers in the night. 'Batting against any type of bowling was an adventure,' Jim Kilburn wrote in the *Yorkshire Post*, 'and the most improbable beginning to the innings was a century partnership.'

In an hour and a half the two of them survived the conditions to put on 105. 'It was batsmanship true to character and of admirable skill. Boycott was resolute and watchful and wary of the illogical. Taylor hoisted all sail and carried the war to the enemy.' With 104 more in the second innings, their two stands were worth 209 runs and, with Ray Illingworth and Don Wilson at their deadliest on the soft turf, the combined total of the two Leicestershire innings was only 202. The game was over twenty minutes after the start of the final day, moments before heavy rain arrived, and Yorkshire had won their fourth championship in five years. Geoff Boycott, their leading run-scorer that summer, was now a vital part of the team.

> Boycs was quite mature when he came into the side. He applied himself, he was very willing to learn and he had a tremendous mental approach. He knew he had to work at his game, and he was prepared to do that.

Ken and he were poles apart temperamentally. In the view of Geoff Boycott, Ken – eager to 'carry the war to the enemy' – was unpredictable, unreliable, too willing to gamble his wicket away on a rash stroke. But for Ken, Geoff – 'wary of the illogical' – placed acquisition of runs above joyous freedom of expression.

> He worked for the Ministry of Pensions, and that's the sort of person he was. From that type of job he brought the same sort of mannerisms. Everything had to be right, everything had to be sorted out. The shots he played had to be like doing his books.
> His whole lifestyle before he came into cricket channelled him into the way he played. He'd got to have it sorted out in his mind and leave nothing to chance.

For Ken the artist, looking for inspiration, there is always an element of chance. And it is the acceptance of that chance that allows the great days to happen.

Your good days are not very often. And when they do happen, you don't know why; they're just happening. It's the same in any profession. When you're painting, there are days when you sit down and graft, and it's rubbish. Then another day, when you're not really thinking, it all happens.

As Alan Thompson wrote in Ken's benefit brochure, 'Ken is a batsman of mood. He possesses neither the single-mindedness of a Boycott, the strength of a Hampshire, nor the patient hard-grafting qualities of a Padgett. From these three, and from many others, one can predetermine the type of innings they will try to play. But with Taylor one cannot, and this is his joy, his secret. He will be out for next to nothing and will make his return to the pavilion with head bowed, fitfully poking at the grass with his bat and wondering what on earth possessed him to offer such a stroke … or he will get a hundred and in so doing the spectator will be permitted to feast on shots seldom seen nowadays on county grounds, shots coached out of batsmen because they carry with them too great an element of risk.'

"Ken had more talent in half his body than Boycs had in all of his," their team-mate Mel Ryan says. "He was a beautiful player. He should never have been overshadowed by Boycs. But he hadn't got Boycs' determination. Boycs was only a home-made player; he played his shots according to what he knew his limitations were. His main thing was, 'Don't get out.' If a half-volley came along, he'd push it for one or two. With Ken, bang, it was four. He was taking the chances. Boycs was a bloody fine player but Ken, with his talent, should have scored far more runs than him."

But Ken was a man of several talents, and he played his cricket as an aspect of his life, not as a singular route through life.

Boycs talked about nothing else but cricket. I often gave him a lift to matches, and he'd talk cricket all the time.
We'd talk about fielding. When he came into the side, he wasn't a great fielder and he wanted to improve. And he did. I think I did help him.
You've got to be balanced when you're fielding and, at a certain point as you're coming in, you've got to anticipate the kind of shot the batsman's going to play. If your instinct tells you that he's going to play a defensive shot, then you move quicker. If he looks as if he's going to play an attacking shot, then you will slow up and think about which way he's going to hit the ball. And to do that you've got to concentrate. I watched the whole of the body and tried to anticipate from that and from experience. It's really quite hard work. You watch Fred come into his delivery stride, but you concentrate on the batsman.

'As a fielder,' Ray Illingworth wrote in 1968, 'Ken has no equal in the country.'

'He is every inch a natural games-player,' Jim Swanton wrote, 'and this sort always show their difference from lesser mortals in the field.'

'As a fielder in the covers I know of no-one better,' Alan Thompson wrote. 'Acting as a substitute for Derbyshire at Chesterfield one year, he cut at least 20 runs off Geoff Boycott's innings – a feat which drew from Geoff at lunch the disconsolate, wry remark: 'It's a good job Ken's not going flat out, or I wouldn't be in double figures yet."

Ken played his part in transforming Geoff Boycott, in Don Mosey's words, 'from a not very good fieldsman into an acceptable one. He gradually developed the ability to anticipate where the ball was likely to run, and this gave him a fraction of a second's start which could disguise the fact that he was a less than sprightly mover.'

They also grew used to batting with each other. In May 1964 they put on 123 against Middlesex at Headingley, then at Old Trafford in the next match they opened the two innings with stands of 236 and 77. Both were in glorious form, and a fortnight later Geoff Boycott was selected for the first Test against Australia. By the third Test Ken was with him in the England team.

But the run-outs still occurred, and in 1965 there were five of them, including one match against the South African tourists when a mix-up in the first innings saw Boycott run out for 4 and another in the second saw Ken run out for 3. Ken's brother Jeff recalls their mother lamenting, "That Boycott's run our Ken out again."

That summer Yorkshire reached the final of the Gillette Cup. It was not a competition they took as seriously as the championship and in the Lord's final, after a delay of an hour and a half, Ken and Geoff Boycott found themselves batting on a wet wicket. That was 12.15 and at one o'clock, when Ken was caught at gully, the innings was in its twelfth over and the score had only reached 22.

Conditions were difficult, and some say that the slow start was part of the Yorkshire plan. Others say that Brian Close, promoting himself in the order to add some urgency, quickly made it clear to his partner that he expected him to play with greater adventure. Whatever the truth, the outcome was an innings of 146 by Boycott which contained such an array of attacking shots that, as John Woodcock put it in *The Times*, 'I shall never again make it an excuse for Boycott that he is unfortunately not endowed with strokes. His magnificent innings contained every shot in the book.'

It just proved what he could do. So there was no reason why he couldn't have continued like that. But it must have frightened him to death, thinking that he had to play like that every innings.

The Cup was won, and the two of them played together for three more summers, in a team which won three more championships. Boycott was by now a regular in the England side, though he was dropped for one match in 1967 after scoring an unadventurous 246 against the Indians when Brian Close had asked him to get on with it.

Boycs was a better player for England than he was for Yorkshire because he had five days. In the three-day game, it's more obvious if you play for yourself.
But in the years we were together at Yorkshire he had a role. You needed one or two like him to stay there. He and Doug Padgett would nudge the ball, play the proper shot to the ball. They wouldn't do anything unexpected. Whereas others like Hampshire and Closey, Phil Sharpe and myself, we tried to score more quickly.

The last time they batted together was on 8 July 1968, against Glamorgan at Sheffield. And their parting was just as it had been at Chesterfield on their first time together at the wicket.

K. Taylor   run out   5

Ken had gone by the time Geoff assumed the captaincy in 1971, but from afar – first South Africa, then Norfolk – he could see that the role that Boycott had played in his side in the 1960s no longer worked.

By then Yorkshire didn't have the bowlers to bowl other sides out. And Boycs was taking so long to get his runs that he wasn't leaving them time to take the wickets.

Their paths would only cross again when Ken's son Nicholas was taken onto the staff at Headingley in 1982. A young fast bowler, educated at Gresham's, the public school where Ken was teaching, he did not fit into the culture of the Yorkshire dressing room.

I know he wasn't an easy lad. He was very enthusiastic. He enjoyed playing. He bubbled enthusiasm to the crowd. And Ray Illingworth told him you don't play cricket in Yorkshire like that. They just squashed him. I thought he'd be accepted, but he wasn't.

They were hard times in Yorkshire cricket, and in Nicholas's second year there the county finished last in the table for the only time in its history.

I asked for his release in July, and they made him twelfth man six matches in a row after that.

Ken and Geoff had never been kindred spirits but, despite their difficulties in negotiating the running, a thread of friendship had passed down the line from those early days in the car when Ken had helped Geoff to improve his fielding. So, when Ken looks back, he no longer dwells on the run-outs.

Boycs was a tremendously successful player. As a batsman he knew his limitations, and he learned to play within them. He became one of the greats of the game.
And when Nicholas was having such a bad time, Geoff looked after him. Not Ray Illingworth who was the manager. Not Doug Padgett who was coach. The only person there who was kind to Nicholas was Boycs.

The loneliest game of them all

Cricket is a game of the most terrifying stresses with more luck about it than any other game, They call it a team game but in fact it is the loneliest game of all.

These are some lines by John Arlott that Ken has copied onto a piece of paper. Several times while we have been working together on this book he has got it out and read it to me, telling me that he would like it included.

Football is a much easier game to play than cricket. The action and movement is happening all the time. You haven't got much time for nerves. You've got a job to do. You know where you should be and where the rest of the players should be. And you're forever shouting at each other. It's far less stressful. You can make mistakes, and you can make up for them. They're more or less forgotten.

But when you go out to bat, even before you go out while you're waiting and thinking, you're on your own. Nobody can help you. If you make a mistake, you've got the rest of the day to think about it.

It made it easier if you got a few runs in the previous game. I never went on the football field thinking, 'Christ, I didn't play well last week.' But you do feel the pressure if you're having a bad run in cricket – and you seem to get more bad decisions from the umpires.

It's all right when you're starting out. But once you get a bit older, you realise that you've got to perform or you'll be unemployed at the end of the season. And when you start to think like that, you do worse – because of the extra pressure.

Cricket came easily to Ken when he was young. He scored runs, he took wickets, he was a brilliant fielder. He had an art training to complete, he had football in winter, and he had little time to dwell on it all.

Perhaps, if he had luck, he might have established himself in the England team while he was still young and innocent. John Arlott and Jim Swanton both thought that that was where he belonged. Late in Ken's career, Swanton penned the following words: 'If anyone were to name a modern cricketer of Test potential who for some reason has just not happened to establish himself on that level, I would soon think of Ken Taylor.'

'Cricket is a game with more luck about it than any other game,' John Arlott wrote. Ken looks back at his Test failures in 1959 in those terms. A bad lbw decision, an unhelpful pitch: the gods had deemed that it was not to be.

Yet perhaps there is a second truth. Ken was a young man with many talents, but it suited him not to give all his attention to one of them. Deep down he lacked that deeper self-confidence that would have brought him greater success. He preferred to go back to football in August or to return to the art studio.

If I didn't get any runs, I would think, 'I'll be back playing football soon,' and that made it easier for me.
I often used to have a dream about going out to bat. I'd get to the middle, take guard, then I'd look down and I'd be holding a golf club. And I'd think, 'Christ, what am I going to do with this?'
It didn't help that Brian Sellers was Chairman of Cricket at Yorkshire. Nothing we did ever seemed to be good enough. We could never be as good as his side of the 1930s. There was one year when we won the championship, and at the pre-season lunch the next Spring he stood up and said, 'The bowling was adequate. The batting was piss poor.'

When it is suggested to Ken that he only narrowly missed being selected for at least two England tours, he shows no regret. "I wouldn't have wanted to play cricket three seasons in a row," he says.

Yet, when he did sacrifice his football in the winter of 1963/64, to coach in New Zealand and to play for Jim Swanton's side in the Far East, he started the following summer in the best form of his life.

He and Geoff Boycott both hit hundreds at Old Trafford in the Whit Bank Holiday match against Lancashire and, if fate had worked out differently, the two of them might have opened the batting for England in the first Test against Australia at Trent Bridge. The selectors opted for the first time for Boycott but his partner John Edrich trod on a ball on the eve of the game and made clear the extent of his injury only an hour before the start. With no other batsman available on the ground, Fred Titmus was drafted in as a makeshift opener, and Ken found himself summoned to the ground to act as twelfth man.

The following week he played for Yorkshire against the Australians at Sheffield. On Saturday night and Monday morning he saw off the new ball without difficulty despite the loss of two wickets at the other end. Then, when the leg-spinner Rex Sellers was introduced, he remembered his upbringing in the Stile Common school yard, used his feet and walloped him for three fours. 'Ten minutes of this treatment might have seen Sellers taking his sweater,' *The Times* thought, 'but McKenzie, at the other end, got Taylor out lbw after a half-hearted appeal when the batsman appeared to edge the ball into his pads.'

After that, the Yorkshire batsmen took to playing Sellers with great care, and he took five wickets as the innings collapsed. By mid-afternoon Yorkshire were following on, and Ken was batting again. By close he had 81 not out.

The next morning Ken found himself once more facing Sellers. The glory of a century against the Australians was in his sights, and he could have been forgiven for working the ball around quietly for a few singles. But instead, in Sellers' first over he swept a four, then in his second he came down the wicket as Wally Heap and Colin Garthwaite had always told him to do, met the ball as it pitched and sent it back over Sellers' head. Three balls, three boundaries – six, four, four – and he was on 99. The long boundary was blocked, so he pushed the next ball for a single instead. 'Taylor made all the bowling look little better than good club standard,' was the verdict of *The Times*, and his final score of 160 fell only seven short of the Yorkshire record against the Australians, set in 1899 by J.T. Brown. And it has not been bettered since.

He was not selected for the second or third Tests, but he was high in the national averages and a clamour was building in the press for his recall. The great West Indian Sir Learie Constantine watched him make 80 against Surrey at Bradford and, under a headline 'Ken Taylor is my boy', wrote of him in the *Daily Sketch* as 'a batsman of Test calibre crying out aloud for Test recognition.'

Jim Swanton sent him a letter on Tuesday 30 June, two days before the third Test at Headingley: 'Just a line to say how sorry I was that you didn't catch the selectors' eye for Lord's or Headingley.' Then, after reminding him that the tour party for South Africa was to be chosen within three weeks and expressing regret that he no longer bowled much for Yorkshire, he concluded, 'Don't bother to acknowledge this – except in the scorebook.'

The letter had not, in fact, arrived when Ken received a call from the selectors to report to Headingley after all. Colin Cowdrey was suffering from a bad back, and they wanted to provide cover for him and not to repeat the Trent Bridge fiasco in which they had had to make do with Titmus as an opener.

On that Tuesday Cowdrey had unwisely played a long innings against Cambridge University, then the next day he drove the 250 miles from Kent to Headingley and on to the team hotel in Harrogate.

Ken was expecting to be twelfth man, but on Thursday morning Cowdrey cried off and, to his great surprise, he was in the team – but not as an opener. As Denzil Batchelor put it, 'he was an opening batsman at the peak of form, and he was due to bat at six.'

It's like playing a left-winger at full-back. You're not geared mentally to hanging about, waiting for wickets to fall. There's too much time to worry.
The whole thing was a bit of a shock. I'd turned up on the morning, thinking that I'd be taking out the drinks.

The match was a disaster for Ken and for England. Early in his first innings, after one splendid drive, the ball chipped the middle finger in his right hand and he became uncomfortable. He lasted for 14 overs, but he had only made nine runs when he edged a catch to the keeper Grout and walked off. It was an unconvincing performance and, according to Denzil Batchelor, 'even the Headingley crowd could hardly raise a clap for him as he retreated.'

England's total of 268 looked a good one when Australia slumped to 178 for seven, but a magnificent innings by Burge took them to a lead of 121 and, when Ken came out a second time, England were five wickets down and only 48 runs ahead.

'They call it a team game, but in fact it is the loneliest game of them all.'

He struggled to 15 before being bowled by Veivers.

I was trying to cut an off-spinner. I don't know what made me do it. You should never cut an off-spinner in your whole life.

His Test career was over.

Football and singing

This is a talk given by Jeff Taylor on the Third Programme in the early 1970s. It began with Maria Callas singing 'Qui La Voce' from Bellini's Il Puritani, followed by commentary on a Bobby Charlton goal in the 1966 World Cup.

Whatever could be the connection between Maria Callas and Bobby Charlton? At first glance the two do seem poles apart.

Nevertheless, I'm pretty sure that anyone who's seen Bobby Charlton in action will admit that there's something very beautiful about the sight of a player of his quality moving smoothly about the field with the ball at his feet, sending an opponent the wrong way with a quick side-step or a slight sway of the hips. There's a grace about it which is balletic; it's almost musical in its rhythm.

This combination of rhythm, poise and balance is common to all forms of sport. In a recent article on Gary Sobers the cricketer I read, 'There's nothing about Sobers that is not beautiful. Lithe and economical, you could have composed music to his run-up.' Here is one writer at least who recognises the link between the balanced movement of a superbly fit athlete and the rhythmic flow of music.

The sight of Bobby Charlton or Gary Sobers in action suggests the music to us. Maria Callas's singing not only suggests it, it is music. Nevertheless, she in her own way needs to be just as athletic as does the professional sportsman. Singing is basically a physical activity, just as much as running or jumping or kicking a football, and has the same fundamental need: for a technique which provides full control of the mechanism involved.

In most sports, the physical effort is pretty obvious and the muscles can actually be seen doing their work. On the other hand, apart from the movement of the diaphragm, the best singers seem to make hardly any effort at all. Don't let's be fooled, though; the work is going on, just the same. But most of the muscles involved in singing are internal and relatively intangible – and can only be set in motion by a thought process. If an athlete wants to put his foot forward, he can actually see it happening. But the singer must think an internal movement and know by the sensations it produces, and the sound that results, whether it has taken place or not. He has to create an imagery for himself which he knows from experience will set off a physical reaction. This may be much more subtle a control than in sport but, for both, muscles are involved. And it is through their development and training that their correct functioning becomes almost automatic.

It is as unlikely for Maria Callas to have to play separately each note in those rapid passages as it is for a centipede to have to decide which foot follows which. She knows full well that, if she sets off a run with the vocal mechanism perfectly poised, the rest will follow – because her muscles have been trained to respond to the slightest thought. In the same way a player doesn't have to think which foot to stand on and which to kick with. Depending on how the ball comes to him, he knows instinctively what to do, and his body reacts accordingly.

The complete control of the physical mechanisms gives both of them a freedom to express their art fully. Such a control demands a great deal of time spent training and practising the respective basic skills: the ability to move smoothly and economically, to change direction and pace at will, to time one's run so as to meet the ball at exactly the right spot and to be able to bring it under control immediately it arrives – or, in the case of the singer, to be able to change smoothly from one tempo or rhythm to another, to be able to poise the vocal mechanism so as to approach each note or sustain each phrase correctly. And then there is for both the great stamina, both physical and mental, to be able to last ninety minutes of non-stop football or complete a long operatic role. For the professional there must be a platform upon which to perform and an audience by whom to be appreciated. There has to be complete commitment on the part of the performer, or the audience will not be convinced. At the same time he cannot allow himself to be too emotionally involved, or he may well end up by being sent off the field or cracking a high note. The professional must be in complete control of himself and the situation.

In both, there is this great need for self-discipline which doesn't confine itself to periods of training and practice but has a habit of spilling over into the rest of his life: careful what you eat, careful what you drink, best not to smoke; early to bed, get plenty of rest, etc, etc. We must be terrible people to live with.

Certainly for me football and singing are not so far apart. Both have been much more than jobs or even careers. One was, and the other is now, my life – and the actual performances, whether on the field on Saturday afternoon or on the concert platform on Saturday evening, exciting highlights of a very enjoyable existence.

Football, cricket and art

Ken matches Jeff's talk by reflecting on his own experiences as a footballer, cricketer and artist, finding a common strand in all three activities.

Cricket and football are, in many ways, very different from drawing and painting. They are much more physical activities. But all three have in common a need for great concentration.

When you're at work in the studio, you're always looking beyond what you actually see, interpreting what you're looking at. And your interpretation will depend on the medium you're working with. If it's a felt pen, then you're looking for line to create the feeling of form. But if it's paint, then the colour has to create the impression. You have to know your strengths and your limitations, but you're at your best when you get beyond thinking, when your concentration is so great that the line just flows. You feel as if you're in another dimension.

A lot of people lose it halfway. With my art scholars at school now, you can tell the ones with a bit extra – because of their concentration. The ones who are fiddling about, dropping their pencils, talking, they may have talent, but they won't get to that point where their work flows.

It is the same with sport. You have to be completely wrapped up in what you're doing at that moment. Your concentration has to be high. It's much easier in football because it only lasts ninety minutes, not three days. But there were times when I batted when I could feel that something else had taken over and I could play shots without thinking. I always enjoyed batting most when I was playing my shots, timing the ball.

In football I was a defender, but it was still all about timing: reading the game, knowing where the other players were, timing your tackle and playing the ball away. You lose yourself in the concentration, and unconsciously you find yourself making the right decision.

The great forwards find positions without knowing why. But the defender has to be creative, too. When you get the ball, you have to use it. You have to click into the system and link up with the forwards.

Waiting to go out to play at a ground like Anfield is a tremendous experience. You stand in the corridor behind the referee, with the police lined up, and you run out of the tunnel onto the field with a great roar all around you. You don't get that with cricket. But, as soon as the whistle blows for the kick-off, you have to shut it all out. I don't think I ever thought about the crowd when I was playing; they weren't there. But, with some players, the crowd got at them. They found that they could play away but they couldn't play at home. They couldn't shut them out. You've got to be focused on what you're doing.

When you're young and you're good at something, it's unusual that you're not going to work at it. But in some ways it's harder for youngsters now. If they have a bad day with something, they can switch to something else. There wasn't much else to switch to when we were kids.

To be a great player, you've got to have the ability to focus completely on what you're doing. The great footballers, people like George Best and Denis Law, all had it. When Denis came to Huddersfield, he was just a little lad in glasses but give him a ball and you could see straightaway that he'd got it.

Gary Sobers had it. He was a completely natural player, and he so obviously enjoyed everything he did.

You would think that Brian Close had it. He had so much ability. But he never achieved what his potential was, and that was probably because he lacked something in concentration. He could be distracted.

Geoff Boycott was different. He had a great ability to concentrate, and he had a lot of talent. But I feel that he didn't let himself go into that other dimension; he was conscious all the time. He was probably more concerned about not getting out than I was.

A lot of people do fail because they approach sport like Boycs, but they haven't got the temperament or the ability to carry through and achieve what he did.

Willie Watson was one who had the ability to concentrate and lose himself. Most of the time he seemed to be in another world. Perhaps I could be a bit like him. But I think it did help me in my sport that I also had to concentrate when I was drawing and painting.

Sport is like art in some ways. To succeed, you have to work hard, you have to understand the tools you're using and what your strengths and limitations are and you have to enjoy what you're doing. And you have got to be creative in both. And all that comes from concentration.

When you do time the ball perfectly and it flies away to the boundary, or your tackle goes in at the perfect moment, or you complete a painting that works, you get this tremendous satisfaction of knowing that you've done something that was good.

Four sportsmen

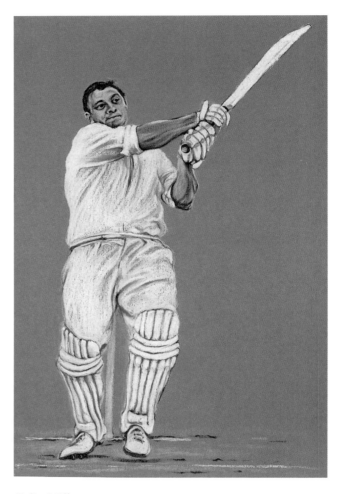

Gary Sobers

He was the greatest of all time. He did the lot. A great batsman, a superb fielder – and not only could he bowl quick but he could bowl spinners, both orthodox and chinamen. A brilliant athlete. I doubt if we'll ever see anybody better.

I got him out in both innings at Middlesbrough once. I bowled him leg stick in the second innings, and I can still see him throwing his head back – as if to say, 'Fancy getting out to that duck-egg.'

Colin Milburn

He was such a nice fellow, a great loss to the game when he had his accident.

As a batsman he stood still and punched from the crease. Not a great deal of movement. But he was very correct. You've got to be correct to survive.

When I was coaching with him at Lord's, I asked him what he used to think about when he went out to bat. I always thought about the ball that was going to get me out. But he never did, he said. He thought about the runs he was going to get. And that's how you should be.

Duncan Edwards

A very strong, all-round player. A hard man. Good in the air, good in the tackle, good distribution of the ball. He had great balance. A bit like Rooney, a similar stocky build. It was a tragedy when he was killed at Munich.

If he'd lived, he would have been a great player. And Bobby Moore might not have got in the England team. But I don't think he'd have been England captain. Bobby Moore was more of a thinking footballer, aware of others around him. The impression I got of Duncan Edwards was that he was a more natural, intuitive player.

But who knows? He was just a young lad. Maybe he would have developed.

David Beckham

He's a great passer of the ball, with good vision. Very similar to Johnny Haynes or Chris Balderstone. Great with the ball. The swerve he gets on free kicks is tremendous – but there's no way he would have been able to do that with the ball we used. You'd a job to get it in the air sometimes.

I like this drawing. It didn't need a lot of packing of colour. I made the line itself create the feeling of form. And it did it very well. Sometimes it does; sometimes it doesn't.

Yorkshire's years of success

Ken played his final season for Yorkshire in 1968, the last summer when the county championship held centre stage in the English domestic game. Already, for an occasional diversion, there was the Gillette Cup, but then in 1969 came the Sunday League and in 1972 the Benson and Hedges Cup. The championship programme rapidly withered from 28 to 24 to 20 games, the rhythm of six-day-a-week cricket was broken, and in recent times the competition has been further undermined by the central contracts that severely restrict the England players from representing their counties.

There have been great teams in the history of county cricket – Yorkshire in the 1930s, Surrey in the 1950s – but it could be argued that, with the proliferation of competitions and the decline in importance of county cricket, the last of the great county sides was the Yorkshire team which won seven championships in the years from 1959 to 1968. Thereafter, with the competition just one of four tournaments, no team dominated to the same extent. Indeed, in the eight years from 1969 to 1976, after Yorkshire had gone into decline, the championship was won in successive years by eight different counties.

The combined table of results for the years from 1959 to 1968 shows Yorkshire's dominance:

Championship Matches, 1959-1968			
	Played	Won	Lost
Yorkshire	292	133	46
Worcestershire	292	106	65
Middlesex	280	88	60
Glamorgan	292	87	89
Warwickshire	292	87	70
Kent	280	86	69
Northamptonshire	280	84	73
Somerset	292	84	96
Hampshire	292	80	65
Surrey	280	78	54
Derbyshire	280	73	82
Gloucestershire	280	73	101
Sussex	292	71	96
Essex	280	67	71
Lancashire	292	67	91
Leicestershire	280	53	116
Nottinghamshire	280	39	112

Throughout these years – whether captained by Ronnie Burnet, Vic Wilson or Brian Close – Yorkshire approached their cricket in the same way. Their bowlers had to win the match by taking twenty wickets while the job of the batsmen was to score quick runs to leave them time to do so. And in this strategy they were blessed with match-winning bowlers.

Yorkshire, Championship Matches, 1959-1968			
	Matches	Wkts	Ave
F.S. Trueman	220	901	16.36
R. Illingworth	231	811	16.74
D. Wilson	251	685	19.42
A.G. Nicholson (62-68)	132	471	16.32
D.B. Close	243	424	23.25
M. Ryan (59-65)	104	294	22.01
R.K. Platt (59-63)	60	190	22.95
R. Hutton (62-68)	76	161	20.99

Fred Trueman was one of the great fast bowlers of all time, and Ray Illingworth was in Ken's opinion the best off-spinner of his generation.

> Better than Fred Titmus because he spun the ball more. David Allen of Gloucester spun the ball, too, but Ray could get runs so you'd prefer him to David Allen. When he played for England, Ray would get upset that he'd come on against three, four, five and Titmus would be brought on against nine, ten, jack. Mind you, Jack Birkenshaw said the same about Illy when Illy was captain at Leicester.

Then there was Don Wilson, whose orthodox slow left-arm bowling put him in the great Yorkshire line that stretched back through Wardle, Verity and Rhodes to Peel.

> Don didn't spin the ball much, but he used flight – like Arthur Booth.

Arthur Booth's career was a remarkable one. Kept out of the Yorkshire team in the 1930s by the great Hedley Verity, he played only one full summer, 1946, when at the age of 43 he topped the national bowling averages. In Ken's early years he helped out with the pre-season coaching in the Winter Shed, and Ken recalls his advice to Ray Illingworth.

> Illy, like all the off-spinners, used to dip his spinning finger into friar's balsam to stop it splitting on the inside. If it did split, you could be out of the game for quite a while.
> One time Illy's finger was all scarred and bloody, and Arthur looked at it. "You don't want to hurt yourself like that," he said. "I never spun a ball in my life."

The spin of Ray Illingworth and the flight of Don Wilson was so often a potent combination in those years, especially when the pitches were recovering from rain.

They were very good in tandem.

Wils had an easy run-up, a nice delivery stride and a high action. And he was so enthusiastic. He expected a wicket every ball, throwing his arms up and widening his eyes. Even if the ball didn't penetrate the batsman, his eyes did.

He was a great team man. Good fun. And a very good fielder.

Another who provided a refreshing contrast to the strain of dourness in the team was Tony Nicholson, who appeared seemingly from nowhere during the summer of 1962. He had had a spell in the Rhodesian police and, according to Mel Ryan, whose place he gradually took, "He looked like a portly village bobby. He used to stand at mid-off with his feet splayed out, and Fred would say, 'F---ing hell, where have we got him from? If the ball doesn't hit him, it's four.' When he first took my place, he came up to me. 'I'm sorry,' he said. 'You're a far better bowler than me.' He actually said that. But of course he got better and, as Fred started to wane, he took the weight off him."

His great asset was his variation. He'd bowl four or five types of ball in an over. And he was very accurate. He bowled to a length you couldn't quite get at; he never gave you anything. He was unlucky that he got injured when he was picked to tour South Africa with England. He would have been a very good third seamer.

He was a great character. He really enjoyed playing. His laughter and his enjoyment were infectious. He and Wils were the same. They made everybody else want to play.

In the early years Ken's gentle seam bowling was a part of the bowling attack, a useful variant for breaking partnerships. "Then Closey became captain. Whenever Illy said to him, 'Why don't you put Ken on?', he'd say, 'I'll have a go.' I hardly bowled."

Behind the stumps in every match was Jimmy Binks.

There wasn't a better keeper in the country. You can only really test a wicket-keeper when he's stood up, and at times Jim would stand up to Bob Platt, Mel Ryan and Tony Nicholson - on uncovered wickets, when the bounce wasn't consistent.

He was a matter-of-fact keeper, no frills. And because he wasn't flashy, he didn't catch the eye of the selectors. His approach was just like he was going to the office each day, or down the mine. Wicket-keeping was his job, and he did it. He had a tremendous pride in the skill with which he did his job.

The fielding was a crucial part of their success and, when they won the championship in 1967, Jim Kilburn in *Wisden* thought that it made the crucial difference: 'Sharpe was outstanding at slip, Hampshire came to brilliance in the leg-trap, Taylor saved runs with athletic artistry, Wilson ranged over ground normally requiring two guardians and the general reliability permitted Close to serve as an extra fieldsman stationed so near the bat that catches could be created, though at an alarming risk of grave injury.'

The batsmen's job was to make quick runs so that there was time in the field for the bowlers to take their wickets, and they did this as a group, most of them prepared to jettison their averages in the cause of purposeful, match-winning cricket.

Yorkshire, Championship Matches, 1959-1968			
	Matches	Runs	Ave
D.E.V. Padgett	270	12,178	30.99
D.B. Close	243	10,554	31.69
P.J. Sharpe	243	10,029	28.99
K. Taylor	206	8,697	26.93
R. Illingworth	231	7,983	30.35
G. Boycott *(62-68)*	108	7,088	46.94
J.H. Hampshire *(61-68)*	169	6,446	26.53
W.B. Stott *(59-63)*	111	5,614	32.08

I think most of us on this list would be disappointed with our individual figures. But at Yorkshire we were always competing for the championship; we were always under pressure to go out and get on with it. There were batsmen at other counties who weren't ever going to win the championship, and they could play every innings how they wanted. So they could play for a Test place.

As a dynamic batsman, brilliant cover fielder and occasional bowler, Ken was a crucial member of one of the most successful county teams of all time, a team that did not depend on star performers but who played with purpose for each other.

The game would be much better if the statistics were not made as important as they are. The object of playing a team game is for your team to win. And we won the championship seven times in ten years.

Doing it again

Ken's last appearance as a first-class cricketer was in Yorkshire's final championship match of 1968: against Surrey at The Circle ground in Anlaby Road, Hull. It was one of the most dramatic matches of his career – but not his favourite of the Yorkshire grounds.

> It was the most miserable place. It was so isolated and always so cold and wind-swept. You felt as if you were playing on the Moon.
>
> We used to visit the Smith and Nephew factory there and get given some free samples. Shampoo and hand cream and things. But, apart from that, it was the deadliest place to play. A good place for me to end.

August 1968. The last match of Ken's career. BBC Television was broadcasting the first series of 'Dad's Army', and the Beach Boys were top of the charts with a happy, summery song with a chorus of 'Let's get together and do it again.'

Yorkshire were certainly doing it again, top of the table and needing just one more victory to clinch a seventh championship title in ten years. And, of all their championships, this one would be the most remarkable because it was the first summer in which overseas players could appear in county cricket without having to qualify. Glamorgan had Majid Khan, Kent had Asif Iqbal while Notts had climbed from fifteenth to fourth, thanks to their new captain Gary Sobers. Yorkshire, however, was still only for the Yorkshire-born.

They were mostly the same team that they had been under Ronnie Burnet back in the heady days of their 1959 triumph. Brian Close, Ray Illingworth, Fred Trueman, Jimmy Binks, Phil Sharpe, Doug Padgett, Don Wilson and Ken. They were not yet Dad's Army, but they had played through the ten summers together and even Richard Hutton, the youngster among them, was nearly 26.

Yet, for all the settled look of the team on paper, things had changed in the side, and Ken – always one to keep his thoughts to himself – was very aware of it.

> Had the atmosphere in the team been as good as it was, we could have kept going for another three or four years. It had been an unselfish side. Everybody had been happy for everybody else to do well. But that feeling was falling away towards the end. It was never quite the same for me once Bryan Stott packed up.

> People were coming in who were more interested in themselves. There were people batting for their averages, to get into the England side. It wasn't just Geoff Boycott. It was like a new generation with a different attitude. It wasn't the way we'd played the game in the past.
>
> It was my benefit year, and there was one member of the team who wouldn't play in the Sunday matches unless he had his expenses paid. That had never happened before.
>
> I'd lost a lot of interest by then, and I made my mind up to retire. I didn't tell anybody; nobody knew till after the season was over.
>
> I was more interested in coaching by then. I know that I was still quite young, but I'd played winter and summer for so many years, and it really is quite hard. It wears you down. You never get a break, you're always having to perform.

There were others who were becoming unsettled. Ray Illingworth was in the England side, but in Yorkshire there were moves to bring the young Geoff Cope into the team in his place. So he went to see Brian Sellers, the all-powerful Chairman of Cricket, and asked him for a guarantee of three more years with the county. Ken can still quote the reply as it was told to him: "You can go, and any other f---er can go as well."

> So I didn't dare let out that I was thinking of retiring. The Yorkshire committee were a peculiar lot. Hardly any of them knew us by name when we met them, and I don't think any of them were at Hull for that final match. They seemed to take it for granted that we would win the championship.

Wednesday 28 August 1968. As the county championship reached its climax, the news on the front pages of the papers was of Russian tanks in the streets of Prague and anti-war riots outside the Democratic Convention in Chicago. Later that day the cricket world would reel from the news that Basil d'Oliveira had been omitted from the MCC party to tour South Africa.

The Circle, Hull. A high north-east wind blew across the ground and, with the pitch greenish and the outfield grass heavy, Surrey's Micky Stewart asked Yorkshire to bat. Twice Ken 'hooked Selvey's short ball mercilessly', but he was caught in the slips for 16 and, with Phil Sharpe and John Hampshire both failing, they were in trouble at 45 for three.

'After a long period of anxiety,' Norman Preston wrote in *The Times*, 'Padgett and Close gradually gained control amid not a few appeals for leg before that were negatived by the two Yorkshire umpires.'

Ron Aspinall and Albert Gaskell. They were the only two Yorkshiremen among the 23 umpires on the first-class list that summer, and by a strange coincidence both had been allocated to Yorkshire's championship decider at Hull.

Ron Aspinall – from Almondbury, near Huddersfield – was a medium-fast bowler who might have played for England in the 1940s, had injury not wrecked his career, and he umpired with a quiet authority. But his partner Albert Gaskell had never played the game at county level. "He was a great big man," Don Wilson recalls. "He drank an enormous amount, and he had this great purple nose. He was from Northallerton, and he was Yorkshire through and through. Everybody seemed to like him so they gave him a couple of seasons on the first-class list."

Eventually Padgett was given lbw, and the Yorkshire innings subsided to 221 for eight. Then a spectacular 61 by Don Wilson – 'hitting three sixes in a whirlwind final hour' – saw Yorkshire to close of play at 327 for nine.

Thursday 29 August. On 'an unpleasant grey and blustering day', Surrey could only manage 189 in reply, with Micky Stewart – out for a duck – one of three Surrey batsmen to be given lbw. In the evening

Ken was going out to bat for Yorkshire for the last time. In gloomy light he reached 16, then drove a half-volley from Robin Jackman to Micky Stewart at mid-on. In 21 overs Yorkshire struggled to 52 for two before 'stumps were drawn in a light that scarcely permitted sight of them.'

Friday 30 August. Norman Preston in *The Times* reckoned that 'Yorkshire will surely have to put forth a great effort today if they are to complete their championship programme with the victory they so desperately wish to achieve.'

With a weak sun breaking through to remove some of the chill, Brian Close demanded 60 runs in an hour from his batsmen, a more reasonable request than the '100 runs in 40 minutes, don't get out, and don't make it look easy.' And on this occasion he got his 60 runs, though at one stage it looked as if they might be all out short of his target.

That left Surrey with 251 to win in 250 minutes and, with Trueman and Nicholson making no impression with the new ball, the visitors looked on target at lunch, with the score on 61 for one.

Then came the collapse, as Illingworth and Wilson set to work. Edwards went for 29, Barrington for 9, and – in the words of Jim Kilburn in the *Yorkshire Post* – 'Stewart was leg before to Illingworth to end a half-hour's agony of attempt to escape a pair of spectacles.'

The Surrey captain still recalls the ball. "It would probably have gone about two feet over the top," he says, struggling to hold back his laughter, "and missed another set of stumps. But Albert Gaskell ... He was a lovely, happy character, always with a smile. He was a real Yorkshireman, and he loved his Yorkshire cricket."

Graham Roope was also given lbw to Illingworth, by the same umpire, and the young Michael Hooper – a talented Old Carthusian, struggling to cope with the various surfaces on which county cricket was being played – was bowled by Don Wilson for four, a dismissal that led – according to Micky Stewart – to a teasing cross-examination outside the pavilion from the great Len Hutton: "You're a batsman, are you? ... How many did you make? ... Four? Well, how were you out? ... Bowled. I see. ... Was it a straight one?"

That was 84 for six, but Surrey's Pakistani import Younis Ahmed was still at the crease and, with Pocock providing watchful company and Younis 'beginning to place the ball at will', the score moved forward to 121.

At this point Ken made his last significant contribution as a Yorkshire cricketer. 'Younis played Wilson towards mid-on and followed his forward stroke down the pitch in search of a single. Pocock delayed response for a fraction of a second that left him short of the crease when Taylor's throw reached the wicket-keeper.'

Michael Carey in the *Guardian* called it 'a nimble pick-up and throw', and it left Surrey 'with only three wickets left and nearly two hours to play.'

At some stage, around this point in the afternoon, Younis swept hard at a ball from Don Wilson, and it cracked into the shin of Brian Close, who – as so often on such turning pitches – was standing perilously close at forward short leg. Ken remembers the scene that ensued.

> John Hampshire was fielding at backward short leg, and the ball rebounded off Closey and hit him, too. And it hit him so hard that he was writhing about in agony, with the pain. Closey told him to get on with it and not make such a fuss.
>
> Then somebody said, 'Brian, look at your flannels', and we all looked down and saw all this blood coming out of his leg.

"There was blood everywhere," Don Wilson says. "But Closey wouldn't go off. 'It's all in the mind, this

pain,' he used to say. He was absolutely mental."

He remained on the field, masterminding operations, but Younis found in Arnold Long a partner able to stay with him. As Jim Kilburn put it, 'Younis was batting comfortably, Long acquired his assurance. Overs passed into extended bowling spells, minutes came to be measured as hours. Yorkshire complacency became Yorkshire anxiety.'

Transistor radios around the ground brought comfort from Cardiff, where Glamorgan were going down to defeat, but at Lord's Kent were taking wickets – and suddenly a title that seemed Yorkshire's at 3.15 was slipping from their grasp by 4.50. Surrey still had only seven wickets down, and there were just four overs remaining. 'As the minutes ticked by, Close began to pace anxiously around like an expectant father.'

It was time to turn to Fred Trueman, for one last burst to break the stand. He was 37 years old now, no longer a bowler of great pace, and he had taken just three wickets in the last 25 days. But he still retained a great aura, and the crowd grew excited as he once more stood at the end of his run-up. "Somebody in the crowd shouted 'Come on, Fred, Yorkshire expects'," Don Wilson recalls. "But he couldn't do it. He just had the one over, and we took him off. It was quite the saddest thing I've ever seen."

'Spin left the sturdy batsmen undisturbed,' wrote Jim Kilburn. 'The speed Trueman could raise brought no alarm.'

These were the last minutes of Yorkshire's championship years. Ray Illingworth was leaving for Leicestershire, and Ken had privately resolved to call it a day. A greater bombshell would explode in November when Fred would announce that he, too, had played his last match. "Time marches on," he told the press. That innocuous over at Hull would be the last he would ever bowl in the county championship for Yorkshire.

Three overs remained on that Friday afternoon, and for the first of them Don Wilson bowled once again to the left-handed Younis Ahmed, now on 75. His second ball was a half-volley on leg stump, and Younis – still playing his shots 'with immense good judgement' – swept it vigorously, only to send the ball crashing once more into Brian Close, who 'had no time to create a catch or crouch to safety.'

"I braced myself," Brian Close says, "as you do when you know a blow is coming, with my arms tight to my sides, trying to make a smaller target, I suppose. The ball hit me somewhere between the side of my arm and the inside of my body, and this time it rebounded in the air."

The blow, according to Michael Carey, 'left an egg-sized lump', but Jimmy Binks the keeper was alert enough to hold on to the ricochet, Younis stood in his crease dumb-founded, and they turned to Albert Gaskell. "You're out," he said, and suddenly there was a glimmer of hope.

Two balls later, when the new batsman Robin Jackman played back and was hit on the pads, Gaskell's finger was up again. "It was Albert's finest match," Micky Stewart jokes, but Jim Kilburn described it as 'leg before, palpably and thunderously'.

With the ground now alive with Yorkshire expectation, Tony Nicholson took over from Fred at the other end. For five balls Long 'fended him off', only for the last to move off the seam and catch the edge of Long's bat. Immediately the ball was in Binks's gloves and, with just one over to spare, Yorkshire had won by 60 runs. With Kent losing at Lord's, the championship was almost certainly staying with them.

It was a moment of joy. In *The Times*, it was the spectators 'amid scenes of delirious excitement' who 'swarmed round the Yorkshire team as they strolled triumphantly from the field.' But in the *Guardian* it was the players themselves who 'leapt and bounded their way from the field like a team of Morris dancers.'

Ken's memory accords more closely with the report in *The Times*.

> We walked off. And I knew as we did that it was the last time I was ever going to play for Yorkshire.

Soon the champagne corks were popping, though Brian Close – completing a hat-trick of championship titles as captain – would not be joining the celebrations. For all the guts of his staying on the field with blood coming out of his leg, he needed attention. "When he got into the dressing room and unlaced his boot," Phil Sharpe says, "there was blood all over the place."

The tannoy called for a doctor, and John Pearce a neurologist volunteered his services. He had to fend off other medical queries in the Yorkshire dressing room before he and Brian Close squeezed into spectator Nigel Pullan's VW Beetle and set off for Casualty. "You know what hospitals are like," Brian Close says. "I missed all of the champagne and most of the party."

'Blood, guts and champagne,' Michael Carey wrote. 'One left the ground thinking that that was an accurate description of Yorkshire's cricket in this match.'

Summer was drawing to a close. Ken had just three more Sunday matches to play in his benefit year, and the Beach Boys' happy sounds of sunshine and sand would soon be gone from the charts.

> *Well, I've been thinking about*
> *All the places we've surfed and danced*
> *And all the faces we've missed*
> *So let's get back together and do it again.*

Yorkshire never would. The era was over – for Ken, for Fred, for Ray Illingworth – and within two years Jimmy Binks and Brian Close would be gone, too.

It would be 33 years before they would win the title again, and by then it would be another age, with an Australian their leading run scorer and no cricket at outposts like Harrogate and Hull.

"I don't think the Yorkshire public appreciated just how good that team was," Phil Sharpe says.

"The tradition went," says Don Wilson, who soldiered on under Geoff Boycott's captaincy till 1974. "We lost the art of winning."

In the summer of 1969 Ray Illingworth of Leicestershire became captain of England, and Fred Trueman developed an after-life as an entertainer and broadcaster. Meanwhile, Ken was in South Africa, quietly developing the career of teaching and coaching that his old headmaster Wally Heap had inspired him to pursue.

> It had been a great ten years at Yorkshire. But I could tell that it was all coming to an end. And I wanted to get on with the rest of my life. I had the opportunity to go to South Africa, to a job at a school where I would be teaching and coaching, and that was exciting. I'd done what I was going to do in cricket and football, and I was ready to start teaching properly.
> I didn't have any feeling of sadness that I'd played my last game. I was looking forward to the future.

South Africa

The wide, open spaces of South Africa appealed to Ken and Avril. They were not politically-minded people, and the offer of a part-time post to teach Art at the Rondebosch High School in Cape Town opened up to them the prospect of an exciting new life.

It was a boarding school with 650 boys, all of them white, and Ken and Avril lived in a flat in the grounds beneath Table Mountain. The headmaster Alec Clarke was a dynamic man, but Art was low on the list of the school's priorities. The pupils' understanding of the subject reflected this.

"I remember Ken coming back from his first lesson," Avril says. "He'd got a boy to sit on a chair and had explained to the others how he was sitting, what he wanted them to notice and how they should go about drawing him. He left them to get on with it for about half an hour and, when he went to look at what they'd been doing, he couldn't believe what he was seeing. He brought the drawings home, and we just rocked with laughter. Some of the figures were like ghosts or aliens, shadowy creatures. One boy had even drawn a tree. Ken was so depressed."

He stayed there for 18 months, and he did make some impression. And now, when you visit the website of the school, the first image you see is of a boy working in an art studio.

But his job was only three days a week, and their

District 6

finances were dwindling. So he applied to be Assistant Secretary for Sport at the University of Cape Town. He reached the final three, and then he was approached by the Rembrandt Tobacco Company, who were keen to appoint him in a newly created role, working with football coaches all over the country. It was an exciting project, sponsored by a wealthy company whose chairman Anton Rupert had a social conscience, and Ken – unable to get an answer from the university job – accepted it.

Apartheid had taken a firm grip in South Africa. A central area of Cape Town, District 6, was declared by the government to be a 'White Group Area', and its 150,000 Cape Coloured inhabitants were moved out to Cape Flats, a desolate, wind-swept area miles from the centre of town. District 6 was renamed Zonnebloem, and its buildings were mostly demolished – though plans to redevelop the area never came to fruition.

Nevertheless Cape Town itself was dominated by the English-speaking whites and was less strict in its application of apartheid than the Afrikaner-dominated areas. Ken's new job required the family to move to a very different part of the country: Pretoria. He remembers what the people at Rondebosch School said. "The Afrikaner up there is not like the Afrikaner down here."

"They were right," Avril says. "The way the Afrikaners spoke about the black people was quite shocking to us. It was nothing like it had been in Cape Town. And there was a strict curfew. The black man had to be off the street at nine o'clock. So they'd creep around at night. It could be quite frightening when you heard these noises in your garden."

Pretoria was the intellectual and administrative capital of the Afrikaner-speaking people. They saw their history as one of oppression under British colonial rule and, as a matter of pride, they insisted on conducting all their business in Afrikaans. Ken recalls that even Jackie McGlew, who had been captain of South African cricket and who was selling insurance, was forced to speak their language.

Ken and Avril felt less at home and, to underline their sense of having made a bad decision, Ken received a telephone call from the University of Cape Town offering him the job. But it was too late. The Rembrandt Company, he was told, had spent a year searching the world for the right man, and they were not going to let him go.

The South African soccer league was an all-white

one, with many former English league players, among them Johnny Haynes who played for Durban. But there were also black leagues. "The townships played each other, but the facilities weren't good. They played without boots."

Ken did not play in the league, and his help was not accepted in the townships. He travelled widely, right up to the diamond mines near the Rhodesian border, and into Lesotho, Namibia, Swaziland and Botswana, coaching all races. At the mines, he remembers watching the men doing step-ups onto benches in great heat as part of a health check. "The mines were deep under ground; you could get the bends down there. They had to demonstrate that they were fit and had strong lungs, and they accompanied these step-ups with a rhythmic chant. It was wonderful to see and hear."

Among those whom he coached at football was the golfer Gary Player's son, and he found himself invited to partner the great man in a four-ball tournament

in Pretoria. Ken was a good golfer, and this was the opportunity of a lifetime. "But Nicholas had a swimming gala at school that day so I had to pull out. Then, when I got to the swimming pool, Nicholas ran up to me. 'I'm reserve, Dad,' he said. 'I'm reserve. What does it mean?'"

A similar sense of disappointment ran through his job. He never felt at ease with the Rembrandt people, they did not speak English in the meetings, and none of his schemes came to fruition in the way that he had hoped. He and Avril became alarmed at the prospect that, when they were 18, the boys would be conscripted into the South African army and that, as English immigrants, they would be sent to the front line. So, after little more than a year in Pretoria, they called it a day and returned to England.

There had been happy times and good friendships were made during their three years in South Africa, but it had not worked out as a way of life.

Coaching up near the mines
"I was teaching him to block the shot more sideways on. People often go down with their chest parallel with the ground, then they can't get the power into the block. You do need to get both hands at the back of the ball."

Arrival in Norfolk

The film of *The Go-Between* was shot in and around Melton Hall in Norfolk. It is a charming yet disturbing portrait of Edwardian England, with a cricket match between hall and village providing one of the central episodes. The original book was set near Salisbury, but North Norfolk in 1970 – with its grand houses and unchanged scenery – had retained more of the atmosphere of that lost world.

> Avril and I watched the film in a school hall in Johannesburg, never dreaming that we would soon be living only a mile or two from where it was filmed.

When the family returned from South Africa in September 1971, they stayed at first with Avril's parents outside Huddersfield. Then Ken, encouraged by a friend in South Africa, applied to schools in East Anglia, and he received an enthusiastic reply from Logie Bruce-Lockhart, the former Scottish rugby international who was headmaster at Gresham's, Holt.

There would be a vacancy as Head of Art the following September, and after interview Ken was offered the position.

"At a public school," Logie Bruce-Lockhart says, "one is always looking for somebody who has something to offer outside the classroom. And to have a trained artist with such a level of achievement in sport was almost too good to be true."

Avril took a job at Beeston Hall, the nearby prep school, and Ken earned what he could in the meantime with part-time appointments. In the summer term he played cricket as a professional for Norfolk, and he did some coaching at schools in Norwich where among his pupils was a 12-year-old Jonathan Agnew.

Norfolk was a county with well-established families going back many generations, and the schools were an integral part of their way of life. Ken was an outsider, a Huddersfield mill-worker's son who had been hired for his artistic and sporting talents, and it took him a while to get used to their world.

It also took him a while to get used to the climate. Returning from the warmth of South Africa to an autumnal Yorkshire had been a shock, but the move to Norfolk required another readjustment.

> It's a very different climate from Yorkshire. The cold there is damp cold, whereas in Norfolk it's dry cold. It comes all the way down from Siberia to the North Sea, and it doesn't go round you. It goes straight through you.
>
> I remember early in the cricket season at Gresham's once, we had a touring side from South Africa. And there was a howling gale blowing. The South African captain decided to field first, and it started to snow. And the snow was coming horizontally across the ground. He turned to me. 'Christ,' he said. 'What kind of weather's this?' I said, 'You should see it on a bad day.'

You might imagine that the flat landscape of Norfolk would not appeal to Ken the artist after the rugged hills of Yorkshire and the dramatic scenes in South Africa, but he soon found much in his new environment to please the eye.

> There are lots of lovely farming villages, with pretty round-towered Saxon churches, made of flint. It's much gentler on your eyes than the West Riding. The churches in Yorkshire are built of stone and tend to be bleak. The Norfolk churches, with their flint, have a more friendly appearance.

They settled, and through a friend they found a plot of farming land in Stody that was available for building.

The lodge gate, Melton Hall, where *The Go-Between* was filmed

Norfolk scenes

The Church of St Peter
in the grounds of Melton Hall
"I did this because it has a continental feel, with the pointed tower. Most of the
Norfolk churches have got round towers because you can't build corners with flint."

Cley Church

"I wanted to create an atmosphere, to make the church as dramatic as possible. Normally, when you drive into Cley, you see the side elevation. You miss this front side, but it is much more interesting."

A cricketer again

Ken's return to England left him with a free summer before he took up his appointment at Gresham's School. He considered a return to county cricket, receiving an attractive offer from Northamptonshire. But in the end he preferred to stay in Norfolk with his young family, securing a position as their professional.

The county was going through a bad patch. In 1969, under the captaincy of the former Surrey fast bowler Richard Jefferson, they were one of the strongest sides in the Minor Counties Championship, with Graham Saville second highest run-scorer in the country and Jefferson himself topping the bowling averages.

But, as captain, the Surrey man struggled to lead a side in which the dominant personality was the veteran England all-rounder Bill Edrich, whom the team still called 'Skipper'. "It was quite impossible," he recalls. "I had a 19-year-old lad making his debut for us the next day, and Bill kept him up in the bar till three in the morning, telling him stories about his bombing raids over Germany in the War."

Jefferson resigned, Edrich retired and Saville returned to Essex. The captaincy passed to David Pilch, of the Norwich sports outfitters family, and, when Ken arrived, he was clearly the star of the team.

Ken had not played any serious cricket in South Africa, and he did not supplement his games for Norfolk with any club cricket. According to David Armstrong, then the Norfolk Secretary, Ken went for a net at Gresham's with Bill Thomas, the master in charge there – and, so the story goes, even that did not give him much practice. "He hit the first ball I bowled him right across the field," Thomas said, "so I packed up."

Norfolk's first match was in late June at March against Cambridgeshire, and Ken was quickly made aware of the frailties of his team-mates. On the first evening, setting off in pursuit of the home team's 246 for five declared, he was ninth out for 36 in a total of 68. The Australian leg-spinner Terry Jenner – who had been bowling against England at Sydney 16 months earlier – was the main destroyer, with six for 21 and, according to Bryan Stevens in the *Eastern Daily Press*, 'Taylor was the only man who had any answer to his wiles.'

The following week at Grimsby Ken faced the West Indian spinner Sonny Ramadhin. There was more support for him this time and – 'demonstrating his vast experience in the way in which he "read" and played Ramadhin' – he was in sight of his first century for the county when he reached 97 out of a total of 171 for six.

Unfortunately, by the time he had scored two singles to take him to 99, there were eight wickets down and he was being joined at the wicket by Tracey Moore.

> He was a fair-haired fellow, a very whole-hearted cricketer, bubbling with enthusiasm. We met in the middle when he came in and he said, 'Run for anything.'

The *Eastern Daily Press* records the outcome: 'Moore, backing up, was still out of his ground when a lightning return from a close fielder shattered his stumps and rebounded to deal him a painful blow on his foot.'

Ken was still on 99 and, with number eleven John Flower now at the other end, he clipped the next ball behind square leg and looked up expectantly. "Theoretically it was my call," Flower says. "We looked at each other and couldn't quite make up our minds. When we did set off, it was too late."

The *Eastern Daily Press* reckoned that, by the time they started, it was 'a single which would have tested the fastest of sprinters.'

Ken was left on 99 not out, and the only compensation as he returned to the pavilion came with the award of his county cap.

However, in the next match, he hit 127 'in a sparking exhibition of free stroke play' at Hertford. Then came consecutive hundreds at Norfolk's own Lakenham ground, against Buckinghamshire and again against Herts. In the closing stages of the latter innings, David Armstrong recalls, he was so in control that three times in one over the Herts captain moved a fielder to where Ken had just hit the ball for four, only for Ken to place another four through the fielding position that had just been vacated.

There were good bowlers in all the sides, yet Ken could pick up a bat after four years and score runs against all of them.

> Playing for Yorkshire, you were always having to go out and score quick runs, because the team was always challenging for the championship. But at Norfolk you could play your own game all the time in every innings. The position of the game never affected the way you performed. You could go in each time and play the game you wanted to play.

Despite poor weather Ken's attractive batting raised attendances significantly and his fielding was, in the words of the annual report, 'one of the sights of the season.' But, with the matches only lasting two days and Norfolk usually batting first, the lack of penetration in the bowling left them without a victory.

David Armstrong remembers Ken as a cricketer who made a greater contribution on the field than in the dressing room or the bar: "He was designing his house at the time and, as soon as he was out and he'd taken his pads off, he'd go off to his car and out would come the drawing board. The game would go on, and he'd be in another world."

The season ended in late August, with Norfolk travelling to Beaconsfield for a return match against Buckinghamshire. After lunch on the second day Norfolk were looking for quick runs to set a declaration, and Ken – partnered by Robin Huggins – cut loose, adding 127 in only 57 minutes. It was 'electrifying', the *Eastern Daily Press* said, and in three overs the experienced Chris Parry was hit for 51 runs with Ken striking four sixes. Three landed in or over the A40; the fourth crashed against the scorebox. He came off with an unbeaten 112, and after the game he told David Armstrong that, if he played at all the next summer, it would be as an amateur.

Away from the pressure of chasing championships at Yorkshire he had prospered – but he had come to feel a different pressure: of being the only professional and being expected to perform.

He had scored 831 runs, and his season's average of 63.92 put him at the head of the Minor Counties list, making him the first Norfolk batsman ever to win the Wilfred Rhodes trophy. Not for eight years had a Minor Counties batsman finished with better figures.

He did not play in 1973, then – when he was persuaded back for two games in 1974 – he hit two fifties, the latter showing him 'at his majestic best as he stroked the ball to all quarters'. Then, in full flow, he got a harsh lbw decision and retired for good. He was 39 years old, and his teaching and his art held his interest.

In those 12 games in Norfolk, played over two summers and after a long break and with no practice, he had shown what so many in the game knew: that he had a rare talent, one that in other circumstances – or with a different temperament – who knows? It might have taken him to even greater heights.

The thatched pavilion at the now disused Lakenham ground

A career in teaching

The world of education has changed so much since Wally Heap encouraged Ken to play cricket against a dustbin in the Stile Common schoolyard. "Wally created Ken's career for him," his brother Jeff says. Out of those years he developed not three passions but four: cricket, football and art but also the desire to become a teacher as Wally Heap was and to pass on his skills to future generations.

In the 1960s he worked part-time in secondary schools around Huddersfield, and there is a part of him that regrets that he did not stay in the state sector – "but only if the schools had been as they were forty years ago," he says, "not as they are today."

Instead, he worked for 15 years at Gresham's, Holt, a public school in Norfolk, where – according to the headmaster Logie Bruce-Lockhart – "his enormous modesty and his dry sense of humour made him very popular in the staff room. He wasn't enough of an extrovert to sell art as a subject to the less interested, but he always got excellent exam results. There are many former pupils who are immensely grateful to him."

The headmaster himself even turned to Ken for advice. "Drawing is something I enjoy, and he helped me greatly. I wasn't getting the sense of perspective right, and he explained to me how the colours in the distance tend to be bluer; the red, brown and yellow come out in the foreground."

In the late 1980s Ken left Gresham's to work with Avril at the nearby Beeston Hall preparatory school. He still helps a little with the cricket, even having coached the Essex batsman Will Jefferson there – "He was a good fast bowler when he was at Beeston" – but mostly, now that he only goes in two days a week, he concentrates his time on the more able art students.

"When I started at Gresham's, it was only the class teachers in the junior school who took Art. And they only took it up to 'O' level. At a big school like that, Art just wasn't considered. It's only in the last twenty years that Art's become an important subject."

Now all the public schools try to attract talented artists with specialists scholarships as well as all-rounder scholarships that take account off artistic ability. In a year at Beeston Hall Ken might work with six or seven such potential scholars, and his record in recent times has been outstanding: three successful pupils in 2005, an unprecedented five in 2004.

For Ken this is rewarding work, and he has been doing it long enough to have seen some of his earlier students grow up to make a successful living in the world of art. One such is Crispin Robjent, a portrait painter in Norfolk; another is Tom Leveritt, also a portrait painter but in London.

"Ken was such a skilled teacher," Crispin says. "I can still remember him teaching me how to look for contrast in the tonal ranges of the still life. We were always drawings things like skulls, and he really brought drawing alive for me. The ideas of tone and depth and contrast, making the drawing look lifelike. I progressed so quickly when I was there. The work that he and Avril did with me was fundamental to my career. I really didn't learn anything more when I went to public school. Without that foundation at Beeston, I don't think I'd have had an art career at all."

"Ken was very kind," Tom recalls. "He was a typically forthright Yorkshireman, a refreshing juxtaposition with the art. I've never seen anybody quite so strong with the pencil – from barely touching the paper to really pressing down on it and back again. He dominated the drawing, like I expect he dominated when he played football. It led me to think that art wasn't a sissy thing to do."

Beeston Hall School has been built up around a substantial residential property on the coast road coming out of Sheringham and is situated in extensive grounds. With a music school and a computer studio, a heated outdoor swimming pool and hard and grass tennis courts, it is a world away from the stone steps and concrete playground of Stile Common School.

Ken is a quiet figure in the school community. Avril staged a 70th birthday dinner for him in the school, and after the meal he stood up to talk about his earlier life as a sportsman. As he told of his encounters with Brian Close and Bill Shankly, the younger members of the audience were spellbound. This was a Ken whom they had never seen or heard before.

It was my task that evening to ask the questions, and afterwards I fell into conversation with the headmaster Innes MacAskill. "You have to work hard to get things out of Ken," I said cheerfully, and he looked at me, rolling up his eyebrows in acknowledgement of the truth of what I had said. But we both agreed that the hard work was always worth it.

And Ken at seventy?

"I've found teaching very satisfying," he says. "It's lovely when you teach kids. You yourself don't feel any older. Anybody over thirty is old to them so you don't have a sense that you're getting older. It's a lovely way of life."

Beeston Hall School

Coaching with Don Wilson

Ken never passed a qualification to be a cricket coach. He attended Lilleshall for the course, but on the final day, a Saturday, he had to play football for Huddersfield Town. Today, when such qualifications are considered vital, he could not have practised as a coach.

His Yorkshire team-mate Don Wilson became MCC's Head Coach at Lord's in 1977, and he was soon calling Ken down from Norfolk to help out at the Saturday sessions for promising young cricketers. Don lived in the flat above the old MCC Shop, and Ken often stayed the night there. "It was a lovely, old building," Ken says, "and they knocked it down and built some glass-fronted monstrosity."

While living at Lord's and working as Head Coach, Don developed a friendship with the actor Peter O'Toole, whose son Lorcan was at school with Don's son Jerrard. There was one Christmas Eve when Don remembers O'Toole turning up at his door with nowhere to go for Christmas. "I'd bought Jerrard one of those steam engines that you fill with methylated spirits and water. I'd only bought it for my sake, because I remembered it from my childhood, and Peter spent the whole morning on the kitchen floor playing with it. It was a wonderful Christmas Day.

"He'd been through a very traumatic divorce, and he loved our nets. When he was in the West End show

'Jeffrey Barnard Is Unwell', he used to come regularly. There was one time when Imran Khan was trying to get fit to go to Australia, and he turned up at Lord's. 'I want to try my legs out,' he said, and we didn't have a batter. So I said to Peter, 'Put your pads on.' 'Who's the bowler?' he asked. I said, 'Don't worry about that.' He was bruised from head to foot, but he loved every second of it. I would have been terrified batting against Imran Khan, but he loved it. It was like he was Lawrence of Arabia all over again."

Don tried to talk about films, always being met with the answer, "I'm here to play cricket". Then one day there was a knock on his office door and in came O'Toole with David Lean, Omar Sharif and Stanley Baxter. "Now you can talk films," O'Toole said. And Don had one of the happiest hours of his life.

O'Toole was a Yorkshireman by birth, his father an Irish bookmaker who lived in Pontefract, and his friendship with Don continued when Don moved back to Yorkshire in 1990, to be Director of Sport at Ampleforth College.

Don was still keen to make use of Ken's services, and in school holidays Ken would travel to North Yorkshire to spend several days coaching. And such was Don's ability to recruit top people that Ken found himself in the company of all sorts of great names:

Ken with
Peter O'Toole

not only Peter O'Toole and Fred Trueman but also the Scottish rugby international Dodie Weir, the Liverpool footballer Alan Kennedy and the one-time Crystal Palace manager Malcolm Allison. It was Allison, of course, who had been the West Ham centre-half responsible for marking Ken on that icy cold Saturday in February 1957 when he had scored four goals.

At the time Don moved to Ampleforth Ken was 55 years old, but he was never afraid to put on the pads and show by example what he was recommending to the young batsmen.

"He was always able to do it himself," Don says, "and that takes a lot of guts when you get to the age of 50 or 55. He would ask anybody to bowl – left-armers, spinners, fast bowlers – and he would show the kids how to play each type of bowling. The turning ball, for instance. He always played it with the spin. Not many people can do that, you know. I remember him telling the youngsters how helmets were ruining the game, because the batsmen weren't watching the ball onto the bat as closely as they used to do. Ken would watch it to the last moment, and they couldn't believe that."

A half-hour video survives of Ken demonstrating the art of batting to a group of boys. Its instruction is simple and clear, well explained, and regularly he asks for a ball to be thrown at him so that he can demonstrate what he is saying. The message of it all is that batting, if done properly, is based on some simple principles.

The coaching sessions at Ampleforth were happy outings for Ken, and the surrounding countryside offered plenty of opportunities for him to slip away and paint, most memorably on the day when

a thunder storm threatened and he went off to the nearby Byland Abbey.

Ken and Don were different types, but they appreciated each other's qualities. For Ken, Don's infectious enthusiasm – with laughter never far away – provided a warmth and an energy that made every day fun, while for Don, Ken's quiet gift of teaching was a precious bonus at his sessions.

"I used to use Ken so much," Don says. "As far as I am concerned, we have the greatest people in the game talking about batting and bowling, but what a pity we didn't use people like Ken a little bit more. Everybody can do the fitness routines, but not everybody can talk about how to get into position to play Shane Warne. He was a brilliant coach."

Don Wilson

All things must pass

On Saturday 30 April 1994 Huddersfield Town played their last ever league match at Leeds Road. The visitors were Blackpool; both clubs now languished in Division 2 – or the third division, as the players of Ken's day would have known it.

How the world had changed since Ken's last match against Blackpool on 27 December 1955. Then the visitors – with the 40-year-old Stanley Matthews still going strong on the wing – had been pressing for their first championship title, and on a wet, muddy day Ken – earning fifteen pounds a week – had played his part in a 3-1 victory that brought cheerful and orderly applause from the 34,619 spectators.

Fewer than half that number were present for the ground's final match, but among them were many of the players whose best footballing days had been there: Ken and his brother Jeff, Ray Wilson, Les Massie, John Coddington, Albert Nightingale and many, many more.

The final whistle blew. Town had won, just as they did back in 1955. But this time the victory was greeted by a rush of supporters running onto the pitch, followed by stewards and policemen on horseback.

Life was moving on. The turf was dug up, and the foundations were laid for a retail park. Where once there was a Main Stand and a 'Cowshed', now there is an Argos, an Allied Carpets and a multiplex cinema.

Ten years later the new stadium down the road would be on its second name, a new sponsor transforming it from the McAlpine to the Galpharm. It is another world from the one in which Ken played.

Ken's photograph after the final whistle is blown at Leeds Road
The game is over. Eddie Boot, far left, the man who succeeded Bill Shankly as manager, looks down for the last time on the ground where he first wore a Huddersfield shirt in 1937.

Picture opposite: **Byland Abbey**
With Fountains and Rievaulx Abbeys, Byland was once one of the three great monasteries of the North. It was home for more than 300 years to Cistercian monks, who established a prosperous living until their way of life was destroyed by Henry VIII.
The first fully Gothic building in the North, its remains are now preserved by English Heritage. Ken's painting dates from one of his coaching visits to Ampleforth. "It was building up to a thunderstorm, and I knew the ruins would look dramatic against the sky."

Half full or half empty?

The world has changed so much in fifty years.

Can you imagine a Premier League footballer today playing four months of county cricket in the summer – or spending every week in winter in an art studio, only meeting up with his team-mates for the match on Saturday?

Ken's story was a remarkable one in 1956. He was 'the most wanted young man in Britain', according to one newspaper. But now it could not happen. We expect our sportsmen to be dedicated professionals, focused completely on achieving success in just one activity.

We live in an age that demands success. Notions of community, public service and decent, honourable behaviour have all become secondary to the achievement of that success. And our sport reflects the change.

"Cricket was a gentleman's game," Ken says. "Players had respect for each other, and unwritten laws were honoured. Umpires were never put under pressure. If you were caught and you knew you'd hit the ball, you walked. And that's gone. Now, if you can get one over on the umpire or you can intimidate the batsman psychologically, then you're doing a good job. All these things have come into the game, and as a teacher I've seen how even the children are copying some of them. They're all in the field, hyping each other up, and that's not the spirit in which cricket should be played."

Ken came from an ordinary working-class family in Huddersfield, and for him these were not values handed down by his social superiors. They were ingrained in the proud traditions of his own culture.

"When I played, you didn't want to be known as a cheat. Now it seems cheating is part of the game. Football is exactly the same. You didn't hold players down at corners. You didn't have your elbows out; you kept your arms down at your sides. And if a forward went past you, you didn't pull them down. It seems in both games now that it's about winning at all costs."

Ken's own life has not been about winning at all costs. He was happy to pursue three careers, knowing that each encroached a little upon the other two, and he was happy to have as a long-term goal the prospect of becoming a teacher.

There were others in the 1950s who played both cricket and football, but none who simultaneously pursued a third career outside sport, a career based on such a very different talent.

Ken owes much of his remarkable life to Wally Heap, the inspirational schoolmaster who, unburdened by key stage tests and league tables, looked for the talent in his pupils and nurtured it.

He owes much to his father, who – in that quiet West Riding way of his – kept Ken's feet on the ground. "You can't play games for ever," he told Ken, insisting that he could do better than clean boots and sweep terraces at Leeds Road. Why not go to college and get a training as an artist?

He also owes much to his brother Jeff, for it was Jeff who combined professional football with a university education and who made it seem quite normal to Ken to move between the worlds of sport and the arts.

A top footballer studying at The Slade? As happy thinking about the pressure of the pencil on the drawing paper as the timing of a tackle? His brother retiring from football to become an opera singer? Hitting a run of notes with the same energy with which he jumped to head the ball into the net?

It says much about the strength of working-class life in Huddersfield at that time, its culture and its values, that the two boys could go out into the world and live such rich and varied lives.

And yet …

According to Jeff, their mother always saw the glass not as half-full but as half-empty. And it is possible to look at Ken's life and to think of how much more he might have achieved: a regular place in the England cricket team, a transfer to Arsenal and a place in the England football team, a completion of his time at The Slade and a successful career as a full-time artist.

Michael Parkinson contributed an article to Ken's cricket benefit brochure. Amidst the memories of his great innings, his brilliant fielding and his uncompromising tackling are some reflections on that top half of the glass:

> I have always envied Ken Taylor. It seemed to me he had everything. Not only a fine cricketer but a good footballer, and not only that, a schoolteacher and an artist to boot. It seemed to me that here was the real all-rounder, a man accomplished at sports and yet versed in the arts, a man as at home with a paint brush as a cricket bat.

I have always felt that Ken Taylor's fault was that he shrugged off the gifts he was granted as if perturbed by their abundance. To be frank, he has been a disappointment to his admirers who, remembering the blossoming of his youth, anticipated a wondrous ripening. This is certainly true of his cricket. That he played only three Test matches is not due to the perversity of the selectors but rather his own inability to give his talents full rein.

He gives the impression of being a well-balanced, contented person, which is more than can be said for his admirers, who spend long sessions in various seedy bars endlessly debating why he doesn't score two thousand runs each season. In terms that he himself will appreciate, we wonder why his career has been sketched in pen and ink and not splashed in vivid hues.

The obvious explanation for this is that Ken did not focus enough on any one of his talents. In the words of EW Swanton, 'As a batsman he looks so good when he is in full spate that it is hard to understand why he is not a more consistent high scorer. But his cricket has suffered from his career as a footballer, giving him a shortened season and possibly somewhat diluting his ambition.' Or, as Ray Wilson put it, 'Ken could tackle as good as anybody, straight on, and he was exceptional in the air for a small man. If he hadn't had the cricket, if there'd only been soccer, there would have been a hell of a chance that he'd have been a good international player. He could have been playing for England with me in the World Cup, but of course cricket called him, too.'

In any case, the physical wear and tear of playing two sports and never having an off-season will have made each of the two games harder. Ken is 70 now, struggling with a replacement ankle and wondering what damage he did himself heading the heavy footballs of his day. "It wasn't easy," he says. "Playing both games, year in and year out, took its toll. It's probably why I finished playing soccer full-time at 29 and cricket at 33."

But there is also a factor of chance in how it all worked out for him, an element of luck that Ken always emphasises when he talks about sport. In the case of Ken's own career, there are some obvious moments when we can look back and ask ourselves, 'What if ...?'

Two minutes from time at Leeds Road in March

1955. The sixth round of the FA Cup. What if the referee had responded to the penalty claims of the Huddersfield forwards, or if moments later Len White's header had hit the crossbar and not the back of the net? Huddersfield Town, with only York City of the Third Division to beat in the semi-final, would have run out at Wembley – and Ken, just 19 years old, would have caught the eye of millions sitting in front of television sets up and down the country.

Saturday 28 April 1956. Town battling for survival in the First Division. What if Aston Villa, their main rivals in the relegation zone, had come up against a team keener to win than their neighbours West Bromwich Albion? Perhaps, with Shankly soon to take the helm, Huddersfield would have stayed in the First Division throughout Ken's career and his claim to an international place would have been more noticed.

The morning of Thursday 4 June 1959. Trent Bridge. Ken's first Test innings. A shaky start, but his confidence was growing as he reached 22. What if it had been another umpire, not Eddie Phillipson, looking down at him when the Indian leg-spinner Gupte made his half-hearted appeal for lbw? Perhaps Ken would have gone on to a score that would have established him in Test cricket. *The Times* thought he had 'more natural class' than Ken Barrington, and Barrington survived in the team to play 82 Tests and to finish with a higher average than any other post-war England batsman.

"You've got to have a bit of luck," Ken says. Then he quotes John Arlott: 'Cricket is a game of the most terrifying stresses with more luck about it than any other game. They call it a team game but in fact it is the loneliest game of all.'

The most terrifying stresses? The loneliest game? Here perhaps is a third explanation.

For one with so much natural ability, Ken did not always find batting to be an easy way of earning a living. It helped that he was such a brilliant fielder; it helped in the early days that he was a useful change bowler. And it helped that cricket was not his only occupation. As he admits, "If I didn't get any runs, I would think, 'I'll be back playing football soon,' and that made it easier for me."

Perhaps, as with his brother Jeff, there has come a realisation as he has grown older that he was not as confident of his talents as he should have been. He was fine when he was 20, starting out on the adventure of life, but by the time he was 27, and much was expected of him, he was prone to worry before he went out to bat, an anxiety that perhaps his team-mates did not always spot beneath his quiet exterior. As the Tarot lady said years ago, after she had dealt out his cards, "People think you're very easy-going, but there's an awful lot of turbulence underneath."

It suited him temperamentally to have a break from it and to play football and to paint. Though his cover fielding and his tigerish tackling were full of commitment, there was something of the dilettante about the way he disappeared to his other activities. But that was his way of enjoying his sport and getting the best out of himself.

Even with his art Ken might have gone further, as his best friend at The Slade, Harry Riley, did. William Coldstream clearly thought that he had the ability, but perhaps he lacked a little in self-confidence and, when it came to the crunch, he put his sport first.

Now he works in the quiet of North Norfolk and rarely exhibits his pictures, drawing much satisfaction from the progress of his pupils at school.

So, if we want to focus on his under-achievement, on the disappointment felt by his admirers in their 'long sessions in various seedy bars', we might ask if it was such a good idea for Ken to have three careers; we might ask if there was indeed an element of bad luck in his not reaching the heights that his talents promised; and we might ask if there was something in his temperament that made him more at ease with life if he took it as it came and did not strive too hard for success.

That is to see the glass as half empty.

But what a life he has had! Here is a man whose talents have taken him from a small terraced house in Huddersfield, where he shared a bed with his brother till the age of ten, to a life in which he has run out of the tunnel at Anfield football ground, opened the batting for England in a Test match at Lord's and developed his artistic skills at The Slade. He has coached cricket in New Zealand, worked with black and white footballers in South Africa and taught generations of young artists in the rural calm of North Norfolk.

He has been managed by one of the great characters of English club football, the inspirational Bill Shankly; he has been led by one of the great captains of English cricket, Brian Close; he has played with Denis Law and Fred Trueman, Ray Wilson and Geoffrey Boycott; and he has been taught by the influential William Coldstream. It is not given to many to enjoy so rich a life.

As a cricketer Ken's greatest achievement was to be an important member of one of the finest county sides of all time, perhaps the last great county side, a side which won seven championships in ten years.

A natural mover, capable of exceptional concentration, he was as good a fielder as any player of his generation. When he patrolled the covers his presence prevented many a run, he could throw a ball further than any of the Australians who toured in 1968, and his catching was safe, even at times spectacular – as with one he held on the boundary in Hong Kong. 'The ball had been hit truly hard and square,' EW Swanton wrote, 'and one felt that Ken could scarcely reach it. As he neared it, going full pelt, a small child ran out from the spectators right in his path – a moment of drama and peril. Ken swerved like a wing three-quarter to avoid the obstacle, straightened, and next second was taking the ball jumping, two-handed, over his head. In a Test match it would have brought the crowd to its feet.'

As a bowler he was a useful option, though he bowled less after Brian Close became captain. Once he dismissed the great Gary Sobers in both innings, and once in the greatest county arena of all – a Roses match at Old Trafford – he took the new ball and, with six wickets, set Yorkshire on the road to their first championship victory over Lancashire for several years.

But his best days were as a batsman. Not for him the Geoffrey Boycott approach: accumulating runs with a minimum of expansive shots or risk. Ken was an artist by calling, and he preferred to take his chance and to enjoy the days when everything went right. There was the 160 he scored against the Australians at Sheffield, when he hit his way cleanly from 85 to 100 in four balls: six, four, four, one; the evening at Leicester when, remembering the coaching of Wally Heap, he danced out of his crease and murdered the slow left-arm bowling of Tony Lock; the 281 partnership with his great friend Bryan Stott at Hove, when – as Bryan puts it – "we ran them into a state of despair"; and his battling 67 out of 101 on a treacherous pitch at Harrogate in the match that clinched the 1962 championship. Rich are the memories left by such innings.

As a footballer he was happy to play at the back, a centre-half whose hard and well-timed tackles were rated by the great Tommy Taylor of Manchester United as the most difficult that he had to encounter. In days when the English game was played with a heavy ball, often on a muddy surface, he was never frightened to challenge for the ball. 'He was one of the hardest men I've ever come across,' Denis Law wrote in 1968, 'and you can include the iron-side players from top continental countries when I say that.'

Bill Shankly might have been suspicious of his art and his cricket, not to mention the handkerchief he sported in the top of his shorts, but he recognised in Ken the same hardness in the tackle that characterised his own game. For all his grumbling about Ken's late arrival for the season, there was always a place for him in Shankly's side.

When an injury kept Ken out of the side for a few weeks in the winter of 1956/57, Shankly fitted him back in at centre-forward, and in only his third outing in that position he went out in the snow and scored four goals against West Ham United.

He has been lucky. In his life after sport he has not only been able to devote more time to his artistic talent, but he has also settled to a teaching career that has brought him much satisfaction.

Cricket, football, art. All three talents were spotted by Wally Heap, and Ken has gained great joy from the three of them. But he has never forgotten the part played by his headmaster, and it has inspired him to find a fresh outlet for his talents as a teacher and coach, passing on his skills to younger generations.

Why should we not accord his teaching the same respect that we do to his England Test caps, his years of footballing success, even his works of art. For Don Wilson, Ken's technical understanding and patient explanations, his willingness to go into the net at the age of 55 and demonstrate what he was saying, made him the best of batting coaches. Also, for the most talented art students at Beeston Hall, their paths to successful careers have owed much to the quiet excellence of Ken's teaching.

The glass is much more than half full.

Ken does not dwell that much on the great achievements of his life. Ask him about his vital championship-winning knock at Harrogate, and he will tell you that he was out first ball in the second innings. Ask him about his four goals in the snow, and he will tell how cold it was and how he nearly walloped into the upright when he scored the last one.

But that is the Yorkshireman in him, happy to have a quiet chuckle about the misfortunes of life. Get below that, and you won't find him with any great regrets about the life he has lived, any tendency to ponder for long on whether he could have done more if he had followed another course.

Jeff and Ken Taylor. They are a remarkable pair of brothers. Two footballers who played with success in the old First Division, an England cricketer, a geography graduate, an artist, an opera singer and two highly respected teachers. They have lived enough lives for five people. "I've got a nice house and a nice car," Jeff says. "I haven't got much money, but I don't owe anybody a penny. And I've never done a proper day's work in my life. It's always been play. It's always been enjoyment. The only hard work has been the striving for perfection."

It is a sentiment that Ken shares.

"When I look back now, I realise what a lucky man I've been. I've had to work hard, but I've always enjoyed what I've done. So it's never felt like work."

And, if he had focused more on one activity, does he think that he could have been more successful?

"Yes, I suppose I might have done better if I hadn't done so many things. There was a policeman up the road from me, when I was still living with my parents in Dalton. He said to me, 'Don't fall into the trap of being a jack of all trades and master of none.' And that's always stayed with me, in the back of my mind.

"To an extent I did fall into that trap. But I don't have any regrets. If you took away any of the three strands of my life – cricket, football or art – it would have meant my missing out on so much pleasure, so much satisfaction. I really have enjoyed everything I've done, and I hope I've given enjoyment to others.

"It's been an absolutely wonderful life. If I had to come again, I wouldn't change it one bit."

Acknowledgements

In the course of writing this book, I have received help from a number of people, for which I am very grateful.

I would like to thank the following for talking to me: David Armstrong, Jimmy Binks, Henry Brown, Logie Bruce-Lockhart, Wilf Charlton, John Flower, Barry Garthwaite, Bruce Heath, Richard Jefferson, Tom Leveritt, Tommy Lyons, Les Massie, John Nash, Nigel Pullan, Harry Riley, Crispin Robjent, Mel Ryan, Phil Sharpe, Micky Stewart, Bryan Stott, Jeff Taylor, Fred Trueman, Don Wilson and Ray Wilson.

Additionally I would like to thank Ron Deaton, David Smith and Peter Rear, all of whom read the manuscript with care and offered invaluable advice, and Ian Thomas, the Huddersfield Town Football Club historian who successfully discovered the identities of some unknown faces in the club photograph on page 55.

I have used a number of reference books, notably:
Wisden Cricketers' Almanack
The PFA Premier and Football League Players' Records 1946-1998,
    edited and compiled by Barry J. Hugman (Queen Anne Press, 1998*)*
Who's Who of Cricketers,
    edited by Philip Bailey, Philip Thorn & Peter Wynne-Thomas (Hamlyn, 1993)
I have also made extensive use of the website CricketArchive.

I have read and sometimes quoted from the following books:
Brian Close, *I Don't Bruise Easily* (Macdonald & Jane's, 1978)
Brian Jackson & Dennis Marsden, *Education and the Working Class*
                    (Routledge & Kegan Paul, 1962)
Denis Law, *The King* (Bantam Press, 2003)
E.W. Swanton, *Sort of a Cricket Person* (Collins, 1972)
Don Wilson, *Mad Jack* (Kingswood Press, 1992)

I have read and quoted from a number of newspapers and magazines. Some of them are articles stuck in scrapbooks in such a way that the identity of the newspaper is not clear, but the following have definitely been used:
The Times, The Guardian, Daily Telegraph, Daily Sketch and News Chronicle; Eastern Daily Press, Huddersfield Examiner, Yorkshire Evening News, Yorkshire Evening Post and Yorkshire Post; Charles Buchan's Football Monthly and The Cricketer.

Most of the photographs in this book have been taken from Ken Taylor's private collection. I would like to thank Susanna Kendall for the photograph on page 9, Mrs K. Kelly for permission to use her late husband's photograph of Ken Taylor's 200th run at Edgbaston on page 15, Albert Booth for the photograph of Joe Carruthers on page 39, Paul Clayton for the cover of the Charlton Athletic programme on page 74, the Huddersfield Examiner for several photographs of Ken Taylor's childhood and playing days, Ross Parry Agency Limited for the photograph of the Harrogate groundsman on page 97, Collins Willow for permission to re-use Ken Taylor's drawing of Brian Close on page 103 and Cameron Taylor for the photograph on page 142.
Some of Ken's drawings are interpretations of old photographs, and I would like to thank Mrs K. Kelly for permission to use her late husband's photograph of Gary Sobers, Bill Smith for the photographs of Colin Milburn and Brian Statham, the *Yorkshire Post* for the photographs of Fred Trueman, Brian Close and Ray Illingworth and the Press Association for the photograph of Dickie Bird. The photographs of Denis Law and Ray Wilson were given to Ken for use in his cricket benefit brochure. The publishers have not been able to establish the copyright owners of the remaining images and, if any photographic source believes that they are theirs, they should contact the publisher to rectify the matter.

Stephen Chalke, Bath, January 2006

Fairfield Books

Fairfield Books was established in 1997 as a specialist publisher of cricket books.

Its full list of publications is as follows:

Runs in the Memory – County Cricket in the 1950s
   by Stephen Chalke, illustrated by Ken Taylor

Caught in the Memory – County Cricket in the 1960s
   by Stephen Chalke, illustrated by Ken Taylor

One More Run – Gloucestershire versus Yorkshire, Cheltenham 1957
   by Stephen Chalke, talking with Bryan 'Bomber' Wells

Fragments of Idolatry – from 'Crusoe' to Kid Berg
   by David Foot

At the Heart of English Cricket – The Life and Memories of Geoffrey Howard
   by Stephen Chalke

The Appeal of the Championship – Sussex in the Summer of 1981
   by John Barclay

Harold Gimblett – Tormented Genius of Cricket
   by David Foot

Guess My Story – The Life and Opinions of Keith Andrew, Cricketer
   by Stephen Chalke

No Coward Soul – The Remarkable Story of Bob Appleyard
   by Stephen Chalke and Derek Hodgson

Born To Bowl – The Life and Times of Don Shepherd
   by Douglas Miller

Charles Palmer – More Than Just a Gentleman
   by Douglas Miller

Ken Taylor – Drawn to Sport
   by Stephen Chalke

Sixty Summers – Somerset Cricket since the War
   by David Foot and Ivan Ponting

Tom Cartwright – The Flame Still Burns
   by Stephen Chalke

For full details of prices and availability, please contact
Fairfield Books
17 George's Road, Bath BA1 6EY
Telephone 01225-335813